Thomas Carlyle, Karl August Varnhagen von Ense, Richard Preuss

Last words of Thomas Carlyle

Thomas Carlyle, Karl August Varnhagen von Ense, Richard Preuss

Last words of Thomas Carlyle

ISBN/EAN: 9783742875440

Manufactured in Europe, USA, Canada, Australia, Japa

Cover: Foto ©berggeist007 / pixelio.de

Manufactured and distributed by brebook publishing software (www.brebook.com)

Thomas Carlyle, Karl August Varnhagen von Ense, Richard Preuss

Last words of Thomas Carlyle

LAST WORDS

OF

THOMAS CARLYLE

LONDON
LONGMANS, GREEN, AND CO
1892

PRINTED BY
SPOTTISWOODE AND CO., NEW-STREET SQUARE
LONDON

CONTENTS

WOTTON REINFRED

CHAPTER I

'Surely,' said Wotton, as he sat by the clear evening fire engaged in various talk with his friend, 'surely, my good Doctor, the poet is wrong; and happiness if it be the aim was never meant to be the *end* of our being.' The old Doctor gave a quiet smile. 'Happiness!' continued Wotton with increasing vehemence, 'Happiness! where is it? The foolish cannot find it, the wisest have sought for it in vain. Not on the towering heights of royalty, not in the houses of the rich and noble, not down in the thatched hut of the peasant does it dwell. The ambitious, be it in the cabinet, the battle-field, or the counting-room, discovers after a thousand mocking disappointments that he is a hapless drudge; the voluptuary dies despicable and wretched, like a putrid gourd; Brutus exclaims "O virtue, I have worshipped thee as a substance, and must I find thee a shadow?" But Science! Yes, Science! And what does Science teach us? The wisdom of living? The nature of our own being, and the art of directing it aright? Alas! alas! on these things she speaks not but in enigmas; for darkness and the shadow of doubt rest over the path of our pilgrimage, and at our journey's end the wisest of us can but exclaim with the old sage: *Foede mundum intravi, miser vixi, perturbatus morior!*'

'Do not forget his prayer,' said the other, meekly.

'Yes! *O causa causarum, miserere mei!*' cried Reinfred, looking upwards, with the tears almost starting to his eyes. '*Miserere mei!*' repeated he, throwing himself down on the table, and hiding his face in his hands.

His cousin looked at him sympathisingly, but spoke not.

'And yet,' cried the other, starting up, and throwing back his head to conceal the wetness of his eyes, 'if He do not hear me? If there *is* no ear to hear me; and the voice of my sorrow peals unreturned through the grim wilderness, and only the echo of the dead rocks replies to me in the gloom! O heaven and earth, what am I or where am I? Alone! Alone! They are dead, all dead, buried beneath the ground or faithless above it, and for me there is no soul that careth! Forgive me, my father,' continued he, after a moment's pause; 'I do you wrong, but I am very weak; and surely these things will kill me soon.'

'Dear boy,' said his friend, 'you are not to blame, you take the matter like a young man as you are;

because hope has hid herself you think she is utterly fled. Tush, I tell you, all this is nonsense, and you will see it yet though you think my words but wind. You were twenty-two last Christmas, and the life of man is three score years and ten. You have much to do, and much to learn in this world; only nature must have her course, nay, she is teaching you even now, teaching you with hard but useful stripes, and you will act your part the better and more wisely for it.'

'It is acted already,' said the other bitterly, 'and the curtain is dropped, and I have nothing more to do but undress, but shuffle off this mortal coil.'

'Dropped? Ay, but not the green one; it is the painted curtain that has dropped, and the first act truly is done, and we have other four to come to. Pity that our interlude of music were not gayer, but we must even put up with it, sighs and groans though it be. O Wotton Reinfred, thou art beside thyself; much learning doth make thee mad. I swear it is even so,' continued he, rising into his usual lively tone. 'There hast thou sat poring over thy Geometries and Stereometries, thy Fluxions direct and inverse, by the Newtonian and the Leibnitzian method, thy Universal History, thy Scotch Philosophy and French Poetics, till thy eyes are dazed with so many lamps, and for very light thou canst not see a glimpse, and so in thy head the world is whirling like a sick man's dream, and for thee it has neither top nor bottom, beginning, middle, nor end! I care not for thy scepticism, Wotton: I tell thee, it will grow to be belief, and all the sounder for thy once having doubted. I say so because thy froward mind is honest withal, and thou lovest truth sincerely. But deuce take it, man! I would have had thee pleading in the courts like a brave advocate——'

'Illustrating the case of Stradling *versus* Styles,' cried Reinfred, hastily, for the talk displeased him. 'Spending my immortal spirit, in vain jangling, for a piece of bread? I have bread already.'

'So much the better! But the honour, the use to others——'

'May be strongly doubted,' cried the youth, still more sharply.

'Well, I grant it would not do,' said the Doctor, hastening to quit this rather thorny province. 'Thou hadst a heart too, but we could not master it; six months of the *Institute* had no whit abated thy aversion, nay, thy horror; and at last, when I saw thee after a resolute night as *Justice of the Peace* absolutely seized with a kind of *tetanus* or *locked-jaw*, I myself was obliged to vote that we should give it up.'—'Heigho!' ejaculated Wotton. 'But now, in Heaven's name,' continued the Doctor, 'what is it that should so overcloud thee, nay for ever benight thee notwithstanding? Are we not here in thy own walled house, amid thy own freehold fields? Hast thou *no* talent that this world has use for? Young, healthy; a proper fellow

of thy inches; learned too, though I say it, for thy
years; and independent, if not rich! Pshaw! Is thy
game lost because the first trick has gone against
thee? Patience, and shuffle the cards! Is the world
all dead because Edmund Walter is a scoundrel
jackanapes, and——'

'Good God!' cried Wotton, starting from his seat,
and pacing hurriedly over the floor, 'can you not
spare me? What have I to do with Edmund Walter?
The tiger-ape!' cried he, stamping on the ground,
'with his body and shoulder knots, his smirks and
fleers! A gilt outside, and within a very lazar-house!
Gay speeches, a most frolic sunny thing; and in its
heart the poison of asps! O the—— But I will not
curse him. No, poor devil! He but follows the
current of his own vile nature, like the rest of us.
God help him—and me!' added he, pausing, with a
deep sigh.

'Yet it is strange,' said the other, 'how this puppy
could muster rhetoric for such a thing. Strange that
for a cap and feather Jane Montagu should have——'

'Doctor!' said Wotton, turning towards him
abruptly, with a look striving to be calm. 'I shall
request of you never to mention that name in my
hearing again.'

'Pooh, think not of her, or think of her as she
merits. A selfish minx after all; brighter talents,
but no sounder judgment or truer heart than the rest
of them; a worthless——'

'Oh, do not blame her! Who knows how much or how little she was to blame? The thraldom of her situation, her youth, that cold cozening cruel woman; all things were against us. No, worthless she was not; and if her heart was false, it was doubly and trebly false, for she knew the light and yet chose darkness rather than light. But could she love that caitiff? She must have loved him! Oh, there is a dark baleful mystery over it which I shall never pierce through. Would she were gone from my thoughts, gone as if she had not been; for here the remembrance of her is but a curse. Was it not hard? One only hope, and that to mock me with the Fiend's arch scoff! The world was dead around me, the last heart that loved me in the cold grave; all efforts baffled, one by one the green places of my universe scathed and blackened into ashes; my whole life one error, a seeking of light and goodness and a finding of darkness and despair. I was to myself as a frightful mistake; a spectre in the middle of breathing men, an unearthly presence, that ought not to be there. And she—oh, fair and golden as the dawn she rose upon my soul. Night with its ghastly fantasms fled away; and beautiful and solemn in earnest shade and gay sunshine lay our life before me. And then, and then! O God, a gleam of hell passed over the face of my angel, and the pageant was rolled together like a scroll, and thickest darkness fell over me, and I heard the laughter of a demon! But what of it?' cried he, suddenly checking himself. 'It was a vision, a brief calenture, a thing that belonged not to this earth.'

He stood gazing out upon the starry night. The old man approached, but knew not what to say. 'Do they not look down on us as if with pity from their serene spaces,' said Reinfred, 'like eyes glistening with heavenly tears over the poor perplexities of man? "Herrliche Gefühle erstarren in," &c. Their bright-ness is not bedimmed by any vapour, the mists of our troubled planet do not reach them. Thousands of human generations all as noisy as our own have been engulfed in the abyss of time, and there is no wreck of them seen any more; and Arcturus and Orion and the Pleiades are still shining in their courses, clear and young as when the shepherd first noted them on the plain of Shinar. Oh, what is life, or why should we sorrow or joy over it when it is but for a moment? What is all the earth, and all that have inherited or shall inherit it? Blot it out utterly and it is not missed from the Creation. Blot *me* out, and shall I be missed? Shame on me, foolish child, to whine for such a toy!'

'Truth, virtue, beauty are in man,' said the other; 'they are older than the stars, and will live when these too have returned to the void night whence they were called forth in the beginning. O Wotton, my son, thou wilt know and feel this at last, though now thou know it not; and affliction will be precious which teaches thee such knowledge.' Wotton

shook his head. 'But I am wrong,' continued he.
'Why do I lead thee to such thoughts? It is a poor
philosophy which can be taught in words: we talk
and talk; and talking without acting, though Socrates
were the speaker, does not help our case but aggravate
it. Thou must act, thou must work, thou must do!
Collect thyself, compose thyself, find what is wanting
that so tortures thee; do but attempt with all thy
strength to attain it and thou art saved.'

'Wanting?' said Wotton. 'Wanting? There is
nothing wanting but deepest sleep, where there were
no dreams to trouble me. Ere long I shall find it in
my mother's bosom. But what of this?' added he,
impatiently. 'Why do we talk, as thou sayest, when
there is nothing to be done? Oh, my old friend, I
abuse your goodness, and load you with griefs which
I should bear myself. Forgive me, forgive me. I
was not always weak. It must alter, for the better or
the worse it must.'

'For the better!' cried the Doctor, cheerily. 'It
must and will. I tell thee help is on the road: it
will arrive when we least think of it. But enough!
Now tell me, to come to business at last, what sayest
thou to Mosely's letter?'

'That travelling will *not* recreate me; that I want
no spiritual leech, for spiritual recipes cannot avail;
that Mosely is a good man, but knows nothing of my
"case" as he calls it; in brief, that I cannot and
must not go.'

'Dost thou know I came hither solely to persuade thee; to offer myself as thy companion?'

'My good, kind, only friend! But why should it be? Why should I intrude upon happy men: to sit in their circle like a death's-head, marring all pleasure by my sepulchral moods? Leave me to fight with my own despicable fate. Here in the mountains I consume my griefs in silence, and except when you in your chivalrous benevolence come over to doctor me, I trouble no one with them.'

'Be my patient then for once,' cried the other: 'what harm can it do? Your books have ceased to please you, and you are learning nothing from them but to doubt. Your long rides among the moors do but feed your melancholy humour. You can neither shoot, nor hunt, nor dine. You keep no race-horses, and the Commission of Supply does not fire your ambition. What have you to do here? Arise, let us mingle in the full current of life, or at least survey it for a season. Who knows what fine things we may see and do? Frank Mosely is a true man, and you will learn to love him; he already loves you. Your case, too, he understands better than you think. Let me read you this,' cried he, taking out a letter and leading Wotton back to the table.

'Oh, I know it already! The old story over again, *be not solitary, be not idle.* And good heaven! what am I that people should quacksalver me with their nostrums? Does Mosely keep a private bedlam for

afflicted scholars ?   Or would he dissect me and ex-
periment upon me ? '

'Patience ! patience !' said the other ; ' he is a
good man, and my friend.   Do but listen.'   He read
as follows :

' *The end of man is an Action, not a Thought*, says
Aristoteles ; the wisest thing he ever said.   Doubt
is natural to a human being, for his conceptions
are infinite, his powers are only finite.   Nevertheless it must be removed, and this not by negation but by affirmation.   From experience springs
belief, from speculation doubt, but idleness is the
mother of unbelief.   Neither is our happiness passive,
but only active ; few men know this, though all in
words admit it, hence their life is a perpetual seeking
without finding.

'Bring thy friend Reinfred hither ; I have long
known him, though he knows not me.   So fair a
nature will not perish in its own superfluity, be its
circumstances for the present never so perplexed.
His state is painful, but in the end it yields peaceable
fruits.   It must at some time be the state of all men
who are destined to be men.   Bring him hither, that
he may see what he has yet but heard of.   Time will
indeed be his physician, be it there or here : but I
would gladly do myself a pleasure in knowing him.
Happy and unhappy two-legged animals about me are
many, but happy or even unhappy men are very
few. . . .'

The discussion of this matter between our friends was protracted to a late hour ; Wotton urging his own misanthropic habitudes, his hatred of change, his inacquaintance with Mosely, and the folly and hopelessness of the whole project; his cousin answering all his cold noes with as many warm yeas, and pleading at last that in this whim of his, if he had ever merited aught, he might for this once be gratified. 'It is a thing I have set my heart on,' said he ; 'and I shall be positively unhappy if thou deny me.' Reinfred loved his cousin ; esteemed him as a man of unintelligible or mistaken views indeed, but of the kindest heart, whose helpful sympathy he had often taken in the hour of need, and who now, sad, lonely, downpressed and darkened as the young man seemed, might almost be said to form the last link that still in any wise connected him with the living and loving world. After long resistance he began to yield, and before parting for the night a faint assent was wrung from him. 'Why many words ?' said he, ' if it really can do anything for thee, mistaken as thou art; against me it can do nothing.'

Next morning the cousin took his leave and rode home to make arrangements for the journey, as the third day was fixed upon for their departure.

CHAPTER II

Reluctantly as Wotton had consented to this scheme, the good effects of it were already beginning to be felt. The preparations and preliminary settlements produced a wholesome diversion of his thoughts, so many little outward cares constraining him to calculation and exertion, the unusual bustle of his still house, all contributed to draw him from the dark Trophonius' cave of his own imagination into the light and warmth of day.

As he rode along through the bright morning to his lawyer, that he might finish, after long loitering, some acts of business relating to his little property, and some acts of beneficence to one or two poor peasants dependent on him, he almost felt as if he were in very deed ceasing to be an alien from the commonwealth of men, as if he too had some duties to perform in his own sphere, barren and humble though it was. The journey itself, though he viewed it with little pleasure, nay in general with a sort of captious regret, was yet a prospect if not a hope, and thus the future, if not filled with inviting forms, was no longer absolutely void. Nay in spite of himself

some promise of enjoyment rose faintly over his
mind; for the plastic vigour of young fancies which
shapes such landscapes in the clouds, though sorely
marred in him was not extinct, and where good and
evil are both possible, there is no such perverse
alchemy as will exclusively select the latter. He
could not deny that he felt some curiosity to know
Mosely and his circle, so enigmatic as it seemed, from
all that he had learned; it may be even that unconsciously some low whisper of his lost Jane Montagu
mingled in his fantasies, some unavowed hope of again
being cast into her neighbourhood, of seeing and
hearing her *once* more, and though not of recovering
her affection, for that he could not even wish, at
least of understanding how it had been for ever lost.

Wotton was one of those natures which it is of
most importance to educate rightly, but also of greatest difficulty, and which accordingly with a capricious
contradiction we often find worse educated than any
other. In early boyhood he had lost his father, a
man of an equal but stern and indignant temper,
soured also by disappointments and treacheries, which
had driven him at middle age from the commerce of
the world, to hide his shattered fortunes, his great
talents, and too fiery but honest and resolute spirit,
in the solitude of his little rustic patrimony. Here
in this barren seclusion he had lived, repelling from
him by a certain calm but iron cynicism all advances
either of courtesy or provocation, an isolated man,

busied only with the culture of his land, amused only by studies of philosophy and literature, which no one but himself understood or valued. To neighbours he was an object of spleen, of aversion; yet on the whole of envy rather than of pity, for he seemed complete in himself, free of all men, fearless of all men, a very king in his own domain. Even happy he might appear, but it was not so, for the worm of pride was still gnawing at his heart, and his philosophy pretended not to root it out but only to conceal it.

In a few years his deep-shrouded chagrin undermined his health, a slight sickness gathered unexpected aggravation, and he sank darkly into the grave with all his ineffectual nobleness, wayward and wilful in himself, mistaken by the world, and broken by it though he could not be bent. Of this parent Wotton recollected nothing, save his strong, earnest, silent figure, and a vague unpleasant impression from him of restraint and awe.

The mother, to whose sole guidance he was now committed, had a mother's love for her boy, and was in all respects a true-minded woman; but for such a spirit as Wotton's no complete though in some points a most precious instructress. She trained his heart to the love of all truth and virtue; but of his other faculties she took little heed, and could take little proper charge. To this good being, intellect, or even activity, except when directed to the purely useful, was no all-important matter; for her soul was full of loftiest religion, and truly regarded the glories of this earth as light chaff; nay, we may say she daily and almost hourly felt as if the whole material world were but a vision and a show, a shadowy bark bound together only by the Almighty's word, and transporting us as if through a sea of dreams to the solemn shore of Eternity, in whose unutterable light the bark would melt like vapour, and we ourselves awake to endless weal or woe.

In her secluded life—for like her husband she was visited by few except the needy and distressed—such feelings gathered strength; were reduced to principles of action, and came at last to pervade her whole conduct, most of all her conduct to her sole surviving child. She never said to him : 'Be great, be learned, be rich;' but, 'Be good and holy, seek God and thou shalt find Him.' 'What is wealth ?' she would say; 'What are crowns and sceptres? The fashion of them passeth away. Heed not the world, thou hast a better inheritance; fear it not, sufficient food and raiment our Father will provide thee; has He not clothed the sparrow against winter, and given it a fenced house to dwell in ?' She wished to have her boy instructed in learning, for though little acquainted with it herself, she reverenced it deeply ; but, judging his religious and moral habitudes of far more conse- quence, she would not part with him from her sight, still less trust him among the contaminations of a boarding-school.

To read and write she had herself taught him; the former talent he had acquired so early that it seemed less an art than a faculty, for he could not recollect his ever having wanted it or learned it. So soon as his strength appeared sufficient, she had sent him to a day-school in the nearest town, a distance of six miles, which, with his satchel at his back, the ruddy urchin used to canter over on his little shelty evening and morning. His progress was the boast of the teachers; and the timid still boy, devoted to his tasks and rarely mingling in the pastimes, never in the riots, of his fellows, would have been a universal favourite in any community less selfish and tyrannical than one composed of schoolboys. It may seem strange to say so; but among these little men a curious observer will detect some almost frightful manifestations of our common evil nature. What cruelty in their treatment of inferiors, whether frogs, vagrant beggars, or weaker boys! How utterly the hearts of the little wretches seem dead to all voice of mercy or justice! It is the rude, savage, natural man, unchecked by any principle of reflection or even calculation, and obeying, like animals, no precept but that of brute giant power.

Poor Wotton had a sorry time of it in this tumultuous, cozening, brawling, club-law commonwealth: he had not friends among them, or if any elder boy took his part, feeling some touch of pity for his innocence and worth, it was only for a moment, and his usual purgatory, perhaps aggravated by his late patron, returned upon him with but greater bitterness. They flouted him, they beat him, they jeered and tweaked and tortured him by a thousand cunning arts, to all which he could only answer with his tears; so that his very heart was black within him, and in his sadness, of which he would not complain, and which also seemed to him as if eternal, he knew not what to do. For he was a quiet, pensive creature, that loved all things,—his shelty, the milk-cow, nay the very cat, ungrateful termagant though she was; and so shy and soft withal, that he generally passed for cowardly, and his tormentors had named him 'weeping Wotton,' and marked him down as a proper enough bookworm, but one without a particle of spirit. However, in this latter point they some-times overshot themselves, and the boldest and tallest of the house have quailed before the 'weeping Wotton' when thoroughly provoked, for his fury while it lasted was boundless, his little face gleamed like a thunder-bolt, and no fear of earthly or unearthly thing could hold him from the heart of his enemy.

But the sway of this fire-eyed genius was transient as the spark of the flint; his comrades soon learned the limits of danger, and adjusting their operations with a curious accuracy to the properties of their material, continued to harass him, more cunningly, but not less effectually than before.

All these things acted on Wotton with deep and

mostly unfavourable influences; fretting into morbid quickness his already excessive sensibility, and increasing the envelopment of his shy secluded nature. His mother and her calm circle, the sole spot in the earth where he could have peace, became doubly dear to him; and he knew no joy till, mounting his pony, and leaving the pavement of the burgh behind him, he could resign himself among shady alleys and green fields to a thousand dreams, which fancy was already building for him in clouds of all gayest hues. In the future he was by turns a hero and a sage, in both provinces the benefactor and wonder of the world; and would weave a history for himself, of dainty texture, resuming it day after day, and sometimes continuing it for months and years. The bleak, monotonous past itself was beautified in his thoughts; its sorrows were like steep rocks, no longer sharp and stern, rising in the distance amid green sunny fields of joy. All forms of his earlier years rose meeker and kinder in his memory; especially the figure of a little elder sister, with whom he had played in trustful gladness in infancy, but whom death had snatched away from him before he knew what the King of Terrors was. Since the departure of this little one, the green knolls, the dells of his native brook had been lonelier to him; indeed, he was almost without companion of his own age, but his mother's bosom was still open to him, and from her he had yet no care which it concerned him to hide.

In the evenings, above all on holidays, he was happy, for then the afflictions of life all lay on the other side of the hill; he wandered over the fields in a thousand gay reveries; he made crossbows and other implements with his knife, or stood by the peasants at their work and listened eagerly to their words, which, rude as they might be, were the words of grown men, and awoke in him forecastings of a distant wondrous world. Old Stephen in particular, the family gardener, steward, ploughman, majordomo and factotum, he could have hearkened to for ever. Stephen had travelled much in his time, and seen the manner of many men; noting noteworthy things, which his shrewd mind wanted not skill to combine in its own simplicity into a consistent philosophy of life. From Stephen also he had half borrowed, half plundered, certain volumes of plays and tales, among these the ever-memorable 'Arabian Nights,' which, not so much read as devoured, formed, with the theological library of his mother, a strange enough combination. These fictions Wotton almost feared were little better than falsehoods, the reading of which his conscience did all but openly condemn, for he believed, as he had been taught, that beyond the region of material usefulness religion was the only study profitable to man. Nor was he behindhand in this latter, at least, if entire zeal could suffice. Ever in his great Taskmaster's eye, he watched over his words and actions with even an over-scrupulousness. His little prayer came evening and morning from a full heart, and life, in the thought of the innocent boy, seemed little else than a pilgrimage through a sacred alley, with the pinnacles of the Eternal Temple at its close.

With increase of years came new feelings, still farther complicated by change of scene. In his fifteenth winter he was sent to college; a measure to which his mother had consented by the advice of her ancient pastor, and the still more earnest persuasion of Wotton's teacher, and to the fulfilment of which the boy himself had long looked forward with unspeakable anticipations. The seminary was in a large town, at a distance of many miles; to Wotton, a pure 'city of the mind,' glorious as the habitation of wisdom, and cloud-capt in his fancy with all earthly splendour.

This new scene might have worked upon him beneficially, but for the present it did not. It was a university in which the great principle of spiritual liberty was admitted in its broadest sense, and nature was left to all not only without misguidance, but without any guidance at all. Wotton's tasks were easy of performance, or, rather, the performance of them was recommended not enforced; while for the rest he was left to choose his own society and form his own habits, and had unlimited command of reading. What a wild world rose before him as he read, and felt, and saw, with as yet unworn avidity! Young Nature was combining with this strange

education to unfold the universe to him in its
most chaotic aspect. What with history and fiction,
what with philosophy and feeling, it was a wondrous
Nowhere that his spirit dwelt in : all stood before him
in indistinct detached gigantic masses; a country of
desire and terror; baseless, boundless; overspread
with dusky or black shadows, yet glowing here and
there in maddening light. To all this, moreover,
the exasperating influence of solitude was superadded; in fact, Wotton's manner of existence was
little less secluded than ever; for though the perse-
cutions of his schoolfellows had gradually died away
as he grew more able to resist them, his originally
backward temper had nowise been improved by such
treatment. Indeed, a keen and painful feeling of
his own weakness, added to a certain gloomy consciousness of his real intrinsic superiority, rendered
him at once suspicious and contemptuous of others.

Besides, in the conversation of his equals he truly
felt little sympathy; their speculations were of far
more earthy matters than his; and in their amuse-
ments, too often riotous and libertine, his principle
forbade him to participate. Only with the little knot
of his countrymen, in the narrowest sense of that
word, did he stand in any sort of relation; and even
of these he often felt as if their intercourse were
injuring him and should be abandoned, as if their
impure influences were contaminating and seducing
him. Contaminate him they did, but seduce him

they could not. Polished steel may be breathed on without being rusted, but not long or often without being bedimmed. Wotton fought hard with evil; for fiercely were the depths of his fiery nature assailed; he was not conquered, yet neither did he conquer, without loss, and these contests added new uproar to the discord within.

Of his progress in the learned languages he himself made little account; nor in metaphysics did he find any light, but, rather, doubt or darkness; if he talked of the matter it was in words of art, and his own honest nature whispered to him the while that they were only words. Mathematics and the kindred sciences, at once occupying and satisfying his logical faculty, took much deeper hold of him; nay, by degrees, as he felt his own independent progress, almost alienated him for a long season from all other studies. 'Is not truth,' said he, 'the pearl of great price, and where shall we find it but here?' He gloried to track the footsteps of the mighty Newton, and in the thought that he could say to himself: Thou, even thou, art privileged to look from his high eminence, and to behold with thy own eyes the order of that stupendous fabric; thou seest it in light and mystic harmony, which, though all living men denied, thou wouldst not even doubt! A proud thought, truly, for little man; but a sad one if he pursue it unwisely!

The *Principia* do but enlighten one small forecourt

of the mind; and for the inner shrine, if we seek not purer light and by purer means, it will remain for ever dark and desolate. So Wotton found to his cost; for with this cold knowledge, much as he boasted of it, he felt in secret that his spiritual nature was not fed. In time, like other men, he came to need a theory of man; a system of metaphysics, not for talk, but for adoption and belief; and here his mathematical logic afforded little help, as, indeed, without other rarer concomitants, it is in such pursuits a hindrance rather than a help. Great questions, the very greatest, came before his mind; with shuddering awe he drew aside the veil from all sacred things; but here, in what he called the light of his reason, which was only a fitful glimmer, there was no clear vision for him. Doubt only, pale doubt, rising like a spectral shadow, was to be seen, distorting or obscuring the good and holy; nay, sometimes hiding the very Holy of Holies from his eye.

Who knows not the agonies of doubt? What heart, not of stone, can endure to abide with them? Wotton's was a heart of flesh, and of the softest; it was torn and bleeding, yet he could not pause; for a voice from the depths of his nature called to him, as he loved truth, to persevere. He studied the sceptical writers of his own country; above all, the modern literature of France. Here at length a light rose upon him, not the pure sunlight of former days, but a red fierce glare, as by degrees his doubt settled in utter negation. He felt a mad pleasure mingled with his pangs, and unbelief was laying waste in scornful triumph so many fairest things, still dear and venerable even as delusions. Alas! the joy of the Denyer is not of long continuance. He burns the city, and warms himself at the blaze for a day; but on the morrow the fair palaces as well as the noisome alleys are gone, and he stands houseless amid ashes and void silence. Thus also it fared with Reinfred.

The philosophy of Epicurus was not made for him; his understanding was convinced, but his heart in secret denied it. Vice and all baseness, which at first it might have seemed to sanction, he still rejected, nay, abhorred. But what, then, was virtue? Another name for happiness, for pleasure? No longer the eternal life and beauty of the universe, the invisible all-pervading effluence of God; but a poor earthly theorem, a balance of profit and loss resting on self-interest, and pretending to rest on nothing higher.

Nay, *was* the virtuous always happiest? To Wotton it seemed more than dubious; for himself, at least, he felt as if truth were too painful, and animal stupidity the surest fountain of contentment. By degrees a dreary stagnancy overspread his soul: he was without fear and without hope; in this world isolated, poor, and helpless; had tasted little satisfaction, and expected little, and in the next he had now no part or lot. Among his fellow-men he felt like a stranger and a pilgrim,—a pilgrim journeying without rest to a distant nowhere. Pride alone supported him, a deep-hid satanic pride; and it was a harsh and stern support. Gloomy mockery was in his once kind and gentle heart; mockery of the world, of himself, of all things; yet bitterest sadness lay within it, and through his scowl there often glistened a tear.

In such inward disquietudes it would have been a blessing to communicate in trustful kindness with other men. However, he kept his secret locked up in himself, judging that if spoken it would meet with little sympathy, perhaps even be but imperfectly understood. By light companions he was now and then bantered on his melancholic mood; but these he despatched with tart enough replies, and himself only withdrew with his alleged imaginary woes still farther from their circle. To his mother least of all could he impart these cares. In his occasional visits, the good woman had not failed to notice some unfavourable change in his temper; but as his conduct still seemed strictly regular, she had taken little heed of this, and imputed it to more transitory causes. Besides, she was becoming more and more immersed in her reli-gious feelings, more divided from the world's cares; and when she counselled her son, it was her sole earnest injunction that he would study to be right with God, and prepared for the change, which for him as for her and every one would be irrevocable, and lay near at hand. Occasionally she may have suspected that all was not right ; but, if so, to rectify it was beyond her sphere ; and she trusted that the same good providence, which had led herself through so many thorny and steep paths, would also be the guide and protector of all that was hers. At last, some two years ago, her health declining, she had moved, by the advice of her physician, into a kinder climate; and was now living far south in her native county, in the family of a widowed sister, where Wotton had never yet seen her. The visit had been unexpectedly protracted from month to month, and seemed at last as if it would not end. Her letters to him were frequent, earnest, and overflowing with sublime affection ; often they brought tears into his eyes; but he could only in return give her false assurances of his welfare, and in sighs thank Heaven that she knew not what had befallen him.

Without associate, however, he was not always to be. In one of his summer rustications, since his mother left him, he had become acquainted with Bernard Swane, or, rather, Bernard Swane had become acquainted with him ; for hearing much of the wonderful talents, the moodiness, and bitter way-ward humours of his neighbour, and being himself a man of influence, warm-heartedness, and singular enthusiasm, he had forced his way into the privacy of this youthful misanthrope ; had accosted him with such frank kindliness, and on subsequent occasions so soothed and cherished him in sympathising affection, that by degrees he had won his friendship, and Wotton had now no secret, economical or spiritual, which he did not share in. To both parties their intercourse had from the first been peculiarly attractive. There was that contrast, and at the same time similarity, in their natures which gives its highest charm to social converse. Bernard was the elder by several years, a man of talent, education, and restless vigorous activity; by profession belonging to the law; already profitably engaged in the public business of his county, and cherishing perhaps, half consciously, hopes of yet rising to some far higher department. For he was a man of a large, if not a peculiarly fine spirit; strong, conscious of his strength; for ever full of practicable and impracticable schemes; and though he flattered himself that the promotion of public good in any sphere was his best or only aim, to all third parties it was clear enough that Bernard had a deep ambition. Nay in his frank and sanguine manner there often appeared the most indubitable outbreakings of vanity; but at the same time of vanity so kindly, social, and true-hearted, that you were forced to pardon it. The truth is, he was of a happy nature ; existence of itself was sweet and joyous to him : he lived for ever in the element of hope ; loving himself, and loving through himself all nature and all men. Rarely could you find a person so superior to others, yet so beloved by them, so calculated to please at once the many and the few. To Wotton in

speculation, as in conduct, he was a perfect opposite.
The former never believed, the latter scarcely ever
doubted; hence, the one acted and concluded, wrong,
even absurdly, it might be, but still acted and concluded, while the other painfully hesitated and inquired.   Both truly loved goodness; of the two,
Wotton more fervently, yet Bernard with more trust-
fulness and effect.   In active courage, the latter was
superior; in passive, the former; who, indeed, had
long lived with pain, and for the better purpose of his
mind had always fronted and defied it.   Not so with
Bernard: he had in secret a deep horror of passive
suffering, so deep that scarcely even conscience could
drive him to brave it; and many times, as it seemed
to Wotton, he would practise cunning subterfuges,
and underhand, nay, unconsciously, play jesuitic tricks
with his own convictions to escape such dilemmas.
That he wished a thing to be true was ever with him
a strong persuasion of its truth.   He sympathised in
Wotton's scepticism; often he seemed, with a deep
sigh, to admit that his objections were unanswerable,
yet himself continued to believe.   Wotton loved him,
for, in spite of drawbacks, he felt all his singular
worth; and Bernard was the only human soul that
knew him, in whose neighbourhood his own exiled,
marred, and exasperated spirit still felt any touch
of peace, still saw afar off, though but for a few
moments, some glimpses of kind sunshiny life.   To
produce such effects, to attract such a spirit, and be

loved by it was no less delightful to the other, for if
he, as it were, protected Wotton, he also admired, nay,
almost feared, him; and, feeling his own superiority
in strength and good fortune, he often felt that in
nobleness and merit the balance might sway on the
other side.

Thus their friendship rested on the surest basis,
that of mutual satisfaction and sympathy; on the
one hand and on the other good offices or good wishes,
pleasure given and received. In their intellectual
discussions, widely as they differed, they by no chance
quarrelled; indeed, except in private they almost
never argued. In society, where, except in the company and by the persuasion of his friend, Wotton
scarcely ever ventured, you generally found them on
a side: Bernard supporting the good and beautiful in
vehement, flowing, rhetorical pleadings; Wotton, in
bitter sarcasms and with keenest intellect, demolishing
the false and despicable, and this, often in the dialect
of his hearers, if no better might be, to whom he
justly enough apprehended his own would many
times have been a stone of stumbling. By such
half displays of his inward nature, poor Wotton's
popularity was seldom increased. Bernard was con-
fessedly a man of parts, by whom it might seem less
disgraceful to be tutored; but who was this Wotton,
this sharp, scornful stripling, whom no one meddled
with unpunished? By degrees, indeed, he established
for himself a character of talent, the more wondered

at perhaps that it was little understood; nay, obser-
vant people could not but admit that in his rigorous,
secluded, gloomy spirit there dwelt the strictest justice,
and even much positive virtue; but still, these things
were conceded rather than asserted. Nay, Wotton
was less than ever a favourite, and the first ineffectual
effort to despise him too often passed into a sentiment of fear, uneasiness, and aversion.

On the young man himself the consciousness of
this was not without corresponding and hurtful influence; but one good effect among many bad was that it
bound him still more closely to his friend. Bernard
was now almost his sole society; a treasure precious,
therefore, both by reason of its rarity and its intrinsic value. Gladly would Bernard have rewarded him
for such exclusive trust; gladly have extracted by
reasonable ministrations the bitterness from his
spirit; truly had he watched over him in many a sad
hour, and much did he long and hope to see his fine
gifts occupied in wholesome activity.

Hitherto, however, his efforts had been fruitless,
or only of transient influence. By his counsel Wotton
had meditated various professions; that of law he had
even for a time attempted. But he was too late; the
young enthusiasm had faded from his heart; there
was no longer any infinitude in his hopes. The
technicalities of the subject dispirited and disgusted
his understanding; its rewards were distant and
dubious, and to him of small value. What was

wealth and professional fame when the world itself
was tarnished in his thoughts, and all its uses weary,
flat, stale, and unprofitable? There had been a time
when, like the rest of us, he was wont to impute his
misery to outward circumstances; to think that if
this or that were granted to his wishes, it would be
well with him. The fallacy which lurked here experience had soon taught him, but not the truth.
He felt that he was wretched, and must ever be so;
he felt as if all men would be so, only that their eyes
were blinded.

He abandoned law and hurried into the country,
not to possess his soul in peace as he hoped, but in
truth, like Homer's Bellerophon, to eat his own heart.
His love of truth, he often passionately said, had
ruined him; yet he would not relinquish the search to
whatever abysses it might lead. His rural cares left
much of his time unoccupied; in mad misdirection
he read and meditated, enjoying hours of wild pleasure, divided by days and nights of pain. It was not
tedium that he suffered, he had too deep an interest
to weary, but light came not to him—no light; he
wandered in endless labyrinths of doubt, or in the
void darkness of denial. With other men his conversation was stinted and irksome, for he had to
shroud his heart from them in deepest mystery, and
to him their doings and forbearings were of no
moment. It was only with Bernard that he could
speak from the heart, that he still felt himself a man;

scanty but invaluable solace, which, it may be, saved him from madness or utter despair.

Such was his mood when a little incident quite transformed the scene. One fine summer evening he had ridden over to Bernard's, as he was often wont; but, finding him engaged with company, was about to retire without seeing him, when Bernard himself hurried out and constrained him to enter. ' It is but some one or two young friends,' said he, ' who have come accidentally to see my sister. There is *one* among them too,' added he with a roguish smile, as they approached the drawing-room; but Wotton had no time to answer till he found himself in the middle of the circle welcomed by the mistress of it, and introduced by name to a bright young creature, the heroine of the evening, whom in his bashfulness he scarcely dared to look at, for the presence filled him with ·painful yet sweetest embarrassment. Jane Montagu was a name well known to him; far and wide its fair owner was celebrated for her graces and gifts; herself also he had seen and noted; her slim daintiest form, her soft sylph-like movement, her black tresses shading a face so gentle yet so ardent; but all this he had noted only as a beautiful vision which he himself had scarcely right to look at, for her sphere was far from his; as yet he had never heard her voice or hoped that he should ever speak with her. Yet surely she was not indifferent to him, else whence his commotion, his astonishment, his agitation now when near her ? His spirit was roused from its deepest recesses, a thousand dim images and vague feelings of gladness and pain were clashing in tumultuous vortices within him; he felt as if he stood on the eve of some momentous incident—as if this hour were to decide the welfare or woe of long future years.

Strange enough! There are moments of trial, of peril, of extreme anxiety, when a man whom we reckoned timid becomes the calmest and firmest. Reinfred's whole being was in a hurricane; but it seemed as if himself were above it, ruling over it, in unwonted strength and clearness. His first movement prospered, and he went on to prosper. Never had his manner been so graceful or free; never had his sentiments been nobler, his opinions more distinct, emphatic, or correct. A vain sophistical young man was afflicting the party with much slender and, indeed, base speculation on the human mind; this he resumed after the pause and bustle of the new arrival. Wotton, by one or two Socratic questions in his happiest style, contrived to silence him for the night. The discomfiture of this logical marauder was felt and even hailed as a benefit by every one; but sweeter than all applauses was the glad smile, threatening every moment to become a laugh, and the kind, thankful look with which Jane Montagu repaid the victor. He ventured to speak to her; she answered him with attention; nay, it seemed as if there were a tremor in her voice; and perhaps she thanked the dusk that it half hid her. The conversation took a higher tone; one fine thought called forth another; each, the speakers and the hearers alike, felt happy and well at ease. To Wotton the hours seemed moments; he had never been as now; the words from those sweetest lips came over him like dew on thirsty grass; his whole soul was as if lapped in richest melodies, and all better feelings within him seemed to whisper, 'It is good for us to be here.' At parting the fair one's hand was in his; in the balmy twilight with the kind stars above them he spoke something of meeting again which was not contradicted; he pressed gently those small soft fingers, and it seemed as if they were not hastily or angrily withdrawn.

Wotton had never known love: brought up in seclusion from the sex, immersed in solitary speculation, he had seen the lovelier half of our species only from afar, and learned in his poetical studies to view them with an almost venerating reverence. Elysian dreams, a fairyland of richest blessedness his young fancy had indeed shaped for him; but it lay far apart from the firm earth, with impassable abysses intervening; and doubting and disbelieving all things, the poor youth had never learned to believe in himself. That he, the obscure, forlorn, and worthless, could ever taste the heaven of being loved; that for him any fair soul should ever languish in fond longing, seemed a thing impossible. Other men were loved;

but he was not as other men; did not a curse hang over him? had not his life been a cup of bitterness from the beginning? Thus in timid pride he withdrew within his own fastnesses, where, baited by a thousand dark spectres, he saw himself as if constrained to renounce in unspeakable sadness the fairest hopes of existence. And now how sweet, how ravishing the contradiction! '*She* has looked on thee!' cried he; 'she, the fairest, noblest; she does not despise thee; her dark eyes smiled on thee; her hand was in thine; some figure of thee was in her soul!' Storms of transport rushed through his heart as he recalled this scene, and sweetest intimations that he also was a man, that for him also unutterable joys had been provided.

Day after day he saw and heard his fair Jane; day after day drank rapture from her words and looks. She sang to him, she played to him; they talked together, in gaiety and earnestness, unfolding their several views of human life, and ever as it seemed glancing afar off at a holy though forbidden theme. Never had Wotton such an audience; never was fine thought or noble sentiment so rewarded as by the glance of those dark eyes, by the gleam which kindled over that soft and spirit-speaking face. In her, hour after hour, a fairer and fairer soul unveiled itself; a soul of quickest vision and gracefullest expression, so gay yet so enthusiastic, so blandishing yet so severe; a being all gentleness and fire; meek, timid, loving as the dove and high and noble as the eagle. To him her presence brought with it airs from heaven. A balmy rest encircled his spirit while near her; pale doubt fled away to the distance, and life bloomed up with happiness and hope. The young man seemed to awake as from a haggard dream; he had been in the garden of Eden, then, and his eyes could not discern it! But now the black walls of his prison melted away, and the captive was alive and free in the sunny spring! If he loved this benignant disenchantress? His whole heart and soul and life were hers; yet he had never thought of love; for his whole existence was but a feeling which he had not yet shaped into a thought.

But human life were another matter than it is could it grant such things continuance. Jane Montagu had an ancient maiden aunt who was her hostess and protectress, to whom she owed all and looked for all. With the eyes of fifty, one sees not as with the eyes of fifteen. What passed between the good maiden and her aunt we know not; the old lady was proud and poor; she had high hopes from her niece, and in her meagre hunger-bitten philosophy Wotton's visits had from the first been but faintly approved of.

One morning he found his fair Jane constrained and sad; she was silent, absent; she seemed to have been weeping. The aunt left the room. He pressed for explanation, first in kind solicitude, then with increasing apprehension; but none was to be had,

save only broken hints that she was grieved for
herself, for him, that she had much to suffer, that he
must cease to visit her. It was vain that the thunder-
struck Wotton demanded, 'Why? Why?' 'One
whom she entirely depended on had so ordered it,
and for herself she had nothing to do but to obey.'
She resisted all entreaty; she denied all explanation:
her words were firm and cold; only by a thrill of
anguish that once or twice quivered over her face
could a calmer man have divined that she was suffering within. Wotton's pride was stung; he rose and
held out his hand: 'Farewell, then, madam!' said
he, in a low steady voice; 'I will not——' She put
her hand in his; she looked in his face, tears started
to her eyes; but she turned away her head, hastily
pressed his hand, and, sobbing, whispered, scarcely
audibly, 'Farewell!' He approached in frenzy; his
arms were half-raised to encircle her; but starting
back she turned on him a weeping face—a face of
anger, love, and agony. She sternly motioned to him
to withdraw, and Wotton scarce knew where he was
till with mad galloping he had reached his own
solitudes, and the town, and the fair Jane, and all his
blessed dreams were far away.

This look of hers he had long time to meditate,
for it was the last. How many burning thoughts he
had to front; how many wild theories he formed of
his misfortune; how many wild projects to repair
it! But all in vain: his letters were unanswered, or

answered in cold, brief commonplaces. At last he received a pressing entreaty, or rather, a peremptory injunction, to write no more. Then hope no longer lingered; thickest night sank over his spirit, and a thousand furies were sent forth to scourge him. They were cruel days that followed. By-and-by came reports that his Jane was to be wedded—wedded to Edmund Walter, a gay young man of rank, a soldier, and, as Wotton rated him, a debauchee, but wealthy, well-allied, and influential in the county. The wedding-day, it was even stated, had been fixed. ' What have I to do with it ? ' said Wotton, as he shuddered at the thought; ' she is nought to me, I am nought to her ! '

But some secret change had occurred, and the public expectation was baulked. The marriage did not take place, no one knew why; only Walter had left the neighbourhood in indignant haste; the aunt, also, and her niece, the latter apparently in deepest sorrow, had closed their house and retired to their friends in London. The talk of gossips was loud and manifold, but no light could be elicited; a curtain of mystery still enveloped the transaction, and one spiteful hypothesis only gave place to another as spiteful and no better founded.

What effect all this produced on the solitary Wotton we need not describe at length. His heart bled inwardly; in solitude he suffered, for his pride and his affection had alike been cruelly wounded; it was long before even Bernard could penetrate into his confidence, and soothe his darkened and exasperated spirit by a touch of human sympathy.

Six months were now gone; the whole incident had removed into distance, and Wotton could now see clearly how it had been and how it was to be with him. He felt that he had loved not wisely, yet irrevocably, and in vain. A celestial vision had entranced him, and now it was all fled away, and the grim world lay round him, sicklied over by ineffectual longing. One little month so fair and heavenly; such a blissful meeting, such a stern good-night! He felt with tenfold force that all hope was lies, that man's life was but a mockery and a fever-dream. By degrees he sank into iron quietude. 'What is the world,' said he, 'but a gloomy vision as the poets have called it? and your fair landscapes, so sunshiny, so green, so far-stretching, are but cunning paintings on the walls. We are captives, but it is only for a season. Death is still our birthright; destiny itself cannot doom us not to die. Strong death, the frowning but helpful and never-failing friend! Cowards have painted him as a spectre; he is a benignant genius bearing freedom and rest to weary, heavy-laden man!'

To all this Bernard listened with regret, yet also with sympathy and firm hopes of better things. This dreary stagnancy he knew would not be final; Wotton's nature was virtuous, it would at length become believing, become active, become happy. For malignant activity it was too noble and moral, for such icy rest too passionate. Nay, even as it stood, was not a burst of fierce tenderness, or far-glancing despair every now and then breaking forth as if in spite of him?

Bernard had half-foreseen his passion for Jane Montagu, and hoped that it might lead him back to life, and in the end make two worthy and beloved beings happy. Painfully as the issue had deceived him, he did not slacken his efforts or abate his confidence. This journey he had diligently contrived and recommended, in the course of which many things, as he hoped, might occur to solace, to excite and instruct the marred and afflicted spirit of the young man, and so in the end to recal him from those regions of baleful shadows into the light of truth and living day.

CHAPTER III

WELL mounted, wrapped and equipped for travelling,
our friends were on horseback at an early hour.   The
sunbeam was still dewy and level as they reached by
a slanting path the brow of the hill-range which
bounded in the valley to the left, and Wotton looked
back for a moment on the blue streak of smoke which
was rising from his own chimney far down in the
bottom, where all that he possessed or delighted to
remember on earth lay clustered together in peaceful
brightness.   The sound of a distant steeple-clock
came faint and saddened through the sunny morning.
‘How trim the burgh stands among its woods and
meadows!’ cried Bernard, looking far across the dale ;
‘how gay its red steeples rise through the fleece of
blue, where many a thrifty mother is cooking breakfast for her loved ones!   The place is alive and astir
and full of busy mortals though you think here you
might cover it all with your hat.   It is speaking to
us, too, with its metal tongue!’

Wotton moved on, for to him it was speaking not
in pleasure but in pain.   It was the sound which had

announced to him in schoolboy years the scene of his daily martyrdom; it was the sound he had often heard beside Jane Montagu; the note of that bell was getting doleful and of evil presage to him.

'I know not how it comes,' said he, 'but to my imagination this journey of ours, simple as it is, seems strangely momentous. It is as if we were leaving our hampered but safe and hospitable ark to venture forth on a world of waters.'

'A sign that hope is not dead in you,' said Bernard, 'since you can still fear. We shall return with olive leaves, I prophesy.'

'Or at least fly to and fro upon the waters,' answered Wotton. 'Well, that is better than pining in the prison. We shall be among the mountains to-morrow,' added he, cheerily. 'Those granite peaks are shining on us as if they were made of sapphire, and near at hand they are but like other rocks. So man was made to be deceived.'

Wotton as a travelling companion, at least to Bernard, was peculiarly delightful. The excitement of a fine exercise, in which he took pleasure and excelled, seemed to shake the vapours from his spirit and awaken in it all beautiful and healthful feelings. In the glow of motion, under the thousandfold benign influences of rural nature, he could many times for a while attain to self-forgetfulness, and pour forth in free and even glad effusion the sensations of the hour. His moody cares retired to the distance and formed

as it were a ground of deepest black, on which the
bright, lovely, nay sometimes sportful imagery of his
mind looked out with double grace. With Bernard
his conversation was at all times, and especially on
such occasions, of the most pleasurable sort. There
was in them that agreement of feeling and disagree-
ment of opinion, that similarity in dissimilarity, which
is justly thought to form the great charm of conversation. Much as they disputed they never quarrelled.

The scene and the lovely weather were of a kind
to maintain the most genial humour. It was a region
as yet unvisited of mail-coaches, traversed only by the
solitary horseman, or some wayworn cadger toilsomely
collecting for city consumpt the minor produce of the
district; a region of knoll and hollow, of modest
streamlet, and lone-lying tree-shaded farm ; the mower
was stooping in the valleys, where as yet the fields were
all of the greenest; and ever, as they mounted any
height, our friends saw before them afar off the long
narrow Frith winding like silver among its craggy
headlands or gray sands; beyond which, over many
an intervening range, towered up in white light in the
extreme distance the world of mountains, with its blue
tops and shadowy chasms shutting in like a land of
romance a land of so many fair realities.

Pleasantly journeying, amid abundant talk, they
had reached before sunset the strand of the Frith ;
where, advancing to the end of one among several long

rude piers of wattle-work, fronted on the other side by several corresponding piers which extended through sand and silt and enabled the ferrymen to ply their trade at all seasons of the tide, their signal was soon answered, and two gnarled weather-beaten rowers, with a helmsman and a huge shapeless boat, had in a few minutes landed man and horse on the farther shore.   Fronting and close by stood a rather gay-looking mansion, which it seemed was an inn and bathing establishment, and where our friends proposed continuing for the night.   During their short voyage Wotton had remarked that the helmsman eyed him somewhat too curiously; he was still further struck, indeed offended, when the same personage, who appeared likewise to be an under-waiter, continued to glance at him, nay, seemed also to have awakened the curiosity of his official superior; for ever and anon as the two were covering with much bustle a frugal enough table, they kept privily casting looks on our hero, who at length determined to end their survey.

'My friends,' said he, 'is there anything especially remarkable in my appearance that you so gaze at me? Have I ever had the honour of your acquaintance for good or bad; or are you apprehensive I may do your establishment here an ill turn?'

'Thousand pardons!' said they of the apron, ducking very low. 'It is nothing, sir,' added the head waiter; 'but you are so *very* like a picture we have here.   You will excuse our freedom, sir!'

' Picture ? ' said Wotton.

' A gold locket with a miniature : an honest countryman found it among the mountains ; thought some of
our guests in their pleasure excursions might have lost
it, so he brought it hither, but no one claimed it ; and
the thing is still here waiting for an owner.   You shall
see it, sir.'

The man left the apartment, and soon returned
with the trinket in question.   It was a pretty enough
piece of work ; a little oval casket of chased gold or
filigrane, on a pink ribbon, which seemed once to have
suspended it over some fair bosom.   It might have
been dropped in riding.   But what most surprised
our friends was, on opening the lid—for the lock had
been broken—to discover in the tiny picture what
really seemed a decided resemblance to Wotton.   As
a painting it was of little value ; neither the individual
tints nor the general finish, though apparently great
pains had been taken with it, betrayed the hand of an
artist ; yet the cast of our hero's features did appear
to have been aimed at, nay, in some points accurately
seized ; the dark gray eyes under their deep decided
brows and high arched forehead, the well-proportioned
nose, the somewhat too shallow chin, the clustery dark
auburn hair, were all more or less correctly Wotton's ;
and about the lips there played a mingled half-painful,
half-lofty expression of scorn, which in some passionate
moments was still more peculiarly his.

Our travellers, it may well be supposed, scarce

knew what to make of this adventure. They examined and re-examined the locket, they questioned and re-questioned the waiter, and all to little purpose. Except that it had been found about six weeks ago, on a mountain road at some fifteen miles distance, he could tell them nothing. Wotton, in particular, with the vague imagination, which at such an age a smaller circumstance will excite, could not help feeling an unusual interest in the matter, and determined if possible at no rate to part with this copy of himself, which chance had so strangely sent him.

'This trinket is not mine,' said he to the waiter, 'yet I question whether you are like to meet with any one who has a better right to it. I will leave you my address, and money to the full amount for the finder; if the picture be ever claimed, you will know where it is to be had; for in the meantime you must let me take it with me.'

The man made little objection, and in return for the deposit of a few guineas the toy was formally made over. For the rest of the evening it formed between our friends the chief topic of conversation, which indeed on Wotton's part was kept up with no great spirit. His mind was hunting over all its domains for some trace of a solution to the mystery, or building on this slender basis all manner of castles in the air. He could not recollect that he had ever sat to any painter, and who was this that had so daintily limned im in his absence? One sweetest possibility he dared not openly surmise to Bernard, scarcely even to himself; yet a light dawned upon him as in the dusky remoteness, and the figure of Jane Montagu came forth in new beauty saddened over by inexpressible longing.

At an early hour he retired to his apartment. His window fronted the sea, over which the moon was peering from her couch of clouds in the far east, while the tide, swelling forth as if to meet her into every creek, was murmuring hoarse and slow through the mellow night. Soft vapours shrouded the other shore; the sea was shipless, for the fisher barks were at anchor in their coves; the moonbeam flickered on a solitude of waters. The thought of life and its mysteries and vicissitudes came over Wotton's troublous but solemn mind. He saw the images of Time as if flitting so fair and transient through the night of Eternity; yet kind scenes crowded round him, and the earth with its stinted joys and man with his marred destiny, seemed but the lovelier that they were weak and without continuance. The picture was in his hand, was already suspended round his neck. 'Why dost thou remember *her*,' said he to himself, ' when she is for ever hid from thy eyes? She came like a heavenly messenger preaching peace to my spirit, and peace was not appointed me. O Jane Montagu! why was the tinsel of the world precious to thee, and its fine gold of no price? Surely, surely

thy heart said nay, nay at that cruel hour ; we might
have been so blessed, so rich, so passing rich !—I will
see her, at least,' cried he, rising ; 'something whispers that she thinks of me, that she loves me ; and
without her will no power on earth or under it shall
part us.'

CHAPTER IV

It was in a pleasurable mood, and with hopes vaguely excited, that our friends entered the mountain region. Mountains were not new to either of them; but rarely are mountains seen in such combined majesty and grace as here. The rocks are of that sort called primitive by the mineralogist, which always arrange themselves in masses of a rugged and gigantic character; but their ruggedness is softened by a singular elegance of form; in a climate favourable to vegetation, the gray shapeless cliff itself covered with lichens rises through a garment of foliage or verdure, and white bright tufted cottages are clustered round the base of the everlasting granite. In fine vicissitude beauty alternates with grandeur: you ride through stony hollows, along strait passes traversed by torrents, and overhung by high walls of rock; now winding amid broken shaggy chasms, and huge fragments; now suddenly emerging into some emerald valley, where the streamlet collects into a lake, and man has found a fair dwelling, and it seems as if peace had established herself in the stony bosom of strength.

All this is not without effect on thinking minds; in Wotton it co-operated with much that he already felt; for the incident of last night, though as if by tacit consent it was not spoken of, still lurked in his thoughts, predisposing him to vague wondrous imaginations and all high feeling. Bernard was full of eloquence; praising the beauty of nature, the benignity of Providence, and the happiness of men; Wotton the while answered him, as a stout sceptic, indeed, but as a sceptic that grieved, not rejoiced to be so; and thus for both parties the conversation was entertaining, for with both such topics, and so treated, were chief favourites. They were in the bottom of a rude solitary glen, engaged so pleasantly, when the tramp of a horse was heard on the left, and presently a rider was observed issuing by a steep side path from a sort of break in the hills, and seemed as if advancing like themselves, though from a different point, toward the head of the valley.

The horseman, in fact, soon joined them, and his courteous salutation being as courteously returned, the commonplace introductions to talk ere long gave place to more interesting topics, and a pleasant feeling of companionship diffused itself over the party. The stranger seemed a man of some fifty years; of a staid, determinate, yet, at the same time, winning manner; at once polished, intelligent, and sociably frank: to look at him and listen to him you felt inclined to assign the man a higher rank than his equipment could have challenged, for he was well and sufficiently rather than splendidly mounted and dressed; and it was only in his clear kind eyes and strong yet calm and gentle look that you read a title to superior deference. Bernard was celebrating the beauty of the scenery; the stranger spoke of it as one familiar with the subject and the district, yet briefly and with judgment rather than enthusiasm.

'A passing traveller,' said Bernard, 'might envy your mountaineers their constant abode among so many noble influences, did not one remember the effect of habit, how it deadens all our impressions both of beauty and deformity.'

'What is grander than the sun?' added Wotton; 'yet we all see it daily, and few think of the heavenly lamp save as a ripener of corn. The moon, too, and the stars are measured in their courses: but astronomy is praised or tolerated because it helps us in navigating ships, and the divine horologe is rated as a supplement or substitute for Harrison's timekeeper.'

The stranger glanced slightly at his vehement companion, yet without expression of displeasure, then answered: 'True goodness of all sorts must have its life and root within ourselves; it depends on external appliances far less than we suppose. The great point is to have a healthy mind, or, if I may say so, *a right power of assimilation*, for the elements of beauty and truth lie round us on all sides, even in the meanest objects, if we could but extract them. Claude Lorraine,

the painter of so many heavenly landscapes, was bred
a colour-grinder; the noble-minded Epictetus was a
slave. As to the effect of natural scenery,' continued
he, 'I think with you that it is trifling. The moun-
taineer has a peculiar way of life, and differs from the
inhabitant of the plains because of it; differs by
reason of the things he has to do, but scarcely of the
things he has to see. No nation has produced fewer
artists than the Swiss.'

'Indeed,' said Wotton, ' this effect, whatever be its
value, lies in a great measure open to all men, dwell
where they may. The bleakest moor I can stand on
is visited by the eye of Heaven, and bears on its bosom
the traces of innumerable years. The pebble I strike
from my path was severed from distant mountains in
the primeval convulsions of Nature, and has rolled for
ages in the depth of waters. This streamlet, nameless
except to a few herdsmen, was meted out by the hand
of the Omnipotent as well as the great ocean; it is
ancient as the Flood, and was murmuring through its
solitude when the ships of Æneas ascended the Tiber,
or Siloa's Brook was flowing fast by the Oracle of
God.'

'Yet surely,' said Bernard, ' there are degrees of
beauty in external things; beauty more direct, and I
will add more pure, than those universal attributes
which my friend here paints so vividly. Is it not the
essence of all true beauty, of all true greatness, that it
makes us forget our own little individuality? That

we mingle for the moment as if in boundless glory, feeling not that we are thus and thus, but only that *we are*; remembering nothing of ourselves, least of all that we are weak and needy and of short duration?'

'Surely,' answered Wotton. 'And if mountain or any other scenery could do this,' added he, pensively, ' it were well worth travelling to see.'

'One thing, at least, you have many times occasion to observe: no topic sooner or more painfully wearies us than description of scenery. Your view-hunter is the most irksome of all articulate-speaking men '

'A proof of the little interest we really take in views,' answered the stranger.

'Besides,' added Wotton, 'if long-winded he is generally in part insincere: there is cant in his raptures; he is treating us not with his subject, but with his own false vainglorious self. At best it is sensations not thoughts that he is describing; and no sensations, except our own, can long fix our attention.'

'Gentlemen,' said the stranger, with a kind smile, 'by your accent I take you to be Scotch, yet your philosophy is not what we call Scotch.'

'Is Scotch philosophy in very bad odour here?' inquired Wotton, somewhat piqued for the honour of his country.

'In bad odour I should not say,' replied the stranger, 'for our little commonwealth is a willing member of the great one; and everywhere, disguise it as we may—in the senate, the press, the pulpit, the parlour, and the market—David Hume is ruler of the world.'

'The pulpit?' cried Bernard.

'I have said,' answered the stranger; 'but it is a subject too long for present discussion. On the whole, I honour the Scotch, and quarrel not with their philosophy. But see, gentlemen,' continued he, 'our roads will soon part; at the corner of that grey cliff I turn to another valley. You are still far from your inn : if a stranger's invitation might prevail, you shall go with me and rest you in the House of the Wold. The path is rough, but the place is tolerable, and good welcome will not fail you. Come with me,' added he, 'I will show you wonders.'

To Bernard, fond of adventures and hopeful of all dubious issues, these were no unpleasant words. He looked wistfully on Wotton, who, rating the speech as little more than a flourish of rhetoric, had no thought of accepting the proposal, no thought that their acceptance of it was desired. But as the stranger pulled up at the parting of the roads, and with the kindest frankness in words and looks that could not be mistaken, assured them that their presence would cause not trouble but much enjoyment; and withal, smiling on Wotton, with whom, as he perceived, lay the hindrance, told him that it were hard to part till they had talked of Scotch philosophy, the latter yielded; and so, after some complimentary formalities, our travellers turned their horses to the right along with him. Their road, or rather track, lay up a winding rocky glen and many times crossed the brook which was gurgling along its bottom to join the larger stream of the main valley.

Ascending the pass, after half an hour's incommodious riding, they found the brook, no longer fed by subsidiary springs, diminished to a rill, which also in a little while ending in a boggy delta disappeared from their side. A rough causeway, which seemed to be the work of man, conducted them across the swamp, still overshaded by craggy heights; till as they proceeded, the bog again drew to a point, and another thread of water began to indent with its tiny channel the bottom of another glen, descending in the opposite direction, but narrow, deep, winding and rocky as the former.

'*Facilis descensus Averni*,' said the guide, smiling: 'the worst of our road is ·past.' Ere long, in fact, the walls of their chasm began to widen and soften; copse wood alternating with verdure mantled the steep, a shepherd's hut rose cheerful and secure in the hollow, and at the next turn our travellers emerged into a scene which no stranger approaching it by such a road could view without astonishment.

'It is the Happy Valley of Prince Rasselas!' cried Wotton.

'It is not Avernus, but Elysium!' cried Bernard.

'It is the House of the Wold,' said the guide, ' where refreshment and rest are waiting us.'

A circular valley of some furlongs in diameter lay round them like a huge amphitheatre, broken only in its contour by the entrance of two oblique chasms like the one they had left; on its level bottom of the purest green stood a large stately mansion, which seemed to be of granite, for in the sunbeams it glittered from amid its high clusters of foliage like a palace of El Dorado, overlaid with precious metal. Behind it, and on both sides at a distance, the hills sloped up in gentle wavy curvature; the sward was of the greenest, embossed here and there with low dark-brown frets of crag, or spotted by some spreading solitary tree and its shadow; in front at a corner of the valley lay the small lake, hemmed in by woody cliffs: and beyond and around all this, ridge after ridge, higher and bluer and wilder as they receded, were seen the peaks of the mountains watching in severe loveliness, like everlasting guardians, over a scene so calm.

Servants hastened out on the lawn to meet our travellers, who a few minutes after found themselves in a large parlour before the lady of the mansion.

'Dorothy, my love,' said the host, 'I have made a capture in the east to-day. Here are two strangers, whom we must change into friends.'

'The beginning of friendship is good offices,' replied she, with graceful courtesy: 'you must be faint and wearied, as pilgrims are wont; and dinner will not come for an hour.'

For the present our friends declined any refreshment; and after some little conversation, which could
not but be general and formal, they gladly retired to
their chambers, under pretext of dressing, a process
which, with the scanty wardrobe of travellers, was soon
enough performed, but chiefly that they might have
time to consider their adventure, and collect their
thoughts, which this rencounter and its unexpected
issue had somewhat put to rout.

The pealing of a gong in a little while summoned
our friends to the drawing-room, from which in a
few minutes a party of some twelve persons moved
down in order to a table tastefully and plenteously
furnished. Sprightly conversation enlivened the re-
past: the company seemed singularly varied for its
number; each an original in his class; men, as it
appeared generally, of intellect and education, rather
than of special rank or breeding; yet all animated by
good humour, and insensibly participating in the
gentle influences of their hosts, whose manners indicated a refinement in every point corresponding
with the highest station. Their fair mistress—for,
though elderly, she still bore traces of a singular
beauty, a woman of the stateliest yet humanest aspect—
presided over them with the graceful dignity of a queen.
To Wotton the sound of her voice was melody; the few
words she spoke were of the most polished, yet expressive sort; her little sentences, so meekly and oppor-
tunely uttered, stood before the mind like living

images, full of loveliness and persuasion. Fain would the poor youth have spoken to her, fain have replied to her courtesies with a copiousness proportioned to his feeling of them : but his heart was pressed together by so singular an environment ; he felt as if he had no right to be so splendidly welcomed, as if it were by mistake that he was here.

Other ladies also there were ; young, beautiful, and blooming ; visitors, as it might be gathered, from no distant neighbourhood ; and not without fit gallants proud to do them service : but these fair ones skirmished only in buckram or from afar ; what manner of persons they might be you did not learn ; and Virgil could only have described them as *pulchram Annam, pulchramque Elisam.* With one of these Bernard entered on a sort of distant flirtation to Wotton's astonishment, who could not comprehend such audacity, or help half-envying the success it appeared to meet with. Though he had loved, he was an utter novice in affairs of love : vain had it been for Chesterfield to tell him and assure him that every woman wishes us to love her ; in his tenfold diffidence and disbelief it never struck him that his approbation could be of worth to any one. He was even threatening to become absent, for sad thoughts were gathering on him : these beauties were blond ; but dark locks clustered round another face far nobler ; and black eyes had told him such things ! Lies they were—perhaps not altogether lies ! yet lovelier than any truth: it was pain to remember them, but to forget them was like a living death.

The cloth being removed, conversation, which had hitherto turned chiefly on the various personal adventures of the morning, began to take a wider range. Public occurrences and persons, glanced at rather than discussed, led the way to topics more strictly intellectual; to abstract views of men and things set forth in criticisms, expositions, comparisons, and the other ever-varying modes by which in social hours our individual *Philosophy of Life* may be so delightfully communicated and apprehended.

To Wotton, much, indeed passionately as he liked such conversation, the tone of the present company was, nevertheless, in some degree alien: the feeling it awoke in him was one of surprise and unrest as well as pleasure. The Attic salt, that air of candour and goodness, those striking glimpses of man's nature and its sufferings and wants, had his sympathy and hearty approval; but he sought in vain for the basis on which these people had built their opinions; their whole form of being seemed different from his. Men equally informed and cultivated he had sometimes met with, but seldom or never had he seen such culture of the intellect combined with such moral results, nay, as it appeared, conducing to them. Here were fearless and free thinkers, yet they seemed not unbelievers, but, on the contrary, possessed with charity and zeal: their affirmations and denials would not harmonise in his conception. It is not always that originality, even when true and estimable, pleases us at first; if it go beyond our sphere it is much more likely to unsettle and provoke us. Of much that he heard, Wotton knew not what to determine; it was a strain of thought which suited not with any of his categories, either of truth or error; in which, therefore, he could only mingle stintedly and timidly, for he felt as if hovering in the vortex of some strange element, in which as yet he had not learned to move.

What, for instance, could he make of such tenets as this, in which, however, several sober-minded persons, their host among the number, seemed partially to acquiesce?

'Demonstrability is not the test of truth; logic is for what the understanding *sees*; what is truest we do not *see*, for it has no form, being infinite; the highest truth cannot be expressed in words.'

'How is it expressed, then?' cried the brisk voice of Henry Williams; a speaker whom, alone of them all, Wotton had from the first understood.

'How is it expressed, then?' cried Wotton and several more, in tones partly of inquiry, partly of cavil.

'It is expressed oftener than it is listened to or comprehended,' said the other in reply; 'for our ears are heavy, and the divine harmony of the spheres is drowned in the gross, harsh dissonance of earthly things. Expressed? In the expiring smile of martyrs;

in the actions of a Howard and a Cato; in the still
existence of all good men. Echoes of it come to us
from the song of the poet; the sky with its azure and its
rainbow and its beautiful vicissitudes of morn and
even shows it forth; the earth also with her floods
and everlasting Alps, the ocean in its tempests and its
calms. It is an open secret, but we have no clear
vision for it: woe to us if we have no vision at all!'

'Kantism! Kantism!' cried several voices. 'German mysticism! mere human faculties cannot take it
in.' Wotton looked at this singular exotic speaker:
he was a man of sixty, yet still hale and fresh; thin
grey hair lay over a head of striking proportions;
the face was furrowed and overlined with traces of
long, deep, and subtle thought, of feeling rather fine
than passionate, and this of pain as much as pleasure;
there was especially a look of strange anxiety in the
eyes; a look at once of vehemence and fear: indeed
the whole man seemed labouring with some idea, which
he longed vainly to impart, for which, while he sought
earnestly some outward form, he knew beforehand
that none would be found.

'My good Dalbrook,' said Maurice (such was the
landlord's name), 'we are hard bested with these gain-
sayers. Do you mean that the sense of poetic beauty
and moral obligation is the highest truth, and to be
apprehended not by conviction but by persuasion, not
by culture of the head but of the heart?'

'There is a truth of the market place,' continued

Dalbrook, attending little to the question; 'a truth of the laboratory, and a truth of the soul. The first two are of things seen and their relations, they are practical or physically scientific, and belong to the understanding; the last is of things unseen and belongs exclusively to the reason.'

'Reason, understanding? Things unseen?' cried the sceptics.

'Laplace's *Mécanique Celeste*, Adam Smith's *Wealth of Nations* are full of understanding,' continued Dalbrook, 'but of reason there is hardly any trace in either. Alas! the humblest peasant reverently offering up his poor prayer to God, and in trembling faith drawing near to Him as to his Father; thus recognising, worshipping, loving, under emblems however rude, the invisible and eternal, has many times more reason, mixed as it is with weakness and delusion, than vainglorious doctors for whose philosophy there is nothing too hard.'

'Then you think with Hutcheson that there *is* a moral faculty, and that taste and virtue are *not* the result of association?' cried a young Oxonian, with a look of glad earnestness.

Dalbrook looked down, arching his eyebrows very high. 'Faculty! Association!' repeated he, with an unspeakable accent. The Oxonian fell back.

Bernard had listened with no ordinary interest. 'Then pray, sir,' said he, 'is not this understanding like what Bacon calls his *lumen siccum*; and reason

like his *lumen madidum*, or intellect steeped in affection?' The old man looked up with an air of partial
contentment, but slightly shook his head. 'Understanding perceives and judges of images and measures
of things,' said he; 'reason perceives and judges of
what has no measure or image. The latter only is
unchangeable and everlasting in its decisions, the
results of the former change from age to age; it is
for these that men persecute and destroy each other;
yet these comparatively are not worth the name of
truth, they are not truth, but only ephemeral gar-
ments of truth.'

'Then what in heaven's name *is* truth?' said an
atrabiliar gentleman, whom, in spite of his politeness,
the whole discussion was too evidently wearying.

'Truth!' interrupted Williams in his gay voice.
'Horne Tooke's is the best of all definitions: *truth* is
simply *troweth*, or that which is *trowed*, or believed.
In this way we have many *troweths*, and my troweth
is very different from thy troweth, and the only rule
is that the one should let the other live in peace.'

'It is not essential to being happy,' observed
our Oxonian from beside the fair Anna: 'the way
to happiness is plain before all men if they like to
follow it.'

'Ay!' said the atrabiliar, who seemed to be his
uncle or some relation.

'But they miss it,' continued the other, 'by
cowardice and indecision.' The clear eyes and buxom

sceptic aspect of this youth seemed to vex his relation.

'My good sir,' replied he, 'we have all had pretty
views of it ourselves in our time. Fair and softly!
There is an age when to every man life appears the
simplest matter. How very manageable! Every
why has its wherefore; this leads to that, and the
whole problem of existence is easy and certain as a
question in the *Rule of Three*. *Multiply the second and
third terms together, and divide the product by the first,
and the quotient will be the answer!* Trust me, friend,
before you come to my time of day, you will find there
is a devilish fraction always over, do what you will;
and if you try to reduce it, it goes into a repeating
decimal and leads you the Lord knows whither. Life
happy!' continued he: 'what thinking mortal ever
found it so? Which of us might not say with Swift:
I have had hours that might be tolerated, but none
which could be enjoyed, and my life in general has
been misery? Show me a man that is happy, and I
will show thee a man that has—an excellent nervous
system. Williams, when you write again, it should
be an essay on the *Comforts of Stupidity*.'

'I have sometimes taken that matter into consideration,' answered Williams, 'but I fear I should
vote rather against you. Much, much depends on the
nerves; but something also on prudence and wise
management. On the whole, too, I think Nature is
kind to us, and it is a blessing to exist: there is more
of happiness in life than of misery.'

'To me the contrary is clear as noon,' said the other; 'and have not all countries and stations recorded opinions in my favour? "Man that is born of a woman is of few days, and full of evil," says the Patriarch. "He is born to trouble, as the sparks fly upwards." "It is better to sit than to walk," say the Indians; "it is better to sleep than to wake; but to be dead is best of all."—When an infant was presented for consecration to the Mexican priest, his address to it was, "Remember that thou art come into the world to suffer; suffer then, and be silent!" What more can any of us say?'

'But there is a fairer land on the other side of the dark waters,' said Dorothy, meekly, 'where pain and sin are banished. This is but a winter day's journey to a home that is glorious and enduring.'

'Alas!' ejaculated he, lifting up his fingers from the bottom of his glass, then slowly restoring them, without farther speech, then looking up with a smile. On the whole, this gentleman had no look of death, but rather of jollity and social well-being. At dinner he had done fair duty, his wine he was sipping, moderately, and not without relish, while he talked in this lugubrious dialect, and to what spleen soever might be lurking about his heart, these speeches were evidently giving comfortable vent.

'Surely, sir,' said Wotton, who, in spite of similarity in thought, sympathised but ill with him, 'if your opinion is correct, there ought to be a change in our social arrangements. Nay, what use is there for social arrangements, or aught else in this life, since life itself is an evil, and there is nothing beyond it? Let us pay off our clergy, pull down our parish churches, and on the ruins of each establish simply a bag of arsenic for the good of the parish. It might be kept up by contribution, and would save us tithes. We could have it suspended on a pole, with this super-scription, "Ho, every one!"'

The atrabiliar himself was forced to join in the laugh, which rose on all sides at his expense. 'A hit! A palpable hit!' cried Williams. 'The arsenic-bag, the arsenic-bag for ever! The death of all blue-devil philosophy!' cried the others.—'Young gentle-man, I must owe you a thrust,' said the atrabiliar, laughing; 'for the present, your arsenic is too strong.'

'Nay, cousin, you deserve it,' said Maurice, 'for the cause is radically bad; even if true, you were wrong to urge it. Does not the adage say, "Speak no evil of your own"? This life, be it what it may, is all that has been given us, to mend or to mar, to hold and to have for better for worse; and not by reviling and contemning what is bad in it, but by arranging, furthering, augmenting what is good shall we ever turn it to account. Fie! would you list under no better flag than the devil's? Your arch fault-finder is the devil; it is no one's trade but his to dwell on negations, to impugn the darkness and

overlook the light; and out of the glorious All itself to
educe not beauty but deformity.'

'I believe,' added Williams, 'there is generally
in this very trite topic one of those ambiguities in
language, which logicians are so frequently beset
with, and this chiefly occasions the dilemma. When
we speak of happiness and being happy, we half
unconsciously mean some extra enjoyment; if I may
say so, pleasure; some series of agreeable sensation,
superadded to the ordinary pleasure of existing, which
really, if free from positive pain, is all we have right
to pretend to. In place of reckoning ourselves happy
when we are not miserable, we reckon ourselves miserable when not happy. A proceeding, if you think of
it, quite against rule! What claim have I to be
in raptures? None in the world, except that I have
taken such a whim into my own wise head; and
having got so much, I feel as if I could never get my
due. It is with man and enjoyment as with the
miser and money: the more he gets the more he
wants.'

'It is our vanity,' said Maurice; 'our boundless
self-conceit. Make us emperors of the earth, nay, of
the universe, we should soon feel as if we deserved it,
and much more.'

'Poor fellows!' added Williams. 'And so when
the young gentleman goes forth into the world, and
finds that it is really and truly *not* made of wax, but
of stone and metal, and *will* keep its own shape, let

the young gentleman fume as he likes; bless us, what a storm he gets into! What terrible elegies, and pindarics, and *Childe Harolds*, and *Sorrows of Werther*! Oh, devil take it, Providence is in the wrong; has used him (sweet, meritorious gentleman) unjustly. He will bring his action of damages against Providence! Trust me, a hopeful lawsuit!'

'We are too apt to forget,' said Bernard, 'that for creatures formed as we are, all permanent enjoyment must be active not passive. Without evil there were for us no good; our condition is militant; it is only in labour that we rest. Our highest, our only real blessedness, lies in this very warfare with evil. Let us conquer it or not; truly an abundant blessedness, but which, as you remark, we seldom take into account in our estimates of life. Weighing the attainment, we find it light, and the search must go for nothing. We would have a paradise of spontaneous pleasures; forgetting that in such a paradise the dullest spirit would and must grow wearied, nay, in time unspeakably wretched.'

'Yes,' added Maurice, 'the lubberland of the old poets in an impossible chimera; impossible, even in the region of chimeras.'

'Yet it is this very lubberland,' said Bernard, 'which so many pilgrims are seeking, and in despair because they cannot find.'

'Most know not what they are seeking,' said Wotton, 'but wander with the crowd, picking sloes

and brambles by the way; others run hither and
thither, now after this gewgaw, now after that.
Pilgrims also we have, walking apart, with their
faces set on distant glorious landmarks; but your
sloe-and-bramble men are the happiest.'

'In spite of your arsenic,' said the atrabiliar, 'I
half suspect you agree with me; in a private corner
you would say, there is little happiness in the world,
and that little chiefly for fools.'

'Happiness is not man's object,' said Dalbrook,
awakening from a muse. 'He does not find it, he
ought not to seek it, neither is it his highest wish.'

'Wish?' cried Williams. 'Nay, Dalbrook, of all
your paradoxes this is the most paradoxical.'

'Pleasure and pain,' continued the other, little
moved, 'are interwoven with every element of life:
to love the one and hate the other is the essence of
all sentient natures, nor for a nature merely sentient
is there any higher law. But was man made only
to feel? Is there nothing better in him than a
passive system of susceptibilities? Can he move
only like a finer piece of clockwork when you touch
this spring and stop when you touch that other? Is
his spirit a quality, not a substance? has it no power,
no will? And is his freedom, that celestial patent of
nobility, the crowning gift of God, to mark him for
the sovereign of this lower world, a mockery and a
lie? O philosophy! O heaven-descended wisdom!
what hast thou been made to teach! In thy name

cozeners have beguiled us of our birthright and sold us into bondage, and we are no longer servants of goodness, but slaves of self. My friends!' continued the old man, with a singular half-natural, half-preaching tone, 'I say to you this is false and poisonous doctrine, and the heart of every good man feels that it is false, and well for him if he pluck it out and cast it away for ever! If not, farewell to all religion, all true virtue, all true feeling of the beautiful and good, all dignity of life, all grandeur beyond it! Nature, indeed, is kind, and from under the basest philosophy some gleams of natural goodness will break forth; nay, thank heaven, righteousness and mercy are everlasting inmates of man's spirit, over-cloud them as we may; but all that any creed can do to banish them, this does.'

'By day and night!' cried Williams. 'This is wondrous strange. Must a man become vicious because he wishes to be happy? Because he wishes to be happy? no; but because he wishes nothing more, yes, doubtless. What is virtue? tell me. A task to be performed for hire? This is not virtue, but profit and loss. If ye do these things that good may come, what reward have ye? Do not even the Pharisees the same?'

'But is not Heaven promised to the Christian as a recompense? Of Heaven and the Christian we might have much to say, but this is not the time for it. One thing I am sure of: no Christian man was ever a Christian because he hoped for Heaven, or would cease to be so, though that hope were taken from him. Nay, hear me: true religion is grounded not on expectation, but on vision; not on paltry hopes of pleasure, satisfaction, happiness, whatever you may name it, but on all-pervading, soul-subduing, infinite love of goodness. Self is self, whether its calculations end with the passing day, or stretch to the limits of eternity.'

'Wire-drawing,' murmured the atrabiliar. 'Metaphysical quibbles,' said he.

'I am afraid,' said Williams, 'if you push matters so far, there are few of us will stand your scrutiny. To say nothing of Utilitarians, Epicureans, and other tribes of the avowed alien; it seems to me that many an orthodox devout person, if tried by this electrometer, might find himself in a shockingly negative state. Self-seeking, if you so understand it, is certainly the staple of human principle; for my share, I will confess, I find it difficult to see how any living creature *can* act on any other. If you told me, "This is and will be pleasant, that is and will be painful," should I not, must I not, reject the latter and cling to the former?' ·

'But if I told you, "The pleasant is and will be vicious, the painful is and will be virtuous"?' said Maurice, hastening to assist Dalbrook, who seemed to be ill at ease in argument.

''Tis an impossible case,' said the other. 'Admit

it for a moment; would you feel no twinge, no compunctious visiting? Nay, if I offered that you should to all eternity be filled and satisfied with pleasure, on condition that you became a villain and a fool, supposing even that I took your conscience from you, and no trace of repentance or remembrance were ever to afflict you again, would you strike the bargain without scruple? Would you plunge into the scene as into your native element? Would you hasten to it as to the bosom of a mother? Would there be no whisper of gainsaying?'

'Perhaps some whisper; but——'

'That little whisper saves us!' cried Maurice.

'It was the voice of your better genius!' cried Dalbrook.

'Perhaps only of my vanity,' said Williams. 'I might not like to be degraded.'

'The voice at least of something which was not love of pleasure; something which the philosopher and I reckon higher, and which you yourself must admit to be different,' said Maurice.

'O good Heavens!' cried Dalbrook. '*Quousque venimus?* Does it require proof that there is something better in man than self-interest, however prudent and clear-sighted; that the divine law of virtue is not a drudge's bargain, and her beauty and omnipotent majesty an " association," a shadow, the fable of a nurse? O Prodicus! Was thy " Choice of Hercules " written to shame us; that after twenty centuries of "perfectibility" are here still arguing? Do you know, sirs,' added he, in a lower tone, 'this doctrine is the curse of Europe in our generation; the bane of all true greatness; the root of sensuality, cruelty, and Atheism? It was the creed of Rome under Nero and Caligula, when the human race seemed lost. Lost, thank God, it was not, and will not be.'

'But on what motive *do* we act then, or *can* we act virtuously?' said the atrabiliar, with impatience.

'Possibly on no *motive* at all, in that sense of the word motive,' answered Dalbrook. 'One of the wisest men now living has told us, as applied to art, "Of what is wrong we are always conscious; of what is right, never." The virtue we are conscious of is no right virtue. But, come,' added he, 'Williams is smiling incredulous, Frank is suspending me *naso adunco*, our young friends are wearied. I move that we exchange our wine for coffee, and the thorns of philosophy for the roses of beauty.'

'One of the wisest things you have said,' cried Williams. 'Will you lead the way?'

CHAPTER V

Before parting for the night it had been settled that
our travellers were not to depart the next day, or the
next; an arrangement to which, entreated as they
were by such friendly hosts, and tempted by so many
fair enticements, they had consented without difficulty.
Bernard in particular was charmed with the valley
and its inmates, and eager to penetrate still farther
into the secrets and affections of so singular and gifted
a household; of whom, as was his way, he felt ready
to believe all good. Wotton, again, with less hope
of the adventure, had perhaps still deeper curiosity
respecting it. On retiring to his room he could not
but wonder in contrasting his present mood with the
mood of yesternight. An unusual, almost painful,
excitement had stirred up many latent energies,
crowds of confused images and all manner of obscure
anticipations and ideas were whirling through his
mind, the very basis of which had been assailed and
shaken; while the gorgeous scenery, as of a new
world of thought which he had only beheld in brief
dreams, seemed now to advance before him in living
reality. The figures of the past, the present, and

future were tumultuously mingled in his head till sleep sank over him like an ambrosial cloud, and hid him within dreamy curtains from his cares.

Next morning he was on the hills with Williams. The rosy precincts of the House in the Wold were out of sight, and the two were pretending to botanise. We say pretending, for neither of them was intent on the matter; to Wotton, at least, the science of botany was uninteresting, indeed, unknown, or known only as a tedious beadroll of names. Williams, however, was a mineralogist also, and a pleasant, lively man.

'The mountain air is pure,' said he, 'and the brown hill-tops in their solitude are a pleasure to look on. We shall go by cliff and tarn, and "interrogate Nature" as well as any of them. Oh,' continued he, 'does it not do your heart good to think of Nature being interrogated? To see some innocent little whipster, with a couple of crucibles, and pith-balls, and other like small gear, setting forth in such gaiety of spirit to cross-question Nature? By heaven! I think Nature must be the queen of dolts if she don't bamboozle him!'

'The Book of Nature,' said Wotton, 'is written in such strange intertwisted characters, that you may spell from among them a few words in *any* alphabet, but to read the whole is for omniscience alone.'

'So each walks by his own hornbook,' said the other; 'and whatever contradicts the hornbook is no letter but a flourish. *As the fool thinks, the bell clinks,* our adage says; and so it is here as well as elsewhere.'

However, it was not to interrogate Nature that Wotton chiefly wanted; but, rather, to interrogate his new acquaintance on matters nearer home.

'I may confess to you,' said he, 'I am in no scientific mood at present. The sudden change of my scene confuses so young a traveller; indeed, this House of the Wold is still a riddle to me; and of much that I saw and heard last night, I knew not and yet know not what to make. Will you give me a little light, for I am wandering in dark labyrinths? Among all our philosophers there was none whom I so well understood and sympathised with as yourself. Can you explain to me what manner of persons I am got among, that so kindly welcome me, and instruct me in such wondrous doctrine?'

'Willingly,' cried his companion, 'so far as may be; but I myself am only a purblind guide, so have a care that we do not both fall into the ditch. You say truly, this House in the Wold is a riddle; we are altogether a surprising household, varying from week to week as visitors arrive and go, yet still differing from all other earthly households. Come when you will, you shall find a circle of originals assembled here; the strangest mortals with the strangest purposes, attracted as by magnetic virtue to the place; in figuration still you might think

Proteus was returned to the world, and had driven
all his flock to visit the lofty mountains, as in the
era of Deucalion. Artists, poets, sciolists, sages,
men of science, men of letters, politicians, states-
men, pedagogues, all find place; one only condition
is required, so far as I can see: that the man be
something, and this something with a certain honesty
of mind; for knaves and scoundrels of the most
amusing cast I have known ere now packed off
decisively enough.

'But to particulars! And first o' the first. Our
noble hosts are persons whom, however we may wonder
at, no one that knows them can speak of without reverence. Maurice Herbert is by possession and descent
the sovereign of this quarter of the mountains; a man
naturally of talent, generosity, and resolution, whom
a life of various activity, not unmixed with suffering,
has moulded into a character of singular composure
and humanity. You will find him well and universally
informed; polished by intercourse with court and
camp; for he has seen the world under both these
aspects; indeed, his natural endowments and connections seemed to appoint him as if from birth for
public life; but his philosophic tastes, joined to a
certain almost haughty inflexibility of spirit, and
also, I believe, to some cruel domestic afflictions,
soon drove him back into retirement. His lady and
he have been wedded some twenty years, most part
of which they have passed in this valley. They have

no children; at least they are now childless; though thereby hangs some secret, for a tale goes of one child having been mysteriously stolen from them while abroad; but on this subject you shall never hear them speak, nor is it safe to question them. For the present they may be said to live, or, at least, to endeavour to live, in the element of intellect and well-doing; their hospitable house is open to all good men; persons of culture, and still more of any worthy purpose or decided capacity, they study to attract and forward by all kind appliances, of which, with such ample means, there are many in their power. With the neighbouring gentry, all this passes for quixotic or even hypocritical; nor will I deny, such is the imperfection of human things, that a certain spicing of vainglory mingles with so much benevolence; but who would quarrel with goodness because it is not perfection? If Maurice Herbert cannot claim the praise of charity and active public spirit, there are few men in England who will deserve it. Far and wide he goes and sends and gives in furtherance of all improvement and useful enterprise; making this, indeed, his occupation, the chosen business of his life. To-day, for instance, he is out with your friend Bernard; if I mistook not, there was something in the wind. It is true, there can no Utopia be realised on earth, and many a time the pure element in which a man like Maurice moves and works will be polluted by baser admixtures; but for constancy of generous endeavour, nay, I may add, for real importance of result, his manner of existence is to be applauded and prized.'

'But does he believe in Dalbrook's mysticism?' inquired Wotton.

'That he believes I should somewhat doubt, though he constantly defends it. But he has a love for all high things, and no darkness or exaggeration·can utterly destroy his favour for them. What his own opinions are you will find it difficult to learn, for he seldom contradicts and never dogmatises, having boundless tolerance for honest speculation, and being himself singularly uncontrollable in thought as well as purpose. Indeed the grand feature of his mind and conduct is this same vigour of will; for meek as you will always see him, Maurice is an autocrat over himself; whatever lies within his sphere must be mastered, cost what it may. It is thus that he has retired from the world of politics and fashion to a world of his own. In morals, also, he is a sort of Stoic, and naturally, for he enjoys little happiness and hopes little — at least, so in spite of his equanimity, I have many times suspected. To such a mind that subtle doctrine of the *summum bonum* may not be so foreign.'

'A goodly gentleman,' said Wotton, 'you have shown me, and one whom it were a pride and pleasure to belong to. But now what of this philosopher, this mystic-Dalbrook? Am I to think him fatuous or inspired? What with his truth and happiness, what with his understanding and his reason, my wits are altogether muddled.'

'I cannot wonder,' said Williams, 'the man does generally pass for mad, and sometimes I fear he will infect us all. For really, if you watch him, there is curious method in his madness, and that huge whirlpool of a mind, with its thousand eddies and unfathomable caverns, is a kind of maelström you were better not to look on lest it swallowed you, unless, indeed, you first cast anchor at a safe distance, which I have now learned to do. Good heavens, how he talks! The whole day long, if you do not check him, he will pour forth floods of speech, and the richest, noblest speech, only that you find no purpose, tendency, or meaning in it! A universal hubbub, wild it seems to you, with touches of seraphic melody flitting through the boundless, aimless din of anarchy itself.

'On the whole, I will confess to you, I cannot rightly understand this Dalbrook. Absurdities innumerable I might laugh at in him, but I see not rightly how his folly is related to his wisdom. Such discord may in part be harmony not understood. He is undoubtedly a man of wonderful gifts, acquirements almost universal, of generous feelings, too; on the whole a splendid nature, yet strangely out of union with itself, and so alloyed with inconsistencies that in action it is good for nothing, and with its vast bulk revolves rather than advances. His very speech displays imbecility of will; he does not talk with you but preaches to you; his thoughts are master of him, not he of them. Accordingly, with all his fine endowments he has effected little, scarcely even the first problem of philosophy, an independent living. Maurice loves and honours him, else matters would go hard. In fact, the man has an unspeakable aversion to pain in all shapes, and among the rest to labour; this, I take it, is the secret of his character. With the loftiest idea of what is to be done, he does and feels that he can do nothing; hence a dreary contradiction in his life, a constant self-reproach, and to help himself he only talks the more. In this way I interpret his exaggerated schemes of virtue, his misty generalities in science, the whole dreamy world where his mind so likes to live. Poor Dalbrook! He was made to be a Brahman or a Gnostic, and he found himself an unappointed English scholar, and the task of living would not prosper with him. Much he talks of writing and teaching, and day after day he reads all manner of supernatural metaphysics and the like; but what will it come to? And yet it is a thousand pities, for there is finest gold in him if it could be parted from the dross.'

'How does his practice correspond with his stoical theories of virtue and happiness?' inquired Wotton.

'Indifferently,' answered Williams; 'idleness is no propitious soil for virtue, and, as we have seen, he cannot work. With all his generous humanity in the gross, you shall often find him spiteful and selfish in detail. Mean men have obtained preferment, and he is unpreferred; then while he despises them, he cannot help half envying. The world has used him ill, and he has no stronghold of his own where he might abide its shocks in peace, nay, love it, pitiful as it is; but wages a sort of Bedouin warfare with its arrangements; an employment in which no one can appear to advantage. Yet certainly he wishes to do well; and his sins are of omission not commission. Let us pity the good philosopher! He was made for a better world than ours, and only in the Heaven, where he looks to arrive, can his fine spirit be itself.

'But now,' continued he, 'I must speak of Burridge whom you poisoned last night with arsenic. Frank, in spite of his atrabiliar philosophy, is no bad fellow; his liver, I believe, is wrong, but his heart is not. A man of birth and wealth, with sense enough to see what is wrong, but scarcely what is right, sits in Parliament legislating after the manner of an English squire; hunts at home or abroad when he is not voting; believes in Hume; curses the badness of the weather, the villainy of men, the derangement of the universe at large; yet, strange enough, feels withal that he must vote with ministers, and Church and State be supported; both are false, but bad might be worse. A Manichean I might call him, or rather an Arimanian, for in theory his *sole* God is the devil, since he worships nothing but necessity; yet such

are the contradictions of human nature, you shall
meet few better men than this same Burridge with
the basest creed; just, frank, true-hearted to a proverb,
nay, as occasion offers, generous if not benevolent, his
life puts to shame many high-sounding professors,
and shows what metal there must be in English
character that can resist such calcination, and still
be metal. Frank is a contradiction; he piques you
into loving him.'

'Maurice called him cousin,' said Wotton.

'They are related, I believe, but chiefly by old
acquaintance, nay, on Frank's side, I might almost
say discipleship; he reverences Maurice, asks his
counsel, and in all domestic arrangements walks by
his light. Every summer he is here with his household; his son, the Hutchesonian philosopher, you saw
last night; his lady and his nephew are expected
to-morrow; they are on a visit in the neighbourhood,
whither Frank would not attend them. You will
mark his nephew, a fellow of some substance, for good
or evil, I know too little of him to say for which.'

'Is he a scholar too?'

'Oh, nowise,' said the other; 'a man of action
this, bred among drums, gunpowder, fire, tempest,
and warfare; he is a soldier, every inch a soldier, has
fought and stormed across the world, and is now
resting with his medals and his laurels and the rank
of major, and fair prospects every way. He is heir
apparent to our landlord, I believe, though Maurice

does not seem to like him over much,—a thing I hardly blame him for, but you yourself shall judge.'

'And his aunt?' inquired Wotton. 'A faded dame of quality, who will not recollect that autumn is no summer. She has been fascinating once, nay, is so still, for she is lively, clever, and by help of the toilette even pretty. She has some real virtues, and many graces; but if old age overtake her, as is like it must, she will surely go distracted, unless, indeed, she take to saintship, or *bluism* which is worse.'

'You are no friend to Blues, then?'

'I profess a kind of enmity to cant, wherever I may find it, but on the whole I think the poor Blues have hard measure among us.'

'We forgive the fashionable woman many follies while she courts distinction in the sphere of common vanity; why should we refuse a similar tolerance to folly in the sphere of literature? The motive is the same in both cases, self-conceit, and undue love of praise, while the means in the latter case are often the more innocent.'

'After all,' said Williams, 'cant is the great cosmetic and enamel of existence, the cheap and sovereign alchemy for making crooked things straight and rough places plain; why should I quarrel with it, I that need it so much myself, nay, so many times am forced to use it?'

'You?' said Wotton; 'surely of all the men I have ever met with, you seem the most free from cant.'

'Ah! how little you know of it,' replied the other; 'few can avow distinctly to themselves what they are aiming at, can weigh in a fair balance the worthlessness of their whole craft and mystery, and see without blinking what pitiful knaves they are. It goes against the grain with one to feel that with incessant bustle, he is doing nothing but digest his victuals! Many a time when I leave our chancery court, and find three bushels of briefs piled up on my table, I say to myself: " Well, Jack, thou art a man useful in thy day and generation, here is much gall peaceably evaporated, much wrong prevented; law is a noble science!" instead of saying : " Well, Jack, thou art a man lucky in thy day and generation, here is much corn and wine converted into ink, much right delayed ; law is a sleek milk-cow whence thou hast thy living." And so it is with most trades that men trade in under the sun. If you viewed them without magnifiers you would find that the result was much the same. Life is a huge treadmill; if you don't step forward, they trample you to jelly ; and if you do step forward for a century, you are exactly where you started. Good Cant! Now she tells us this is a journey towards a noble goal with prospects of this and that on the right and left; it is a journey, as I tell you. Long life to Cant! If it were not she, we might hang and drown ourselves, and with her one can live in surprising comfort.'

The conversation of his new acquaintance could

not but amuse our hero, however little it might satisfy him.

To be spoken to with such attention, and so confidentially treated by a man of influence and talent was in itself gratifying, and still more so by its rarity in Wotton's previous experience; for it was seldom that his hap had led in the way of such people, and much seldomer that he had found them so divested of vanity as to give their minds free play and forget in his presence that he being little and they being great, it behoved them to trample on him, or at least to astonish and overawe him. Williams was none of those painful persons; he cared too little about anything on earth to vex himself or others for it; the basis of his philosophy was: Live and let live. With a gay kind guileless heart, and the clearest and sprightliest perceptions, he was the most attractive of all unbelievers. Intelligence and courteous pleasantry sparkled in his eyes; he was of quick sensation, yet not irritable, never deliberately vindictive; for nature had so blandly tempered him, that he could wish no injury to any living thing. Without effort, he habitually forgot self and the little concerns of self, and mingled with trustful entireness in the feelings of the place and hour, even while his judgment despised them. Nothing could be kindlier than his contempt, which indeed extended far and wide, embracing with a few momentary exceptions the whole actions and character of man, his own not excluded,

nay rather placed in the foremost rank of pettiness.
For moral goodness and poetical beauty, save only as
pleasurable sensations, he had no name; yet few men
had a keener feeling or a better practical regard for
both; he was merciful and generous, he knew not
why; and a great character, a fine action, a sublime
image or thought struck through his inmost being,
and for an instant gleaming in every feature with
ethereal light, the gay sceptic had become a worshipper and a rapt enthusiast. These, however, were
but momentary glows, reflexes of a strange glory from
a world which he had never dwelt in, which he knew
not, and soon lost in the element of quiet kindly
derision and denial where he lived and moved. They
consorted ill with his philosophy of life, and might
have made him doubt it, had he taken time to search
it to the bottom; but time was wanting in his busy
sphere, jostling for ever among selfish men and their
pursuits, he believed as they believed, and such contradictions pleasant or painful with which his own
kinder nature now and then warned him of his error
he heeded little, or loosely referred to that unknown
infinitude which encircles all human understanding,
mocking it with phantasms and inscrutable paradoxes
which, thought Williams, he is wisest who heeds least.
In this way had the man grown up to middle age,
the light and not unlovely product of benignant
nature striving with perverted culture, professedly a
sceptic, unconsciously a believer and benefactor : all

men wished him well, and if more serious critics missed in Williams any earnestness and true manliness of purpose, they too were often captivated in his gay fascinations, and forced to prize him as a thing if not as a man, and to like if they could not love him.

In manifold narration and discussion the hours passed swiftly on, till without singular advancement to the science either of botany or mineralogy, but with the consciousness of having spent a pleasant day, our two friends found themselves again descending into their hospitable valley, under some fear of being stayed for by their company. Burridge had caught several wonder-worthy fishes; his son had been listening to Dalbrook lecturing under the elm-rows and shady garden-walks, as in the groves of a new Academe; Bernard and Maurice were returned from a visit in some neighbouring valley. All seemed contented with their morning's work; the Lady Dorothy with her two fair secretaries, studious like her of household good, found that they had laboured for no unthankful guests.

On this occasion, it was moved and agreed that the party should withdraw with their wine and coffee to the garden-house, not quitting the dames, whose harps and melodious voices were to heighten and as it were vivify with music the other charms of a scene and evening so lovely. Embowered in the richest foliage, in front of them the fair alternation of lawn and thicket, of bush and fruit-tree, and many-coloured flower-bed, stretching far and wide, cut with long winding walks, in mellow light, and silent, save when from his green spray the thrush or blackbird was pouring his gushes of harmony in many a linked bout, around them towering clusters of roses, and the hues and odours of a thousand flowers, and beyond all, in the remote distance, the slopes and peaks of the mountains sparkling in the glow of evening, our friends were soon sociably seated in their little garden-house, the front of which had been thrown open to admit so many kindly influences.

In such hours, when all is invitation to peace and gladness, the soul expands with full freedom, man feels himself brought nearer to man, and the narrowest hypochondriac is charmed from his selfish seclusion and surprised by the pleasure of unwonted sympathy with nature and his brethren. Gaily in light graceful abandonment and touches of careless felicity, the friendly talk played round the table; each said what he liked without fear that others might dislike it, for the burden was rolled from every heart; the barriers of ceremony, which are indeed the laws of polite living, melted into vapour, and the poor claims of me and thee, no longer parted and enclosed by rigid lines, flowed softly into each other; and life lay like some fair unappropriated champaign, variegated indeed-with many tints, but all these mingling by gentle undulations, by imperceptible shadings, and

all combining into one harmonious whole. Such
virtue has a kind environment of circumstances over
cultivated hearts. And yet as the light grew yellower
and purer on the mountain tops, and the shadows of
these stately scattered trees fell longer over the valley,
some faint tone of sadness may have breathed through
the heart, and in whispers more or less audible reminded every one by natural similitude, that as this
bright day was coming towards its close, so also must
the day of man's existence decline into dusk and darkness, and the night come, wherein all image of its
joy and woe would pass away and be forgotten.

In the fair Anna, at least, we cannot but suspect
the presence of some such intrusive thought, for by
degrees she had withdrawn her contribution, nay her
interest, from the conversation; her look, still and
pensive, was lost in the remote landscape; it seemed
as if in the long eyelashes a tear were trembling. It
was her turn to sing; she started from her reverie,
flung her hand hastily over the harp-strings, and
after short preluding in a melody half longing and
plaintive, half sad and contemptuous, thus began—

What is Hope? A golden rainbow, &c.

All listened with attention, and still for a few
instants after the music ceased there was silence,
while the fair singer, glancing rapidly between tears
and smiles over the company, then hung down her
head, and seemed busy rectifying some error with
her strings.

' Surely, my good Anne,' said Williams, ' you mean
not as you sing; these dismal quatrains are fitter for
a likewake than to greet so fair a banquet, amid sunshine and roses, and plenty of brave young gallants to
boot ! '

' Women go by the rule of contraries,' answered
the lady, with a smile, but rather of concealment than
of gladness. ' Do you know,' added she, ' I have
work within doors, and must beg the fair banquet's
pardon, sunshine and roses and brave gallants, young
or old, notwithstanding. My blessing with you all ! '
cried she, tripping through the bushes towards the
house, and making signs that she was not to be followed.

' A strange young lady,' said Burridge, ' and
more full of crotchets than ever.'

' But did you like her song ? ' inquired Dorothy.
' Was it not in the spirit of your own bitter creed,
cousin ? Why the rhymer may have meant not ill ;
the spirit as you say was willing but the flesh was
weak. There is no pith in this balladmonger ; his
wires are slack and have a husky jingle. Besides, I
doubt he is an imitator.'

' Neither is the spirit of his verse unexceptionable,'
said Williams. ' His is a conclusion in which nothing
emphatically is concluded, save perhaps our old friend
the bag of arsenic, Frank ! Really one tires of your
death's head when it grins at one *too* long. This
sweet singer, as you hint, is but a faint echo of Lord
Byron.'

' Say rather of the general tone of our time,'

observed Maurice. 'Lord Byron was the loudest harper, but not the first or the best of this arsenical school. The keynote was struck in Goethe's *Werther*, and Europe has rung ever since with the tune and its variations.'

'It is the want of the age,' said Wotton. 'Thousands on thousands feel as Byron felt; and his passionate voicing of emotions hitherto shapeless and crushing with a force vague and invisible was a relief to the heart that could not speak them. He was a spirit of Heaven, though cast down into the abyss; and his song, like that singing of the fallen seraphs,

> was partial, but the harmony
> (What could it less when Spirits immortal sing ?)
> Suspended Hell, and took with ravishment
> The thronging audience.'

'An apt enough allusion,' said Maurice, ' for the unbelief of men, their sickly sensitiveness and vociferous craving for enjoyment, have made the world a sort of hell for every noble nature that is not delivered from the baleful greed of the day. Our longing is towards the Infinite and Invisible : but for these our time has no symbol; nay, rather it denies their existence; substituting in their stead the shadows and reflections of a merely sensual and mechanic philosophy; and thus the highest faculties of the spirit are shut up in painful durance, or directed into false activity; thought cannot be converted into deed; what should have been worship and blessing becomes idolatry and malediction; for Self is a false God, and his rites are cruel, and end in the destruction of his votaries.'

'Moloch and Juggernaut,' said Dalbrook, 'could but kill the body; but this, with long doleful agonies, or worse, with craftier opiate poisons, kills the soul.'

'But surely,' said Dorothy, 'there is a truer poetry possible even for us than this frightful sort, which is built not on love but on hatred, and for all the wounds of humanity acknowledges no balm but pride.'

'Which is a caustic and no balm; may corrode, but cannot cure,' added Bernard.

'Oh, call not by the name of poetry,' cried Dalbrook, 'such fierce disharmony, which is but infuriated, not inspired! The essence of poetry is love and peace, but here is only rage and disdain. Is the poet gifted with a finer sense only to feel with double anguish the stings of pain? Was his creative faculty bestowed on him to image forth and falsely ornament deformity and contradiction? Is it *he* that should mistake the discords of the poor imperfect part for the diapason of the glorious all, and hear no fairer music in this symphony of the creation than the echoes of his own complaining? must *he* hover through existence, not like a bird of paradise, feeding on flowers, nay sleeping with outstretched wings in middle air, but like a hungry vulture, searching for the carrion of selfish pleasure, and shrieking with baleful cry when he does not find it? Shame on us!

When the very high priests in this solemn temple of the universe have become blasphemers, when they deny their God, and love not the worship but the incense ! '

'Bravely said, philosopher ! ' cried Burridge. ' With your rhetoric you might persuade one that black was white ; but we must not let your figures of speech mislead us. If people do feel in pain, and vexed with these same discords, how can they help it, and help complaining of it ? What is your glorious all which lies far enough away, when a man has got a scurvy fraction for his own whole allotment, and can draw from it neither sense nor profit, but only trouble and grief for his life long ? Was it the poor soul's own blame that he came no better off; or must he be denied the small privilege of complaining ? And is he not obliged to the poet, who utters for him in soul-subduing melodies a feeling which in his own mouth would have sounded harsh and trivial ? '

'If untrue, it could not sound too harsh or be too little heeded,' observed Maurice.

'Nay, but true or untrue,' cried Williams, 'it is the general feeling of mankind at present, and will express itself in spite of us. Now the poet is a citizen of his age as well as of his country. It is his proper nature to feel with double force *all* that other men feel, as to give this back with double force, ennobled and transfigured into beauty, is his proper business.'

'There are many things men feel,' said Maurice,

'which he should suppress and war against, for he has no alchemy which *can* so transfigure them. If his age is worthless and sunk, he must make for himself another; let him strive to change his degraded brethren into *his* noble likeness, not deface himself into theirs.'

'But the means?' said Williams.

'By deep worship of truth and a generous scorn of falsehood, however popular and patronised. Let no momentary show of things divert him from their essence. Let him not look to the idols of the time, but to the pure ideal of his own spirit; let him listen not to the clamours and contradictions from without, but to the harmonious unison from within.'

'And how will the time relish this?' said Burridge.

'Badly, it may be,' answered Maurice, 'but all hope is not therefore lost. Fit audience he will find though few, let him speak where he will; and if his words are sure and well-ordered they will last from age to age, and the hearing ear and the understanding heart will not be wanting. *Cast thy bread upon the waters, thou shalt find it after many days!* So it is with true poetry and all good and noble things. The wheat is sown amid autumnal vapours, and lies long buried under snow, yet the field waves yellow in summer, and the reaper goes down to it rejoicing.'

'Then it is not the poet's chief end to please?' said Wotton.

'His means not his end,' replied Maurice; 'on the

whole, in art as in morals, it seems to me, we must guard ourselves against the love of pleasure, which, admitted as a first principle, may lead us in both cases far astray. The first poets were teachers and seers ; the gifted soul, instinct with music, discerned the true and beautiful in nature, and poured its bursting fulness in floods of harmony, entrancing the rude sense of men ; and song was a heavenly voice bearing wisdom irresistibly with chaste blandishments into every heart.'

'But what of Homer, or Shakespeare ?' cried Burridge. 'Methinks their science was of the meagrest ; what did they teach us ?'

'Much, much,' answered Maurice, 'that we have not yet rightly learned. They taught us to know this world, cousin, and yet to love it ; a harder science, cousin, and a more precious than any chemistry or physics or political economy that we have studied since. Look with their eyes on man and life ! All its hollowness and insufficiency, and sin and woe, are there ; but with them, nay by them, do beauty and mercy and a solemn grandeur shine forth, and man with his stinted and painful existence is no longer little or poor, but lovely and venerable ; for a glory of Infinitude is round him ; and it is by his very poverty that he is rich, and by his littleness that he is great.'

'I have heard the poet's spirit likened to an Eolian harp,' said Dorothy, ' over which the common

winds of this world cannot pass but they are modulated
into music, and even their anger and their moaning
become kindly and melodious.'

'Yes,' cried Dalbrook, 'there dwells in him a
divine harmony, which needs but to be struck that it
be awakened. His spirit is a spirit of goodness and
brotherhood; anger, hatred, malignity may not abide
with him, will not consort with his purer nature.
Wherefore should he envy; where shall he find one
richer than he? While the vulgar soul, isolated in
self, stinted and ignoble alike in its joy and woe, must
build its narrow home on the sand of accident, and
taste no good but what the winds and waves of accident
may bring it, the poet's home is on the everlasting rock
of necessity, the law which was before the universe, and
will endure after the universe has passed away; and
his eye and his mind range free and fearless through
the world as through his own possession, his own
fruitful field; for he is reconciled with destiny, and in
his benignant fellow-feeling all men are his brethren.
Nay, are not time and space his heritage, and the
beauty that is in them do they not disclose it to him
and pay it as their tribute? What do I say? The
beauty that is in them! The beauty that shines
through them! For time and space are modes not
things; forms of our mind, not existences without us;
the shapes in which the unseen bodies itself forth to
our mortal sense; if we were not, they also would
cease to be.'

'God help us! whither are we going now?' cried Burridge.

'It is in this unseen,' hastily continued Dalbrook, 'that the poet lives and has his being. Yes, he is a seer, for to him the invisible glory has been revealed. Life with its prizes and its failures, its tumult and its jarring din, were a poor matter in itself; to him it is baseless, transient and hollow, an infant's dream; but beautiful also, and solemn and of mysterious significance. Why should he not love it and reverence it? Is not all visible nature, all sensible existence the symbol and vesture of the Invisible and Infinite? Is it not in these material shows of things that God, virtue, immortality are shadowed forth and made manifest to man? Material nature is as a *fata-morgana*, hanging in the air; a cloud-picture, but painted by the heavenly light; in itself it is air and nothingness, but behind it is the glory of the sun. Blind men! they think the cloud-city a continuing habitation, and the sun but a picture because their eyes do not behold him. It is only the invisible that really *is*, but only the gifted sense that can of itself discern this reality!'

'Now, in Heaven's name,' cried Burridge, 'what is all this? Must a poet become a mystic, and study Kant before he can write verses? I declare, philosopher, you are like to turn one's brain.'

Dalbrook only smiled and shook his head, but Maurice answered: 'Nay, cousin, let us abide by

things, and beware of names, above all of nicknames,
which are mint-stamps not metal, and should make
brass and pewter pass for gold and silver not among the
wise few but among the simple many. Much of this
which you call Kantism seems but the more scientific
expression of what all true poets and thinkers, nay,
all good men, have felt more or less distinctly, and
acted on the faith of, in all ages. Depend on it, there
are many things in heaven and earth which you
believe in, though you can neither see them, nor make
a picture of them in your head. What is all religion
but a worship of the Unseen, nay, the Invisible ?
Superstition gives its God a shape, sometimes in
marble or on canvas, oftener in the imagination ; but
religion tells us that with Him, form and duration are
not ; for He is the same yesterday, to-day, and for ever.
Time is an eternal now, and no eye hath seen Him nor
can see.'

Burridge shook his head. ' Ah, Frank, you are a
heretic in understanding, and if your heart did not
know better, I really think we should have you burnt
by the first *auto da fè*. But tell me why do you fight
duels ? No, it is not out of disgrace or fear, for you
would let yourself be shot equally in the island of
Juan Fernandez, nay, in another planet, if need were,
and though you were never more to see a human face ;
but it is because you also worship the spirit of honour,
which is your invisible deity, before which all other
feelings, all earthly joy and pain, fly away like light

dust before the whirlwind. Thus you too believe in the reality of the invisible, nay, in its chief or sole reality; yes, you and all of us, else were we machines not men; more cunningly devised steam-engines, to manufacture and to be impelled; not reasonable souls, to make and to will.'

'But what has this to do with poetry?' said Williams.

'In our view it has much to do with moral goodness,' answered Maurice, 'and therefore with the poet who is the interpreter and shadower forth of goodness. Except on some such principle, consciously or, it may be, unconsciously adopted, I see not how he is to find firm footing; for it is only by a sense of the invisible that we can clearly understand the visible, that we learn to tolerate it, nay, to love it and see its worth amid its worthlessness.'

'These are hard sayings,' rejoined the other, archly: 'Who can understand them? I question but that blackbird that sits on the hawthorn-tree, singing its carol in the red sunlight, is a better poet in its way than any of us.'

'The perfection of poets,' answered Maurice, 'would be a man as harmonious and complete in his reasonable being as that bird in its instinctive being.'

'The blackbird, at least, *is born not made*,' said Williams; 'is it not so also of the poet?'

'Born *and* made were perhaps truer of the poet,' answered Maurice. 'Nature in her bounty gives him much, but her most precious gift is the wish and aptitude to cultivate himself to become what he was capable of being.'

'Are not all men, while under strong excitement, poets?' said the Oxonian.

'Scarcely,' answered Burridge; 'the hen does but cackle when you excite her, she will not sing.'

'A false simile!' cried the other. 'The hen's cackling may be musical to hens; for it is the law of nature that all living beings sympathise with beings organised like themselves. Human passion is poetical to men, and makes men poets. The rude Indian defies his fellow savage in gorgeous tropes; the peasant is a poet when he first sees the wonders of the city, a poet when he trembles at the moonshiny churchyard, a poet when he goes to church in sunlight with his wedding company and his bride.'

'Umph!' inarticulated Dalbrook.

'Now the poet is simply always what these are only now and then,' continued the other, ' and his fine frenzy, when he utters it, is poetry.'

'Yet this frenzy, you observe, must be fine,' said Wotton, 'and therein lies the puzzle of the problem. The poet is an artist and does not sing from any Delphic tripod; he has need of forethought as well as fury, and many times, I doubt, finds it no such smooth matter.'

'True, he is an artist,' said the other; ' his mind is stored with imagery and beautiful remembrances;

these he unites, omitting what was trivial or repulsive in them, and thus is formed by degrees an ideal whole in his mind. When the painter would create his Venus, does he not borrow the eyes from this fair woman, the nose from that, the lips from another; and uniting so many separate beauties, form them into one beauty, which is indeed all taken from nature, yet to which nature has and can have no parallel ? '

' When the mantua-maker would create a kettle-quilt,' cried Williams gaily, ' does she not borrow the patch of taffeta from this bright remnant, the lustring from that, the sarcenet from another, and so produce a kettle-quilt, which is indeed all taken from Spital-fields, yet to which all Spitalfields can show no parallel ? I declare to you, my friend, I could never for an hour believe in this theory, though Akenside himself took it under his wing, nay, for aught I know, first hatched it.'

' Why do we not in good earnest set up Gulliver's poetical turning-loom,' said Wotton, ' and produce our poetry in Birmingham by steam ? '

' It is surely a false theory,' said Dalbrook, ' but of a piece with our other false mechanical philosophy. All things must be rendered visible or they are not conceivable: poetry is an internal joiner-work, but what of that ? Virtue itself is an association or perhaps a fluid in the nerves ; thought is some vibration, or at best some camera-obscura picturing in the brain ; volition is the mounting of a scale or the pressing of a spring; and the mind is some balance, or engine, motionless of itself, till it be swayed this way and that by external things. Good Heavens! Surely if we have any soul there must be a kind of *life* in it? Surely it does not hang passive and inert within us, but acts and works; and if so, acts and works like an immaterial spirit on spiritual things, not like an artisan on matter. Surely it were good, then, even in our loosest contemplations, to admit some little mystery in the operating of a power by its nature so inscrutable. With our similitudes, we make the mind a passive engine, set in motion by the senses; as it were a sort of thought-mill to grind sensations into ideas, by which figures also we conceive this grinding process to be very prettily explained. Nay, it is the same in our material physiology as in our mental; animal life, like spiritual, you find is tacitly regarded as a quality, a susceptibility, the relation and result of other powers, not itself the origin and fountain-head of all other powers; but its force comes from without by palpable transmission, does not dwell mysteriously within, and emanate mysteriously in wonder-working influences from within; and man himself is but a more cunning chemico-mechanical combination, such as in the progress of discovery we may hope to see manufactured at Soho. Nay, smile not incredulously, John Williams! It is even as I say; and thus runs the high road to Atheism in religion, materialism in philosophy, utility in morals, and flaring, effect-seeking mannerism in Art. Art do I call it ? Let me not profane the name! Poetry is a making, a creation,' added he, ' and the first rising up of a poem in the head of the poet is as inexplicable, by material formulas, as the first rising up of nature out of chaos.'

'I have often recollected the story of Phidias,' said Wotton, ' when in his exile he had retired to Elis, and, to punish his countrymen, had resolved to make a Jupiter still grander than their Minerva. The thought he meant to express was present to him, all the strength and the repose, the kingly omnipotence of the Olympian; but no visible form would it assume, no feature to body itself forth; and the statuary wandered for days and weeks in the pain of an inward idea which would cast itself out in no external symbol. Once he was loitering at sunset among the groves, his heart sick in its baffled vehemence; his head full, yet dark and formless; when, at the opening of some avenue, a procession of maidens, returning from the fountain with their pitchers on their heads, suddenly uplifted the evening hymn to Jove; and, in a moment, the artist's head was overflowed with light, and the figure of his Jupiter started forth in all its lineaments before his mind, and stood there visible and admirable to himself, as afterwards, transferred to marble, it was for many ages to the world.'

' Yes,' said Dalbrook, ' a strange wind will some-times rend asunder the cloud-curtains from the soul, and the fair creation, perfected in secret, lies unexpectedly before us, like the gift of some higher genius.'

'Some such process,' said Maurice, 'some such influence as this of Phidias's, in one manner or another, most poets seem to have felt. What else is it that they call their inspiration?'

'Well!' cried Elizabeth, 'the sun is going down here also; our groves on such a night are little worse than those of Elis. If I should sing you some song to my harp, we might have the scene of this same Phidias moderately realised; and then,' added she archly, 'if any of you geniuses had a heart, who knows but you might *make* somewhat yourselves by winds of inspiration?'

'Do let us try, Elizabeth!' cried several voices.

Elizabeth, complying, sang handsomely enough, with sweet accompanying harp-tones, a not ungraceful song to evening; but none of our friends, as would appear, played Phidias to it, but retired to the house, and by degrees to their rooms, without creation of any sort; nay, rather, with destruction, for certain of them consumed some supper.

CHAPTER VI

The inmates of the House in the Wold were a fluctuating brotherhood; now coming, now departing; so that week after week, often day after day, a new assortment of characters appeared upon the scene. Bernard had not yet returned; and Wotton was spending the morning in a richly-furnished picture-gallery, under the conduct of his fair hostess, who had herself proposed this indoors occupation, less with the view of instructing her new friend in pictorial art, for which, however, she was well qualified, than of gradually dispelling his reserve, and winning her way into more free communication with him. For such an object, which besides she carefully kept out of sight, this place was not ill chosen. Wotton knew little of art, but his susceptibility for it was deep and keen ; these noble pictures could not but pleasantly engage him; and while under the clear and graceful commentary of one speaking from the heart and to the heart, many a figure rose with fresh loveliness before his eyes, and revealed to him in glimpses the secret of its beauty, he felt as if acquiring some new sense, and distant anticipations of unknown glories finally predisposed him for giving and receiving, at intervals, some friendlier expression of personal feeling, with which the pictorial lesson might be intermingled. He began to be at home with his fair critic, and had the satisfaction to perceive that here and there an observation which he hazarded was partially approved of, and given back to him by new examples, and in new elucidation and expansion. The thought of being interrupted could not have been welcome to either, when the rolling of a carriage rapidly approached the house, and terminated in as loud an explosion of sound as the gravel would admit of before the main door.

'It is Isabella and her nephew,' said the lady. 'We shall by and by resume our lecture. Meanwhile let us go and meet them.'

The gallery extended from the drawing-room, which they had reached by a side entrance, when the door flew open, and a servant ushered in the new guests. The airy lady and her gay voluble compliments, as she floated in with her silken travelling attire, obtained little notice from Wotton, for his whole being was fascinated in strange pain, at another name and aspect. Figure his mood, when he found himself introduced in form to Captain—— Edmund Walter! For one suffocating moment no force of ceremonial principle could hide the fierce alarm which pealed through his soul; but he stood motionless, and the wild dilated eye, the quiverings

or quick stormful flushes of the face must have be-
tokened mystery to the least heedful witness.   Over
Walter's darker countenance there also passed, but
with inconceivable rapidity, a twinge of sternest recog-
nition; but it vanished as it rose; and with courteous
composure he approached his new acquaintance,
affably expressing his happiness in meeting with a
countryman of whom he had often heard; and sub-
joined this and that complimentary remark, passing by
easy transition to more general topics, and this with
a frankness, nay, a kindness, which irresistibly rolled
back the tempest into Wotton's heart, and with gentle
influence smoothed him into calmness.   Thus was
serenity restored almost before it had been missed;
the company were at their ease, and Wotton wondered
to find himself socially exchanging indifferent thoughts
with this man, both hearts meanwhile, it is like, shut
up in enmity; as soldiers from two hostile camps may
for a time mingle in some common market, and traffic
peaceably, though their artillery is not destroyed, but
only slumbering within the trenches, and to-morrow
they must join in battle.

Some such thought was lurking in the background
of Wotton's mind; but Walter's thoughts seemed not
of war, for nothing could be friendlier and gayer than
the temper he showed. Dorothy alone glanced at him
now and then, as if she had observed the effect of his
entrance, and not forgotten it; as if she suspected
somewhat. To Wotton, again, deeply as he reckoned

himself entitled to detest and dread this Walter, there was a singular dominion in his presence; a power which, whether it were benignant or the contrary, you could not but in part respect. He seemed a man of thirty, military in his air rather than his dress; his compact, sinewy frame impressed you in its soldier-like repose with an idea of strength beyond his stature, which, however, was tall and portly; while the thick black locks clustering in careless profusion round that face, so still and massive, burnt by many suns; the broad brow; the calm, quick eyes, fearless, not defiant; the lips, firm without effort, and curved in manifold yet scarce perceptible expression: all bespoke a character of singular vehemence and vigour, a striking union of passionate force with the strictest self-control. Yet this self-control did not invite you, but rather silently beckoned you away; for this, too, seemed passionate, the result not of love, but of pride; not of principle, but of calculation; its very strength seemed dangerous. You would have said, the man had lived in wild perils and wild pleasures; mingling stormfully in both, but surrendering himself to neither; acting among multitudes, nay, ruling over them, yet apart and alone when in the midst of them; it was as if no difficulty could discompose him, no danger make him tremble, but, also, no pity make him weep. To Wotton there was something alienating and oppressive in this look of quietude, of sufficiency, and unsuffering isolation; he gazed on the man, sitting there, thrown negligently backwards, speaking with such vividness and penetration, yet so cool, so indifferent; and there were moments when, had it not been for a softer gleam, perhaps of sorrow, now and then blending in the steady fire of those dark eyes, he could almost have fancied him a man molten out of bronze.

In a little while, the gay Isabella had retired to her room, and Walter, who professed an unabated love for art, volunteered to attend our two students in a farther survey of the gallery. Wotton was again among his pictures; his eye still followed that of his fair instructress; but the pleasure of the lesson was now in great part gone. His late growing frankness, checked rudely enough by this rencounter, had given place to a certain irksome estrangement, which, indeed, Walter himself by many little attentions, the more artful that they seemed involuntary, was the readiest to attempt removing. Walter's feeling of art appeared much more distinct, but also much coarser and narrower, than Wotton's; you would have said he admired in the picture little more than some reflex of himself. For the still beauty, and meek, graceful significance of Raphael he expressed no love; he lingered rather over the scenes of Gaspard Poussin and Salvator, as if enjoying their savage strength, as if in art in general the superiority of beauty to force had not been revealed to him. But what he chiefly dwelt on were portraits, by eminent masters, of

eminent men. For the merit of these his taste
seemed true; yet his partialities were regulated by
the former principle, and appeared to depend as much
on the subject as on the painter.

'Cousin,' said Dorothy, with a smile, 'I grieve to
see you are still an idolator and no true worshipper in
art; with the clearest sense of what is good you do
not prefer the best; it is not the pure ideal, but the
exciting real that you look for; you want devoutness,
cousin; you reverence only power.'

'I am without critical taste,' said Walter; 'but I
tell you honestly what I enjoy and what I do not.
Here, for instance,' continued he, 'here is my old
friend again; can I help it if I like him?'

'It is Cromwell's portrait,' said Wotton. 'Truly a
striking picture; and, if I mistake not, physiogno-
mically expressive of the man.'

'Old Noll, as he looked and lived!' said Walter.
'The armed genius of Puritanism; dark in his
inward light; negligent, awkward, in his strength;
meanly apparelled in his pride; base-born, and yet
more than kingly. Those bushy grizzled locks, flowing over his shoulders; that high, careworn brow;
the gleam of those eyes, cold and stern as the sheen
of a winter moon; that rude, rough-hewn, battered
face, so furrowed over with mad inexplicable traces,
the very wart on the cheek, are full of meaning. This
is the man whose words no one could interpret, but
whose thoughts were clearest wisdom, who spoke in

laborious folly, in voluntary or involuntary enigmas, but saw and acted unerringly as fate. Confusion, ineptitude, dishonesty are pictured on his countenance, but through these shines a fiery strength, nay, a grandeur, as of a true hero. You see that he was fearless, resolute as a Scanderbeg, yet cunning and double withal, like some paltry pettifogger. He is your true enthusiastic hypocrite; at once crackbrained and inspired; a knave and a demigod; in brief, old Noll as he looked and lived! Confront him in contest with that mild melancholy Stuart, who eyes him in regal grace and order from the other wall, and you see that royalty is lost, that it is but withered stubble to devouring fire.'

'Yet the *grey discrowned head*,' said Dorothy, 'has something of a martyr halo round it in feeling minds; and our thoughts dwell rather with the ringdove in his nest, than with the falcon who made it desolate.'

'I confess I am for the falcon,' said Wotton, 'only he should fly at other game than ringdoves. And for this martyr of ours, we love him chiefly, I believe, because he was unfortunate; otherwise in his history there is much to pity, but little to admire. Surely, indeed, to quit our figure, it is wrong to reverence the spirit of power, considered simply as such; yet power is the sense of all sublimity, and does not this of necessity captivate the mind; nay, is it not the chief element of religion itself?'

'Scarcely of the highest religion, our philosophers would tell us,' answered she. 'Perfect love casteth out fear. To a true worshipper, the omnipotence of God is lost in His holiness; in other words, sublimity is swallowed up in all-comprehending beauty. You will observe, too, how much easier it is to homage the former than the latter attribute. In every thunderstorm we see the very beasts fall prostrate with a sort of terror-struck, slavish worship, and dumb cry for mercy; such, likewise, has been, and in great part still is, the devotion of most men; but for the pure soul that, without thought of self, worships the beauty of holiness, fears not and yet reverences, we still look as for a jewel in the common sand; and in ourselves we are glad if we can trace any vestiges of what in its complete sovereignty should form the crowning glory of our culture. For is it not our chief glory that the strong can be made obedient to the weak; that we yield not to force but to goodness; that we walk under heavenly influences, which are mild and still, not under earthly desires, which are fierce and tumultuous? Nay, that while these incessantly assault us, those alone should quicken us, alone be felt and regarded. Of you, my friend, I shall one day make a convert; but for our cousin here,' added she, with a grave smile, 'he is wedded to his errors.'

'And a stormy matrimony we have had of it,' said Walter, 'before the household could be brought to peace. But positively, cousin, you do me wrong; I have my lucid intervals as well as another; only in a life of storm and battle our philosophy will sometimes step aside, and many things must be left as they can be, not as they should.'

Dorothy, with a faint smile, shook her head. On the whole it seemed to be an object with the soldier to stand well with her; an object which, under a show of candour and indifference, he was not imperceptibly pursuing with unusual eagerness, and in which with all his mastery in such arts, he appeared by no means completely prospering. In the piercing eye of such a woman, the craftiest dissimulation brings no perfect concealment; in pure souls there is an instinct which, in the absence of vision, warns them away from the bad, and as if in obscure beckonings declares: 'There cannot be communion between us.' Much more when this instinct, the product of the heart, has been allied to quickness of intellectual perception, and its dim intimations become clear in the light of long observation and experience of men and their ways. Walter's secret might be hidden, but the hiding of it was not hidden; under this smooth smiling expanse his fair cousin felt that there were rocks and cruel abysses; that whoso trusted to its calmness might find it a treacherous element, and in its strength make shipwreck.

But in a little while the Lady Isabella flitted in, new and glittering like a pheasant after moulting-

time; in whose gay, graceful discursiveness all sober
study, all serious purpose, whether of aversion or
affection, necessarily found its turn. She was one of
those souls to whom Heaven has denied the power of
any perseverance. Sharp, rapid in her understanding,
keen and many times correct in her tastes, she had,
indeed, the elements of much worth within her, but
these so loosely combined, and intermixed with such
a quantity of light alloy, that generally their influence
was ineffectual, nay, often their existence altogether
invisible. She looked upon the world as a vain show,
for such to her it really was; without serious interest
in it, without hope, or, indeed, wish of any abiding
good, she flickered through it gracefully and carelessly
as through the mazes of a masquerade, neither loving
any of her brother figures nor hating any, content if
this or that individual among them could transiently
amuse her with his talent, and all would gratify her
with due admiration. Nor was it men only that she
viewed as masks, but, indeed, all things; in her conceptions no object was, properly speaking, of more
than two dimensions, length and breadth, without
thickness; so she dwelt not among things, but among
hollow shells of things, mere superficies, of more or
less brilliancy in truth, but without solidity or value,
and which thus deserved no care from her, thus
obtained none. For with all her susceptibility it was
nearly impossible to fix her mind on aught; greatness, goodness of any sort, would bring a tear into her

bright eyes, but next moment she was thinking how very singular this greatness or this goodness *looked.* She believed in Heaven and Hell; yet always after the first thrill of wonder or terror, she insensibly figured them like more extended meetings at Almack's; the first, a bright assemblage, gas-lit, harmonious, fantastic, and unspeakably amusing; the last, some obscure chaotic medley, horrid, it is true, but chiefly by its dulness and vulgarity, an intensation merely of the horror suffered in a maladroit 'At Home.' Thus all things in her were like Sibyl's leaves; her opinions, purposes, moods, at the breath of every accident, were in continual flux and reflux, and if with her gaiety and grace she was delightful for an hour, her dominion for a day was well-nigh insupportable.

To Wotton, in his present humour, such entertainment was peculiarly unsolacing: this sparkling, fitful, levity, which he could neither rule nor obey, distressed him; but if Walter's presence had been like a nightmare, which he thought not to withstand, this was a continual dropping, which in its annoyance reminded him of escape. He seized the first fit opportunity; said something of his customary morning ride; and with hasty compliments took leave.

His morning ride was a ceremony of no binding nature; but a new light rose on him while his horse was a-saddling. 'Would I were with Bernard!' thought he; for his heart was weighed down with a crushing load, and he felt as if free speech would be an inexpressible relief to him. Leaving a proper message with the groom, he accordingly inquired his way across the hills; learned that in two hours of good riding he might reach his friend; and so at a brisk pace, which soon became a gallop, he left the happy valley.

Such furious speed seemed at once to express and in some degree assuage the internal uproar; but in his mind there was neither peace nor clearness, all was yet imagination and sensation; its forms had not given birth to thoughts, but in their greater stillness were only growing more complicated, more gigantic; and ever as he pulled up, in ascending some rough steep, or from his ledge of road looked down into the shaggy chasm, it seemed amid the sound of waterfalls and moaning woods and hoarse choughs, as if deep were speaking of him to deep in prophetic words full of mystery, sadness, and awe. The journey itself was soon and safely accomplished, but it proved ineffectual. Bernard was from home; he had gone with the nobleman, his landlord, to attend some meeting in the market town of the district, and was not expected till the morrow.

With difficulty, Wotton, bent on continuing his quest, yielded to friendly entreaty and alighted, that so clearer direction and brief rest and refreshment might enable man and horse to pursue their route with more convenience. The town was at some

twelve miles distance, and two roads led to it; of
which our traveller preferred the horseway through
the mountains, as shorter and more solitary; for in
this mood the waste stillness of such regions was
friendly to him. For the rest, the mansion being
empty, save of servants, no unessential delay was
called for: in a little while, Radbury Park with its
groves and lawns had disappeared, and Wotton was
again mounting the uplands in vain eagerness to reach
what he half knew could little avail him. The declining sun shone softly on him through the foliage
of the glens; the brooks gushed loud and cheerful
by his side; and often from some open eminence his
eye rested on stern blue ranges, or caught here and
there the glitter of a lake or streamlet in the distance.
But his heart was heavy and alone as in old days; the
dreamy hope which had mingled with so much in-
quietude in the morning, seemed to die away and
retire into littleness, as the scene of it retired; and he
asked himself: 'What art thou to this man Walter,
or what is he to thee, that thou shouldst either shrink
from him or seek him? Dost thou still love, still look
for blessedness, outcast as thou art? Art not thou
poor and helpless; are not the gates of human activity
inexorably shut against thee? Have I an aim that is
not mad, a hope of peace but in the chambers of
death! O thou bright form, why lingerest thou still
in the desert of my life? Vanish, fair treacherous
vision, vanish and mock me not. If I have been unwise

I bear it, and darkness and desolation are my lot for ever.'

In this humour, little would have tempted him to turn his horse suddenly; to snap asunder these new-formed ties, and, without leave-taking, hurry back to his native solitudes with blank despondency for his guide. But shame and a little remnant of hope still urged him forward: 'After all,' said he, 'what have I to lose? My integrity is mine, and nothing more. Who fears not death, him no shadow can make tremble;' and reciting this latter sentence with a strong low tone in the original words of Euripides, its author, he rode along as if composing his soul by this antique spell into forced and painful rest.

In a short while his attention was called outwards from these meditations, for the valley he had been ascending closed in abruptly on a broad, rugged mountain, stretching like a wall across the whole breadth of the hollow, the high sides of which it irregularly intersected, forming on both hands a rude course for the winter torrents, and on the right a path, which suddenly became so steep and stony that Wotton judged it prudent to dismount while climbing it. Arrived with some labour at the top, he again found himself in the western sunlight, which had been hid below, and he paused with the bridle in his hand to wonder over a scene which, whether by its natural character, or from the present temper of his own mind, surpassed in impressiveness all that he had ever looked on.

It was an upland wavy expanse of heath or rough broken downs, where valleys in complex branching were, openly or imperceptibly, arranging their declivity towards every quarter of the sky. The hilltops were beneath his feet; the cottages, the groves, and meadows lapped up in the folds of these lower ranges and hid from sight; but the loftiest summits of the region towered up here and there as from their base; gray cliffs also were scattered over the waste, and tarns lay clear and earnest in their solitude. Close on the left was a deep chasm, the beginning of another valley, on the farther side of which abruptly rose a world of fells, as it were, the crown and centre of the whole mountain country; a hundred and a hundred savage peaks attracting eye and heart by their form, for all was glowing like molten gold in the last light of the sun now setting behind them, and in this majestic silence to the wanderer, pensive and lonely in this wilderness, the scene was not only beautiful but solemn. Wotton was affected to his inmost soul; he gazed over these stupendous masses in their strange light, and it seemed to him as if till now he had never known Nature; never felt that she had, indeed, a fairy and unspeakable loveliness; nay, that she was his mother and divine. And as the ruddy glow faded into clearness in the sky, and the sheen of the peaks grew purple and sparkling, and the day was now to depart, a murmur of eternity and immensity, a voice from

her worlds, stole through his soul, and he almost
lt as if the earth were not dead; as if the spirit of
he earth might have its throne in this glory, and his
vn spirit might commune with it as with a kindred
ing. ''Ορεστέρα παμβῶτι Γᾶ!' internally exclaimed
e in Doric words; ''Ορεῦτέρα παμβῶτι Γᾶ, thou
igged all-supporting earth!'

But what words can express our feeling in such
ours? It is as if the spirit for a moment were
elivered from the clay; as if in Pisgah vision it
escried the gates of its celestial home, and tones of
diviner melody, wafted from beyond this world, led
aptive our purified sense. And the thought of death,
s in all scenes of grandeur, steals over us, and of
ur lost ones that are already hid in the narrow
ouse, and of all the innumerable nations of the
ead that are there before them, the great and
amous that have gone thither since the beginning
f time. Their multitude affrights us; the living are
ut a handful; one wave in the boundless tide of
ges. Who would grieve for his own light afflictions in
his universal doom? Who could envy, who could
ate or injure any fellow-man? Frail, transitory
nan! we weep over him in fondest pity, for the
shadows of Death bound in our brightest visions,
nd mingling in the jubilee of Nature is heard a
voice of lamentation!

Wotton was aroused from his strange reveries by
the tramp of approaching riders. Starting round, he

observed a cavalcade emerging from the dwarf thickets that skirted the base of a neighbouring cliff, and advancing towards him at a brisk pace; or, rather, perhaps, towards his track which winded forward through the wolds obliquely to their present one. The evening light shone full on the group, which consisted of two men gaily mounted, and a lady between them managing a light Arab with the skill and elegance of a complete equestrian. Long folds of a dark riding-dress flowed over her feet and the side of her horse; black locks waved in graceful clusters from beneath her gold-banded fur *barrette*; but, as she approached, the first glimpse of her features struck our hero with a nameless feeling. His presence also in these solitudes at such an hour seemed to give surprise in its turn, for the whole party simultaneously pulled in as they noticed him; and the lady drew back and hastily dropped her veil.

' A good evening, fair sir ! ' said one of the riders, advancing near him. 'You linger late on the moors. Has anything befallen ? '

Wotton was instinctively clinging to his horse, which this new arrival had disturbed; but in his confusion he scarcely knew what the stranger had said, much less how to answer him with courtesy; he answered merely with a slight bow and an inquiring ' Sir ? '

' Nay, Jack, you are wrong, 'tis another ! ' cried the second horseman, also coming up. ' Pardon us, sir!' continued he, addressing Wotton. 'The sight of a traveller at sunset on these wolds, and not in motion but at rest, surprised us, and we have forgotten good manners in interfering with your privacy. We crave your pardon.'

'The wilderness has privileges of its own,' said Wotton, who had now recovered himself. 'In such solitudes every human face is friendly. No pardon, for there is no offence, but a favour. I am a stranger among the mountains, a passing pilgrim; the wild light of these fells detained me in spite of haste. If our roads go together, I shall be proud of such company. I am riding northwards.'

'*We* ride alone,' said the first horseman in a somewhat surly voice.

Wotton looked in his face; the man, naturally nowise truculent, had an aspect of elaborate resolve, almost of menace.

'You have leave, sirs,' answered Wotton coldly, and bending his eyes towards the path they had quitted.

'And we go armed,' said the other, glancing at his holsters, and evidently piqued by this indifference.

'*Defensively*, I may presume,' said Wotton, in a still chiller tone. 'But for the love of God, madam,' cried he with utmost earnestness, and advancing a step towards the lady, whose horse had now joined the rest, 'tell me, are not you——?'

'Ah, yes!' faintly interrupted the sweet silver voice of Jane Montagu. 'But——'

'Gracious God!' exclaimed he, almost sinking in the unspeakable conflict of his feelings. 'Oh, my friend! my friend!'

'Wotton Reinfred,' said she, in a livelier tone, as he grasped her hand, 'if you are indeed my friend, you will not quarrel with my guardians, nay, my blood relations. Here is no time for ceremonies and the point of honour. This is no recreant, but a true knight, and loyal to me. Of caitiffs we have enow besides; there, give him your hand; and for you, sir, mount, if you will, and come along with us.'

The surly rider brightened up into frankness as she spoke in this tone; readily apologising for his over-hastiness, he proffered cordial reconcilement; and thus, in the singular vicissitudes of a few moments, was Wotton riding forward through the desert, at the side of one whom he had long bitterly mourned as lost, and yet could scarcely in his tumultuous bewilderment believe that he had found.

The rapid pace at which they rode was unfavourable to talk or explanation, which, at any rate, the lady seemed desirous to avoid; she did not lift her veil; she answered briefly, and in a voice from which its first liveliness, perhaps only a transient gleam constrained for the occasion, had disappeared. She was evidently thoughtful, earnest, and, it might be, her thoughts were of sorrow rather than of joy. As for Wotton, his mind was as in a maze; the past would not join with the present or the future; and at times, as he dashed along in silence with the rest, the dusk sinking deeper and stiller over the mountains in their horizon, and the crags near at hand growing whiter, huger, and almost spectral, and the quick footsteps of the horses alone sounding through the waste, or mingling in echoes with the rush of distant waters, he could have fancied that his senses were deceiving him; that he should awake and find this vision, so full of sadness and of rapture, only a dream-picture, a pageant of the mind.

'But is it really you?' whispered he, with melting heart in the ear of his loved one, as he approached her for a moment. 'Is it really you, the Jane whom I have sat with and talked with of old? For here in the wizard solitude I begin to doubt it, and feel that I were too happy.'

'God knows,' said she, 'times are altered, and we with them; but surely I was once Jane Montagu, and had a friend called Reinfred. That you may believe.'

The two horsemen were silent also, or spoke only at intervals, and of their distance from the town, the qualities of the road, or the rare performance of their horses. In another hour the foreground of the scene grew darker, and the track began to slope. At last, far down, rose the light of the burgh, gleaming peacefully in hospitable sheen against the sky, like a beacon to the wayfarer. Our party descended into the valley, and soon a smooth shady road conducted them to paved streets and their inn.

CHAPTER VII

Jane Montagu had with brief good-night retired directly to her apartment, an example which her two attendants, wearied by a hard day's journey, seemed not disinclined to follow. Their supper with our friend was short, and in regard to table-talk laborious rather than exhilarating; they yet knew not rightly on what footing he was to stand, or how far he might safely be admitted to their secrets, so that cheerfulness and trustful communing gave place on all hands to politeness and cautious generalities. From their conversation, which he could but watch not lead, he had gathered only that they were naval officers, that Jaspar, the elder and blunter of the two, was in fact the cousin of Jane, with whose character and late history, however, he appeared nowise personally familiar, nor did either he or Elton his comrade seem to be her lover, though in her fortunes both testified a true interest. For the rest, the party was evidently in a state resembling flight, though whence or whither was not so much as hinted, only a pressing entreaty for silence and concealment taught Wotton that they still reckoned themselves within the sphere of pursuit, and dreaded being overtaken as a great evil. To their request he gave a strict and prompt assent, and so with expressions of good will, and of hopes that what was dark would to the happiness of all become light, the company broke up, and Wotton like the strangers withdrew to his room.

From the servants he had learned that Bernard was in the town, nay at that very hour in the inn, but to speak with him, much as he had longed for it, he now carefully avoided. What could he speak of, when all concerns were swallowed up in one, of which he could not yet divine the mystery, or thousandfold importance, and must not even whisper his surmises. But what, now in his seclusion, was he to think of this strange day? What had befallen Jane Montagu, that she was crossing the mountains, a fugitive, encompassed with anxieties, and under such dubious escort? The men seemed honourable men, and of the friendliest feelings to her; but whither was she hastening with them, what was she flying or in search of? Was it in fear or hope; was she driven or allured? To all which questions, with the utmost strain of his invention, he could answer nothing, but he only in baffled efforts at conjecture increased the weariness which was already stealing over him like the advance of night.

Did she love another, then; did she trust another more than him? Her manner had been kind, confiding, nay for moments almost tender. No! She did not love another! Gracious Heaven! She still loved him! And was she unfortunate? Did she need *his* help? Could he assist her; could his heart, his life, have value to her? And this thought, like a little point of splendour, by degrees tinged in wild hues of beauty the whole chaos of his mind; the cruel became meek, the impossible easy; all harsh discordant shapes, expanding into infinitude, coalesced in friendly union, and his spirit sank into sleep as into a sea of many-coloured lights.

At an early hour he awoke from vague gorgeous dreams, but depressed and heavy-laden, and with the feeling of a man who has much to do and suffer. Looking forth from his window across the wide court-yard with its grooms in their miscellaneous occupation, he observed in the alleys of the garden two men walking to and fro and earnestly conversing, one of whom he directly recognised for Bernard. The air of his friend seemed anxious and busy; he was bent forward and moving his hand as in the endeavour to persuade, while his companion, apparently a man of rank, seemed listening kindly rather than replying. Wotton drew back, for at present he dreaded inter-ruptions, even from Bernard.

He was scarcely dressed, when a servant whom he had summoned for some other purpose delivered him a note. The handwriting Wotton knew of old: it was Jane Montagu's! 'To Wotton Reinfred, Esquire.' He opened and read:—

' A new day has risen, and like the Wandering
Jew I must again set forth with the morning. Come
and wish me good speed ere I go ! A strange chance
restored me a friend, and in two hours I must part
with him, perhaps for ever.'

Wotton made no loitering; in few minutes, with
proper guidance and announcement, he found himself
in a trim, quiet, little parlour, where Jane Montagu,
already in her travelling attire, received him with
smiles, beautiful in their sadness as a cloudy summer
morn. Both parties looked embarrassed, as they
naturally felt, while there was so much demanding
utterance, and no words in which it could be uttered.
What change since these two had last met face to
face ! What a chasm now separated them, over
which, in the pale dusk of memory, hovered past joys,
mournfully beckoning them from afar, and as if
weeping that there was no return ! Those times were
now gone, that blissful community of life had been
all rent asunder, and yet still her right hand was in
his, and they again stood near in space, though in
relation so widely divided ! A tear was gathering
in the bright eyes of Jane, which she fixed on the
ground, and through Wotton's heart were quivering
wild tones of remembrance and hope, wailing as of
infinite grief, and touches of rapture rising almost to
pain. He gazed silently on that loved form; there
was no motion in her hand, but she timidly raised her
face, where over soft, quick blushes tears were stealing,

and next moment, neither knew how it was, but his arms were round her, and her bosom was on his, and in the first pure heavenly kiss of love two souls were melted into one.

It was but for a moment. She sharply, almost angrily withdrew herself and cried, hiding her face: 'Forbear, sir! If you hope to see me another minute, no more of this!' Wotton stood confounded at his rashness, yet glorying in its celestial fruit: he attempted in broken words to apologise.

'Beware, sir!' said she. 'It was not to hear love declarations, which I must not listen to, that I sent for you hither. My life is made of sterner stuff; they are far other tasks that await me. Alas!' continued she, 'I have no friend in this world, if you be my lover. I am an unhappy girl, an orphan wanderer!' She burst into weeping.

'Jane Montagu!' said Wotton, in a voice striving to be calm, 'I have hoped, I have wished for no other happiness, but to be your friend and brother through all time. If there was ever any vestige of goodness in me, believe that I am yours, to live and die for you as you shall desire. Weak, unworthy I am, but not wicked; trust in me, O trust in me! Can I betray your trust? Can I give it in exchange as a thing less precious? O what else could my life have in it worth keeping!'

'My wish and purpose is to trust you,' said she, giving him her hand, which he modestly pressed to his lips. 'I am parting from you, but I would not part from your good wishes, from your estimation. But come, why all this tragedy?' continued she, in a lighter tone, and summoning a smile through her tears. 'Sit down, and speak with me, for I have much to inquire and say, and it will be long before we meet again.'

'In Heaven's name,' cried he, 'whither are you going? Why did I lose you, and in what strange scenes have I found you after long waiting?'

'You have right to ask,' said she; 'but I cannot answer in a word. Have patience with me; I have longed to tell you all; longed to unfold the sad per-plexities which encompass me, to give them voice and shape to any mortal that was not false-hearted, who, if he could not offer me help, would faithfully offer me pity, the solace of all the wretched. I have been alone in my grief, alone! Perhaps it were wiser to continue so, but it is otherwise determined; listen to me, you shall hear all.'

Wotton sat in breathless attention, and the fair Jane, with a resolute effort at indifference and com-posure, thus proceeded:—

'I might well say with Macbeth, My May of life is fallen into the sear and yellow leaf, were it not that little sunshine visits one at any time, and as for my life, I think it has been cast in some Nova Zembla climate, where, however it might be May by the calendar, by the sky it was December. Bright blue hours I have had too, and one always hopes the weather will mend!

'Of my childhood I can say little. Something whispers me that in the earlier part of it I was happier, for I have faint recollections of a pleasant home and kind nurses, and one that used to weep over me and kiss me, perhaps she was my mother. But an obscure, confused period succeeds; of which I have no remembrance, except a certain vague impression of tumult and distress; and this first scene stands like some fair little island, divided by wild seas from my whole after life. I had lost my parents, how I have never known, some baleful mystery hangs over their fate, a gloomy secret, which when I have inquired into I have been answered only in hints and dark warnings to forbear inquiring. Unhappy father! It seems he must have died miserably, sometimes I have feared by his own hand. And she too, the good mother, she that fondled me and laid me on her bosom, was for ever hid from my eyes. Alas! was she my mother? or is this also but a dream which I mistake for a reminiscence? Father or mother in truth I have never known.

'You have seen my aunt, and something of her character, which therefore I need not describe at large. Surely I owe her much, she was my sole benefactress; herself a widow, she found me a helpless orphan, for with their ill-starred life the fortune of my parents had also gone to wreck, and had it not been for her affection, I was destitute as well as orphaned. Affection I may call it, though of a strange sort, and made up of mere contradictions. She has shared her all with me; though poor she has shunned no cost in procuring me instruction and improvement ; indeed day after day she has watched over me with the solicitude of a mother; yet scarcely a day has passed but I have had to doubt whether her feeling towards me was love or hatred. In my childhood often she would hold me in her arms, and gaze over me till her heart seemed melting with saddest tenderness, then all at once I have seen those swimming eyes flash into fury, and she would spurn me from her as an accursed thing. A tempestuous life we had of it, and sore many times was my little heart oppressed and vexed. I had none to trust in, I wept in secret, and were it not that childhood is naturally forgetful and inclined to joy, I must have been often quite wretched.

'My aunt is certainly no common person ; she has the most decisive opinions, a firm and speedy resolve, high feelings also, indeed a certain taste for all excellence. Yet these fine elements of goodness have in her come to no good; she is proud, vindictive, jealous, she does even kindness unkindly, and her temper is changeful as winter winds. It seems as if some malign influence had passed over her nature, and thwarted into perverse direction so many possibilities of virtue. Poor lady! For if she makes others suffer, she herself suffers still more. It is long since I discovered that she had no happiness, no peace, but rather the gnawing of an inward discontent, which never dies, and often I have thought its source lay deeper than mere worldly disappointment. Perhaps her marriage was unfortunate, she will not speak of it, she sternly avoids it, and to Jaspar her son she shows less affection than even to me. Perhaps— But alas! Do not mystery and mischance environ me and gird me round? My whole history is a riddle, which he were a cunning seer that could read me! Disquietude of conscience my unhappy relative may have or not, disquietude of some kind she too evidently has. No system of circumstances, no scene, no circle of society can long please her, nowhere can she take up her permanent abode, but she wanders from place to place seeking that rest which she knows beforehand is not to be found. Of late years her misery seems increasing, there are times when she shrinks from human presence, for days she will sit secluded in her room, refusing all sympathy or trustful communication, and her look when it falls on you is cruel and cold. Poor lady! Her heart will break one day, for she is too strong-willed to end in madness.

'My native place and hers is this North of England, but directly on the death of my parents she retired with me to Vevey in Switzerland, where she had before resided. Thus French became a second mother-

tongue to me, and the Leman Lake and the wild
mountains of Savoy are the earliest scenes of my
memory. Our way of life here was sombre enough;
except with certain clergy of the place, and one or
two sedate persons chiefly of literary habits, my aunt
had no society; the English travellers, of whom many
passed, she carefully avoided, nay repelled if they
sought her. Jaspar was not with us but in England
at a boarding-school; one grave old woman was our
only servant. Yet this solitude was not lonesome to
me, nor with all my little griefs did I feel myself
unhappy. What wealth is in childhood, how that
morning sun makes a very desert beautiful! One
has yet no consciousness of self, one is a thought, an
action, not a thinker or an actor. They praised me
for diligence at school, the whole world was indeed a
school to me, where day after day I was learning new
wonders, and forming new ties of love. What joy
when I could escape to bound over the meadows with
my little sister maidens! But still deeper joy I felt
when in solitary castle building I shaped out the
future, and saw myself not a princess with kneeling
knights—no, no!—but a Corinna, a poetess, an
intellectual woman! For towards this goal, whether
by natural temper, or the influence of our literary
visitors, my whole soul was already bent. Blame
not my mad whim! I cannot blame it, though I
know its emptiness; this poor vision has come before
me in its brightness, and been a city of refuge to my

soul in all troublous seasons. Vevey is still dear to me, and the great Mont Blanc with his throne of glacier-rubies still visits me in sleep and shines in the background of many a dream.

'It was not without bitter tears that I left this first home and all that I had ever loved or known in life. But I was now in my twelfth summer, and my tears soon dried, for England and London were before me. What a world of hopes! England the land of my nativity, where in some lone churchyard, which I often figured, were the graves of my parents, over which I should indeed weep, but tears so soft and blessed! London, the city of wonders, where I was to see and learn so much! My heart leapt at the thought, in spite of all perversities, caprices, nay cruelties, I was the happiest little soul alive. Not so my aunt; her gloom seemed to deepen as she approached the English shore, and I was more than once reminded that but for me and my interests she would not have set foot on it again; but in kinder hours she told me I might now be happier, if I were good; I was to complete my learning; by and by I should meet friends, be introduced to society, of which, however, I ought rather to beware than expect much good. I was too young to understand her fully, but my images of danger and enjoyment were alike gorgeous and almost alike attractive, and her ideas I still rocked to and fro on the wildest waves.

'London fulfilled neither my expectations nor hers.

The deafening, never-ceasing tumult of that monstrous city, its aspect of power and splendour for a while intoxicated me, but the charm of novelty wore off, and I looked back to my little room at Vevey, and its book-shelves and rose-festoons and studious quiet seemed doubly precious. Of masters I had abundance, but they taught me only female accomplishments, and what I most wanted was knowledge. In public our relations, gay, grand people, saw me and caressed me, but I soon found that their kindness was from the lips only, while in secret at home I had more to suffer than ever. My aunt had become a stranger among her kindred, in every circle her place had long ago been filled up, or rather in so many years of absence the circle itself had disappeared, and now she saw herself superfluous, nay, it may be, regarded with distrust, for her way of life had long been involved in a certain mystery, from which it was not difficult for many to draw spiteful inferences. She felt all this and smarted under it in her proud spirit. I too was unhappy. Alas! I was now awakening to life, I was now looking on the world with my own eyes, and sad enough were my surveys and forecastings! I saw myself alone; I saw my aunt, as she was, desolate, gloomy, if not malignant; sometimes I secretly accused her, sometimes I almost hated her, this aunt that had been a mother to me. I was still gay, sportful, but no longer from the heart, which, when I thought of it, was often full of fear and sorrow. The future lay

T

before me, so vast, so solemn, and often all gloomy; except in my darling vision, my old dream of intellectual greatness, I had no strength or stay, and this was but a trembling hope which I hid from every one almost as a guilty thought. The fate of literary women, the ridicule I saw cast on them had grieved me deeply, yet in the end nowise effaced my first project; nay perhaps, for there is a spirit of contradiction in us, rather added strength to it. Foolish girl! But soon I had more pressing matters to reflect on.

'We left London finally after a residence of three years; my aunt mortified and disdainful; I neither glad nor sorry at the change which, indeed, I foresaw would not be lasting, for dissatisfaction and unrest had now taken firm hold of my unhappy relative; she had ceased to be devout, she was at once violent and aimless, and bad days seemed to await me beside her wherever we might live. It was in the south of Wales, whither a pleasant situation and some distant connections in the neighbourhood had invited her, that we next settled. Our way of life here you can figure: why should I trouble you with the poor repetition of frivolity and spleen which with only superficial varieties now this now that new abode has witnessed? One circumstance there is, however, which makes these scenes for ever memorable to me. It was here that I first saw the being whom I may justly call my evil genius; for since that hour his influence has pursued me only to my hurt, and still hangs like a baleful shadow over my whole life. Oh, my friend! This man, this demon! Why did he ever behold me? Why must the black, wasting whirlwind of his life snatch him into its course? But I will be calm.

'Edmund Walter, the first time I saw him, thought right to treat me with a distinction which could not but be visible to everyone. It was a rather numerous assembly: Walter was among the cynosures of the night, and perhaps the poor bashful girl was somewhat envied such attention. In my own mind, God knows, it caused little joy: on the contrary, this man with all his pomp and plausibility of aspect was positively distressing to me, or if I had for the moment some touch of female vanity in his flatteries, I received them but as fairy-money and with a half-criminal feeling, for dread and aversion, as to a wicked soul, were my impressions of him from the first. My impressions, however, it appeared, were not to regulate our intercourse; nay, perhaps this indifference, this repulsion, accustomed as he was to prevail over all hearts, rather piqued him into new assiduity. He followed me, at least—followed me from that hour with continual civilities, the more questionable as they could not be rejected, for so dexterously did he go to work that his conduct expressed at once everything and nothing, wavered like a changing colour; seen on this side, all softness and beguilement; on that, mere acquaintanceship and common social courtesy. With such craft was he studying to spin his nets about me, but it profited him little. If for moments I might trust to the voice of his charming, and feel only that a person of such talents and commanding energy was profitable as a transient companion, especially to one who had so few that could instruct her in aught, I failed not with all my inexperience to see habitually what and how dangerous was our true relation, nay, the more his conversation pleased, instructed, fascinated me, the stronger in my mind grew a dim persuasion that he was selfish and worthless, that it behoved me to break off from him, once for all to be open and decided and, with whatever violation of ceremony, for ever forbid him my presence. This, indeed, had I been mistress of my own actions, I should have done.

'But my aunt said nay, and my part was submission. Her conduct in regard to this man had all along been a puzzle to me. At first she vehemently objected to him, received his visits with coldness, sometimes scarcely even with a polished coldness; it was plain that she watched for opportunities of hurting him—that she strove, by all means short of open incivility, to harass him into retreat. Nevertheless, he was not to be so baffled: with a strange patience he submitted to her injuries, or by cunning turns of courtesy evaded them, and so persevered with a thousand wiles in paying court to her, that by degrees

he insinuated himself into tolerance, nay, ere long
into highest favour. By what new arts he had
effected this I knew not, but so it was, for the two
were evidently on the most trustful footing; they had
private interviews, the purport of which I did not
learn; only I could see by abundant symptoms that
secrets were between them—secrets of what they
reckoned weighty import, and from which it seemed I
was to be carefully shut out.

'This mystery surprised and sometimes alarmed
me; I hate mystery at all times, and in the present
case I had signs that it concerned myself. My aunt
had now changed her dialect with regard to Walter;
she no longer spoke of him with bitterness, but
zealously, with affection, nay, with admiration. She
daily introduced the topic; asked my opinion of this
and that feature in his character; defended him
where I disliked, and warmly confirmed my judgment
when it was favourable. She descanted at large on
his looks, his talent, his manliness of mind; the
polished strength, the elegance, the perfect nobleness
of his whole bearing—in short, whatever quality she
knew me to approve of, with that in full measure she
strove to invest him. I had much to object; I failed
not to point out in contrast her own prior view of
him. She owned that she had been mistaken; a
fair outside was not always a false one; she understood this man better than I and could answer for
his integrity, nay, more, for his intentions towards

myself, which she had at first doubted, but now knew to be generous. As she saw me shrink from such applications, she did not pursue them, but talked in general of the charms of wealth and high station, and how precious it was to be loved for one's own sake. The drift of all this I could not but divine; in fact, her whole being seemed possessed with the project; a glad animation sparkled in her looks when she spoke of it, a hope and ardour such as I had never seen there before.

'Of my own feelings on the matter I could give little account. By such influence, with which his own treatment of me skilfully co-operated, a sort of false glory had been thrown round this man; yet surely, thought I, this is not love? For I felt, or might have felt, that I feared and did not trust him, that we were still divided, must for ever be divided. The thought of wedding him was frightful to me, but his asking me to wed him seemed a thing, with all the hints I had heard of it, so utterly unlikely that it gave me little trouble. On the whole I was mazed, dazzled, and knew only that in this bewilderment I knew nothing.

'Walter disappointed my calculations; in a letter full of cunning rhetoric he declared himself my lover, and offered me his hand; my aunt had already given her consent, and he waited only for mine to be the happiest of living mortals! What could I do? what could I say? I wept and sobbed, for there was a fearful contradiction within me. On the one side lay a life of dependence and chagrin, now threatening to become more galling than ever, without sympathy, without a friend, but one relative whom by my refusal I should bitterly afflict, nay, as it seemed, I should rob of her last earthly hope ; and here, on the other side, stood the tempter, bright and joyful, stretching forth his hand and beckoning me with smiles to a scene so different ! A man who loved me, of so many graces, too, and really splendid endowments ! For some instants I could have yielded, but a secret voice, in tones faint, yet inexpressibly earnest, warned me that he was false and cruel, that it should not and must not be. This warning I at last resolved, come what come might, to obey.

'After two sleepless nights, and days exposed to a thousand influences of entreaty, menace, and persuasion, I rose with a decidedness of purpose such as I had never before felt ; briefly, in words as distinct as were consistent with politeness, I penned my refusal, and, without speaking a word, laid the note before my aunt. Contrary to expectation she showed no anger, but only sorrow ; she wept and kissed me ; said that my happiness was hers ; that if I so wished it, so it should be. Such tenderness melted me ; I burst into tears and expressed in passionate language my unhappiness at distressing her. She renewed her caresses and encouragements, only at the same time hinting as a question, if perhaps my note was not too vigorously worded? Why should we offend a man so powerful, so friendly to us? Were it not better if I excused myself on simply the score of youth, and, without peremptory denial, left the matter to die away of itself and Walter to change imperceptibly by force of time from a lover into a friend? Eager for conciliation, glad by any means to purchase peace for the present, I consented; in an unlucky hour the new letter was written and despatched; and so the evil which I should have fronted when it came postponed into vague distance, where it gathered fresh wrath against me for a future day.

'Walter renewed his visits almost as if nothing had happened, only glancing once and from afar at the occurrence, to which he adroitly contrived to give a light turn, so that matters soon settled on their old footing, and I blessed myself that the storm was blown over. Of love for me he had never spoken and did not now speak, but strove rather with all his resources, which were nowise inconsiderable, to make our conversation generally interesting and profitable in particular for my intellectual culture, which he saw well was the object I had most at heart. By such means my suspicions were certainly quieted if not dispersed; I again began to look on him with some degree of satisfaction, at least, with thankfulness for what he taught me; nor could I hide from myself that dubious, nay, repulsive as his inward nature might appear to me, I had seen few men of

such endowments, few who had so quickened my
faculties and, though with somewhat alien influence,
given me so many new ideas and so much incitement
to improve.

'In this favourable mood he left us, his regiment
being ordered to the North, where it was to be reduced, perhaps broken. He took his leave quietly,
with friendliness, but no show of tenderness, and in
the manner of a man who hoped yet without anxiety
to meet us again. War, he observed, was a trade for
the present as good as ruined, and of which at any
rate one would in time grow tired; he had thoughts
of slackening his connection with the army and set-
tling on his own soil; who knew but the Cincinna-
tulus, when his sword had become a ploughshare,
might tempt his fair hostesses to a long journey, or
at least meet them in their wayfarings and renew the
memory of so many happy days? In this fashion we
parted; with my aunt he was in dearer esteem than
ever; even I could not but wish him good speed, and
sometimes afterwards not without regret contrast his
sprightly sense with the laborious, often malicious,
inanity of most that remained in my sphere behind
him.

'A brisk correspondence had commenced between
my aunt and Walter, in which she seemed to find her
chief, or rather sole pleasure, for ever since his
departure a double discontent had settled over her.
About this time Jaspar, her son, paid us his first

visit; a gay, rather boisterous, but on the whole true-hearted young man; with him, as with the only one of my relations who had ever shown me much affection, I by degrees established a pleasant friendship, which has remained unbroken through various vicissitudes, and now, indeed, forms my last confidence in the future. His regiment had returned from India, where he had fought and wandered, of all which he had much to tell us, or rather, to tell me, for his mother manifested little interest in this or aught that concerned him, and, strange as it may seem, her own only child had now come to see her, for the second time since infancy, not by her solicitation, but by her consent, and that unwillingly bestowed. Of these things he sometimes complained to me, yet with pity towards his mother rather than with anger; indeed, my cousin is of so jocund and buoyant a temper that nothing painful abides with him.

'Walter he knew by old acquaintance: they had been fellow-students at the military college, but as Jaspar spoke of him with dislike, the mother, to avoid quarrels, rarely mentioned this subject, and to me it was now become well-nigh indifferent. Jaspar and I had family concerns and much that interested both to talk of. On the history of my parents he could throw no light, but he wondered with me at my aunt's mysterious silence; encouraged me under so many painful circumstances, and often with unusual warmth declared that he would be a friend and brother to me always, befal what might. I had never had a brother, but I felt towards this man something like what a sister may feel. Undistinguished by any great quality, nay, with many faults and a certain coarseness of nature, he was good and kind to me, and in his company I felt so glad and safe, so affectionate yet so calm! These five weeks flew away too quickly; my new brother left us and I again remained alone, my aunt by some unaccountable perversity refusing even to let me correspond with him.

'Her days were indeed become days of darkness; she was wasting in unexplained sorrows; her soul wrapt up in mystery and often also in the terrors and mortifications of superstition; she felt no hope in life, no sympathy with the living. With the social circle of our neighbourhood she was displeased, herself likewise displeasing, and had almost ceased to correspond; except when she heard of this stranger, her face was seldom brightened with any smile. What I suffered from her why should I describe to you? But I foresaw that some change of place would soon follow, and with it perhaps some alleviation. Meanwhile I kept retired within my old fortress, where, quiet and diligent, I felt as if for the sake of knowledge I could suffer all this and much more.

'What I had anticipated failed not to happen. Early next spring we moved northwards, and, after a short residence among these fells, still farther northwards into Scotland, to the spot you know so well! Dear land!'

EXCURSION (FUTILE ENOUGH) TO PARIS;

AUTUMN 1851:

THROWN ON PAPER, PEN GALLOPING, FROM SATURDAY TO TUESDAY, OCTOBER 4–7, 1851.

Chelsea, Oct. 4, 1851.—The day before yesterday, near midnight (Thursday, Oct. 2) I returned from a *very* short and insignificant excursion to Paris; which, after a month at Malvern Water-cure and then a ten days at Scotsbrig, concludes my travel for this year. Miserable puddle and tumult all my travels are, of no use to me, except to bring agitation, sleeplessness, horrors and distress ! Better not to travel at all unless when I am bound to it. But this tour to Paris was a promised one; I had engaged to meet the Ashburtons (Lord and Lady) there on their return from Switzerland and Homburg, before either party left London : the times at last suited; all was ready except will on my part; so, after hesitation and painful indecision enough, I did resolve, packed my baggage again, and did the little tour I stood engaged for. Nothing otherwise could well be more ineffectual, more void of entertainment to me; but, in fine, it is done, and I am safe at home again.   Being utterly weary, broken-down, and unfit for any kind of work, I will throw down my recollections of that sorry piece of travel, then fold the sheet or sheets together, and dismiss the business.   *Allons donc.*   I will date, and be precise, so far as I am able.

Monday, Sept. **21.**—Brother John still here; he and I went to Chorley to consult about passports, routes, conditions, the journey being now, and not till now, resolved upon.   John was to set out for York-shire and Annandale on the morrow, and so had special business of his own to attend to.   For me Chorley recommended the route by Dieppe and Rouen; got me at the Reform Club a note of the packet and rail-way times (the former of which proved to be in error somewhat); could say nothing definite of passports. We are consulting Fk. Elliot at the Colonial Office.   I was instantly taken across to the Foreign Office, close by in Downing Street, and there for 7*s.* 6*d.* got a pass-port, which, in spite of rumours and surmises, proved abundantly sufficient.   Did no more that day that I can remember.   Next morning early John awoke me, shook hands, and rapidly went, leaving me to my own reflections and opposite airts of the sky.   How we come and go in this world!   A rumour had arisen that my passport would require to be *visaed* (if that is the word); that I must go to the City for this end; that, &c.:

I called on Chorley to consult; Chorley, his old mother having fallen suddenly ill, could not get away to see me even for a minute : laziness said, however, 'Not to the City, don't!' At Chapman's shop, I learned that Robert Browning (poet) and his wife were just about setting out for Paris : I walked to their place—had, during that day and the following, consultations with these fellow pilgrims; and decided to go with them, by Dieppe, on Thursday; Wednesday had been my original day, but I postponed it for the sake of company who knew the way. Such rumours, such surmises; the air was thick with suppositions, guesses, cautions ; each public office (Regent's Circus, Consul's House, or elsewhere) proclaimed its own plans, *denying*, much more, ignoring, that there was any other plan. For very multitude of guide-posts you could not find your way ! The Brownings, and their experience and friendly qualities, were worth waiting for during one day. *Thursday, September* 24, at 10 A.M., I was to be at London Bridge Railway Station ; there in person with portmanteau, and some English sovereigns : *das Weitere würde sich geben.*

Up accordingly on Thursday morning, in unutterable flurry and tumult of humour,—phenomena on the Thames, all dreamlike, one spectralism chasing another ; to the station in good time ; found the Brownings just arriving, which seemed a good omen. Fare to Paris, 22*s.*, wonderful ; thither and back ' by return ticket ' was but 1*l.* 12*s.* according to this route

—such had been the effect on prices of this ' Glass Palace,' and the crowds attracted towards it.   Browning with wife and child and maid ; then I ; then an empty seat for cloaks and baskets ; lastly, at the opposite end from me, a hard-faced, honest Englishman or Scotchman, all in grey and with a grey cap, who looked rather ostrich-like, but proved very harmless and quiet : this was the loading of our carriage,— and so away we went, Browning talking very loud and with vivacity, I silent rather, tending towards many thoughts.   To Reigate the country was more or less known to me.   Beautiful enough, still green, the grey cool light resting on it, occasionally broken by bursts of autumn sun.   Some half-score miles from Brighton our road diverges to the left ; we make for ' Newhaven,' the mouth of a small sea-canal, divided from Brighton by a pretty range of chalk hills.   Chalk everywhere showing itself, grass very fine and green ; fringings of wood not in too great quantity ; all neat, all trim, a pretty enough bit of English country, all English in character.   Newhaven, a *new* place, rising fast as ' haven ' to the railways : our big solitary inn, the main building in it ; other dwelling-houses, coal-wharves, &c., chiefly on the opposite side of the channel—a channel of green, clear sea-water, hardly wider than a river : everything in a state of English trimness, and pleasant to look upon in the grey wind while we had nothing to do but smoke.   Browning managed everything for me ; indeed there was as yet nothing to manage. Our company numerous, but not quite a crowd ; mostly French : operations (as to luggage, steamer, &c.) all orderly and quiet. At length, perhaps about half-past one P.M., we got fairly under way.—I should have said, a man with religious *tracts*, French, German, English, came on board ; I took from him in all the three kinds (which served me well as waste paper); many refused, some (chiefly of the English) with anger and contempt. On the deck were benches each with a back and hood covered with well-painted canvas, impenetrable to rain or wind ; these proved very useful by and by. Steward's assistants enough ; especially one little French boy, in fine blue clothes and cap, who was most industrious among his countrywomen ; *bigger* French gawky (very stupid-looking fellow this) tried to be useful too, but couldn't much.

Our friends, especially our French friends, were full of bustle, full of noise at starting ; but so soon as we had cleared the little channel of Newhaven, and got into the sea or British Channel, all this abated, sank into the general sordid torpor of sea-sickness, with *its* miserable noises, ' Hoahah—hotch ! ' and hardly any other amid the rattling of the wind and sea. A sorry phasis of humanity. Browning was sick, lay in one of the bench-tents horizontal, his wife, &c., below ; I was not absolutely sick, but had to lie quite quiet, and without comfort, save in one cigar, for seven or eight hours of blustering, spraying, and occasional rain. Amused myself with French faces, and the successive prostration of the same—prostration into doleful silence, then evanition into utter darkness under some bench-tent whence was heard only the 'Hoahhah-hotch!' of vanquished despair. Pretty enough were several of them, not perfectly like *gentlemen* any one of them :—indeed that character of face I found of the utmost rarity in France generally. 'Bourgeois,' in clean clothes, if civil, rather noisy manner. One handsome man of forty, olive complexion, black big eyes and beard, velvet cap without brim, stood long wrapped in copious blue cloak, and talked near me; at length sank silent and vanished. Other, of brown hair and beard, head wrapt in shawl, rather silent from the first, protruded his under lip in sick disgust, and vanished a little sooner. Third, of big figure, blind and with spectacles, strikingly reminded me of Jeffrey of *Cierthon* ('Robin Jeffrey,' long since dead) : he sat by the gunwale, spoke little, in preparation for the worst, and staid there. Inside the tent-benches all was 'Hoahoh—hotch!' and more sordid groaning and vomiting. Blankets were procurable if you made interest. Many once elegant Frenchmen lay wrapt in blankets, huddled into any corner with their heads hid. We had some sharp brief showers : darkness fell; nothing but the clank of the paddles, raving of the sea, and 'Hoah-oh-ho-ahh!' Our Scotch ostrich friend stood long afoot, hard as stick; at length he too disappeared in the darkness, and we heard him asking about '*Dipe*' (Dieppe) whether it was not yet near. Hard black elderly man came to smoke on the gunwale seat, near me ; Captain forbade, stopped him ; long foolish controversy in consequence ;—this was in daylight, and the ostrich had assisted : now it was only ' *Dipe ?* ' in the seventh or eighth hour from starting. At length lighthouses appeared, and soon the light-house at the end of Dieppe pier ; and we bounded into smooth water, into a broad basin, and saw houses and lamps all round it. Towards nine P.M. by English time :—put your watch *forward* a quarter of an hour, for that is French time which you have to do with now.

Hôtel de l'Europe, near the landing place, proved to be a second-rate hotel ; but we got beds, a sitting-room, and towards 10 P.M. some very bad cold tea, and colder coffee. Browning was out in the *douane :* we had all passed our persons through it, guided in by a rope-barrier, and shown our passports; now Browning was passing our luggage ; brought it all in safe about half-past ten; and we could address ourselves to desired repose. Walked through some streets with my cigar : high gaunt stone streets with little light but the uncertain moon's ; sunk now in the profoundest sleep—at half-past ten. To bed in my upper room, bemoaned by the sea, and small in-cidental noises of the harbour ; slept till four ; smoked from the window, grey cool morning, chalk cliff with caves beyond the harbour—France there and no mis-take. If France were of much moment to me ! Slept

gradually again, a little while; woke dreaming, confused things about my mother: ah me! At eight was
on the street, in the clear sun, with my portmanteau
lying packed behind me; to be back for breakfast at
nine. Dieppe harbour is the mouth of a river, broad
gap in the general chalk cliffs (bounded to *east* by the
chalk of 'caves' aforesaid; westward it stretches into a
level *down* of some extent beyond Hôtel de l'Europe
and the other houses); basin big, I know not how
deep, has fine stout quays, drawbridges, few, very few
ships; range of high quaint old houses border it on
two sides, the west (ours) and south where is a market
of fish, &c., and then the main part of the town;
eastward is innocent fringed undulating green country
(cliff of 'caves' goes but a short way inland), northward is the sea. Walked south, with early cigar, into
the interior of the town. Good broad street with
trottoirs, with fair shops and decent-looking population; very poor several of them, but none ragged,
their old clothes all accurately patched—a thrifty
people. Ragpickers; a sprinkling of *dandies* too;
London dandy of ten years ago, with hands in coat
pockets, and a small stick rising out from one of them!
Bakers, naked from the waist, all but a flannel waist-
coat and cotton nightcap; *horse-collar* loaves and of
other straighter *cable* shapes, all *crust* and levity.
Streets of fair cleanness, water flowing in the gutters.
Beards abundant. Rue *d'Écosse*: thought of old
Knox, how he was driven to 'Deap' and from it. A

château, with soldiers, is in the place; the *down* is fortified, and shows big cannon. Several big old churches; many fountains, at one of which I drank by help of a little girl and her *carafe*. Besides the chief street (continuation of our Hôtel de l'Europe), there break off at least two others from the southern part of the harbour, and join with chief street in the interior; one of these is Rue d'Ecosse, very poor and dead, which I did not far survey. Near the harbour, between chief street and next, is a square, and general market-place (fruit, herrings, &c.); big old church, new statue of Duquesnoy (? 'ancien marin de cette ville,' said a snuffy, rusty kind of *citoyen* to me on my inquiry): a quaint old town of 10 or 15,000: fairly as good as Dumfries; immense *roofs*, two or sometimes three *stories* in them; many houses built as *courts* with a street door; each house in its own style: all very well to look upon, and good for a morning stroll.—Breakfast was not much to brag of; tea cold, coffee colder, as before; butter good, bread eatable though of *crusty-sponge* contexture. Browning and I strolled out along the quay we were upon, very windy towards the sea; sheer chalk cliffs some mile or two off, downs and straggly edifices close by.—House given by 'Napoléon le Grand' to somebody there named: we inquired of three persons in vain for explanation of the inscription legible there; at length an old fisherman told us. The M. somebody had saved many persons from the sea: a distinguished

member (or perhaps servant) of the Humane Society,
which had its offices there within sight. *Très bien.*
An immense flaring crucifix stood aloft near the end
of this quay : sentries enough, in red trousers, walked
everywhere ; a country ship, with fresh fish, came
bounding in : we strolled back to pay our bill, and get
ready for our start to Paris. Browning, as before,
did everything ; I sat out of doors on some logs at my
ease, and smoked, looking over the population and
their ways. Before eleven we were in the omnibus,
facing towards the *débarcadère* (rail terminus), which
is at the south-east corner of the harbour, a very smart,
airy, but most noisy and confused place.

Maximum of fuss ! The railway people, instead of
running to get your luggage and self stowed away
quàm primum and out of their road, *keep* you and it
in hall after hall, weighing it, haggling over it, marching you hither, then thither ; making an infinite hubbub. You cannot get to your carriages till the very
last minute, and then you must plunge in head foremost. 'They order these matters *worse* in France ! '
Browning fought for us, and we—that is, the women,
the child, and I—had only to wait and be silent.
We got into a good carriage at last : we four, a calm
young Frenchman in glazed hat, who was kind enough
not to speak one word, and a rather pretty young lady
of French type, who smiled at the child sometimes,
but sat thoughtful for the rest and did not speak
either. There was air enough, both my window

and the other down; the air was fine, the country beautiful; and so away we rolled under good auspices again.

This rail, all but the terminus department, is managed in the English fashion, and carried us excellently along. Country of bright waving green character, undulating, our course often along brooks, by pleasant old country hamlets; many *manufactures* (spinning, I guessed), but of most pleasant, clean, rustic character; wood enough on the hill sides, far too thick-planted; stations not *named*, you can only guess where you are. 'Junction' by and by—from Havre probably —an open space without buildings as yet: an altogether beautiful, long, manufacturing village town to the left near by; without smoke or dirt visible, trees enough— might really be a model in Lancashire; the Glos'tershire railway scenes offer nothing much superior Country all made of chalk, as in England (to near Paris, I think); fine velvet grass, *meadow* culture mainly; fine old humble parish churches; wood enough still, but twice or even thrice as thick as we allow it to be. Rouen in two hours: long tunnel, still stronger signs of cotton, bleaching, spinning, &c., then the big black steeples, thick heavy towers of cathedral and the rest— and here is Joan of Arc's last resting place and the scene of many singular things. Distinguished still by the clearness of its air, the trees and gardens and pleasant meadow-looking places, which extended to the very entrance. No smoke to speak of; a lovely place

compared with Manchester or the others of that region!   It is true the press of business seemed a great
deal more moderate.   Our railway station, roofed
with glass, was equal to the Carlisle one; '*buffet*'
(refreshment room), &c., all in order; and they let us
smoke under conditions.   In twenty minutes some other
train got in to join us; and we took our flight again
through space.

Country still chalk: we cross and again cross the
Seine river, swift but not bigger-*looking* than the
Thames at Chelsea: fine hills, fine villages, with due
fringing of wood; a really pleasant landscape for many
a mile.   Pass 'Vernon,' battle-scene of Convention
with Charlotte Corday's people: not notable farther.
Town of [   ] visible, all in white stone and rural
purity, on my right.   At Mantes we stop ten minutes;
fine houses with their French windows and blinds
hung over our station: 'Mantes, je crois, Monsieur!'
and away we go again.   A 'swift' method of travelling; swift and nothing more!   The land, I observe,
is all divided into *ribbons; petite culture* with a
vengeance.   Beans and *légumes* probably the chief
growth.   Ploughing shallow and ill-done: certainly
the Seine valley, which ought to be one of the richest
in the world, was not *well* cultivated, nor by this plan
could it be.   Copses are pretty frequent; at length we
get into vineyards.   But still the ribbon subdivision
lasts; pleasant to the eye only, not to the mind.
Towards four P.M. see symptoms of approach to Paris:

blunt height with something like a castle on it—
guess to be St. Cloud : big arch of hard masonry to
left of that—guess to be l'Arc de l'Étoile : right in both
cases. At length Paris itself (4 P.M.), and we are safe
in the terminus at our set hour.

Alas, it was still a long battle before our luggage
could be got out ; and a crowding, jingling, vociferous
tumult, in which the brave Browning fought for us,
leaving me to sit beside the women. It is *so* they
manage in France : there are *droits de l'octroi* ; there
are—in fine, there is maximum of fuss, and much ado
about almost nothing! Some other train was in the act
of departing, as our poor women sat patiently waiting
on their bench ; and all was very fidgetting and very
noisy. I walked out to smoke ; one official permitted
me, another forbade ; I at length went into the street
and sat down upon a *borne* to smoke ; touters of hotels
came round me: I am for the Hôtel Meurice, inflexibly
fixed ; *de grâce, Messieurs, laissez-moi en paix* ; which at
last they did. Cigar ended, I went in again, Browning
still fighting (in the invisible distance) about nothing at all. Our luggage visible at last upon a distant counter, then Browning visible with report of
a hackney coach : we think it is now over ; rash souls,
there is yet endless uproar among the porters, wishing
to *carry* our luggage on a truck ; we won't, they will :
even Browning had at last grown heated ; at length
I do get a cab for myself and little trunk, certain
French coins hastily from Browning, and roll away.

Halt! Browning has my *key*; I have to turn back, and get it : happily this proves the last *remora*, and now I do get along and reach Meurice's—at five instead of four P.M.: Friday, the 25th September, 1851.—And here, it being now two o'clock, and the sun inviting, I will draw bridle, and stop for the present day.

A brisk, bright autumn evening as I rolled through the streets of Paris ; recognise my route first on the Boulevard, still better in the Rue de la Paix and Place Vendôme ; cigar nearly done, we are at the door of Meurice's in the Rue de Rivoli, a crowd of cabs and other such miscellanies loitering there. Concierge, old good-humoured woman with black eyes and clean cap, knows the number of the Ashburtons, knows not whether they are at home : my cabman, an old, poor, good-humoured knave of the whip, is defective in *petite monnaie*; at length by aid of the concierge we settle handsomely. Mason, too, Lord Ashburton's servant, appears, and I get aloft into my appointed bedroom, 'No. 22,' a bare fantastic place, looking out into the street—bad prospects of *sleep*—though I am at the very top of the house for that object. Both Lady and Lord have gone out, not finding me at four as covenanted; dinner is to be 'at six precisely.' Walk on the streets, finishing my cigar ; dress, have melancholy survey of my bedroom ; dinner in the dim *salle à manger*, seasoned with English news ; after dinner to the Théâtre Français, where Lord Normanby has been pleased to furnish us his box. Very bad box,

' stage-box,' close to the actors ; full of wind-draughts, where we all took *cold* more or less. *Parterre* in stalls; a clever energetic set of faces visible there (far superior to such as go to Drury Lane) ; among them, pointed out by Lady Ashburton, who had met him, the figure of Changarnier. Strange to see such a man sitting sad and solitary there to pass his evening. A man of placid baggy face, towards sixty ; in black wig, and black clothes ; high brow, low crown, head *longish* ; small hook nose, long upper lip (all shaved), corners of which, and mouth generally, and indeed face generally, express obstinacy, sulkiness, and silent long-continued labour and chagrin. I could have likened him to a retired shopkeeper of thoughtful habits, much of whose savings had unexpectedly gone in railways. Thomas Wilson of Eccleston-street resembles him in nose and mouth ; but there was more intellect in Changarnier, though in a smoke-bleared condition. A man probably of considerable talent ; rather a dangerous-looking man. I hear he is from Dijon, come of reputable parliamentary people. Play was called *La Gageure Imprévue,* or some such name ; worthless racket and cackle (of mistaken jealousy, &c., in a country château of the old régime); actors rather *good*; to me a very wearisome affair. Lady Ashburton went to her mother's at the end of this; Lord Ashburton and I staid out a trial of the next piece, *Maison de Saint-Cyr*: actors very good here again, play wretched, and to my taste sadder and sadder—two *roués* of Louis XIV. time, engaged in seducing two Maintenon boarding-school girls, find the door of Saint-Cyr *locked* as they attempt to get out ; find at the window an Exempt '*de par le roi*,' are carried to the Bastille, and obliged to marry the girls : their wretched mockeries upon marriage, their canine libertinage and soulless grinning over all that is beautiful and pious in human relations were profoundly saddening to me ; and I proposed emphatically an adjournment for tea ; which was acceded to, and ended my concern with the French theatre for this bout. Pfaugh !—the history of the day was done ; but upstairs, in my naked, noisy room, began a history of the night, which was much more frightful to me. Eheu ! I have not had such a night these many years, hardly in my life before. My room had commodes, cheffoniers, easy-chairs, and a huge gilt *pendule* (half an hour wrong) was busy on the mantelpiece ; but on the bed was not a rag of curtain, the pillow of it looked directly to the window, which had *battants* (*leaves*, not sashes), no shutters, nor with all its screens the possibility of keeping out the light. Noises from the street abounded, nor were wanting from within. Brief, I got no wink of sleep all night ; rose many times to make readjustments of my wretched furniture, turned the pillow to the foot, &c. ; stept out to the balcony four or five times, and in my dressing-gown and red night-cap *smoked* a short Irish pipe there (lately my poor mother's), and had thoughts enough, looking over the

Tuileries garden there, and the gleam of Paris city during the night watches. I could have laughed at myself, but indeed was more disposed to cry. Very strange: I looked down on armed patrols stealthily scouring the streets, saw the gleam of their arms; saw sentries with their lanterns inside the garden; felt as if I could have leapt down among them—preferred turning in again to my disconsolate truckle bed. Towards two o'clock the street noises died away; but I was roused just at the point of sleep by some sharp noise in my own room, which set all my nerves astir; —I could not try sleep again till half-past four, when again a sharp noise smote me all asunder, which I discovered now to be my superfluous friend the heterodox *pendule* striking (all wrong, but on a sharp loud bell, doubly and trebly loud to my poor distracted nerves just on the act of closing into rest) the *half-hour*! This in waking time I had not noticed; this, and the *pendule, in toto*, I now stopt; but sleep was away; the outer and the inner noises were awake again; sleep was now none for me—perhaps some hour of half stupor between six and seven, at which latter hour I gave it up; and determined, first, to have a tub to wash myself in; secondly, not for any consideration to try again the feat of 'sleeping' in that apartment for one. My controversies about the tub (*baquet* as I happily remembered to call it) were long and resolute, with several successive lackeys to whom I jargoned in emphatic mixed lingo; very

ludicrous if they had not been very lamentable :
at length I victoriously got my *baquet* (a feat Lord
Ashburton himself had failed in, and which I did not
try again while there) : huge tub, five feet in diameter,
with two big cans of water, into which with soap and
sponges I victoriously stept, and made myself
thoroughly clean.   Then out—out, thank heaven—to
walk and smoke ; an hour yet to breakfast time.

Rue de Rivoli had been mainly built since my
former visit to Paris ; a very fine-looking straight
street, of five or six storey houses, with piazza ; French
aspect everywhere, otherwise reminding me of Edinburgh New Town,—and only perhaps *three* furlongs
in length.   Streets straight as a *line* have long ceased
to seem the beautifullest to me.   Population rather
scanty for a metropolitan street ; street-sweeper,
cantonniers, a few omnibuses with Passy, Versailles,
&c., legible, a few straggling cabriolets and insignificant vehicles,—it reminded you of Dublin with its car-
driving, not of London anywhere with its huge traffic
and its groaning wains.   Walkers anywhither were
few.   Tuileries Garden (close on my left) seemed to
have grown *bushier* since my visit ; the trees, I thought,
were far larger ; but nobody would confirm this to me
when I applied to neighbours' experience.   I did not
enter Tuileries Garden yet : sentries in abundance ; uncertain whether *smoking* was permitted *within* ; judged
it safest to keep the street,—westward, westward.
Place de la Révolution (Place Louis Quinze) *altogether*

altered : Obelisk of Luxor, asphalt spaces and stone pavements, lamps all on big *gilt* columns, big fountain (its Nereids all silent) : a smart place, and very French in its smartness, but truly an open airy quarter ; Champs-Elysées woods (or shrubs and brushwoods), broad roads, river, quais, all very smart indeed. Cross the bridge (Pont de la Concorde, I think, a new-looking bridge), Palais Bourbon or National Assembly House on the south side of it,—*No*, I did not now cross these, I crossed by the next bridge eastward (Pont Royal), that was my route, so important to myself and mankind ! Quais rather rusty and idle-looking ; river itself no great things either for size or quality,—bathing-barges mainly, and nothing very clean, or busy at all. Re-cross by the Pont des Arts ; Louvre getting itself new-faced, its old face new *hewn*, complicated scaffoldings and masons hanging over it,—rather *cobwebbish* in its effect. Much of the interior is getting pulled down ; Carrousel, Tuileries, Jardin des Tuileries, Palais Royal, &c., all looked *dirty*, unswept, or insufficiently swept,—the humble besom is not perhaps the chosen implement of France. Home at nine : *all* our party ill of cold, Lady invisible ; my room to be next night a much better, curtained and quite elegant, but still *not* quiet one, on this same floor (the third I think ; directly above the pillars and the first entresol), looking out into the interior court : there I will try again, one night at least. Lord Ash-burton to see ' Museums ' or some such thing with

two French 'gentlemen of distinction;' I decline to
go;—lie down on a sofa, covering my face with a
newspaper, address two stamped Galignani's *Journals*,
to Chelsea, to Scotsbrig, and decide to do nothing
whatever all day but lie still and solicit rest. *Si
fait*;—but very little rest may prove discoverable? I
lay in one place at least,—having first made a call on
the Brownings, whom I found all brisk and well-rested
in the Rue Michodière (queer old quiet inn, *Aux Armes
de la Ville de Paris*), and very sorry for my mischances.
After noon, Lord Ashburton returned, out to make
calls, &c.; I with him in the carriage, into the *Pays-
latin* and other quarters; lazily *looking* at Paris, the
only thing I care to do with it in present circumstances.
Did me good, that kind of 'exercise,' the hardest I
was fit for. *Nimm Dich in Acht.*—At four o'clock
home, when two things were to be done: M. Thiers
to be received, and a ride to be executed,—of which
only the former took fulfilment.

A little after four Thiers came. I had seen the man
before in London, and cared not to see him again; but
it seemed to be expected I should stay in the room, so,
after deciphering this from the hieroglyphs of the scene,
I stayed. Lord and Lady Ashburton, Thiers and I:
a sumptuous enough drawing-room, yellow silk sofas,
pendules, vases, mirrors, Turkish carpet, good wood
fires; dim windy afternoon: *voilà*. Royer-Collard,
we heard, once said: 'Thiers est un polisson; mais
Guizot, c'est un drôle' Heigho, this was Prosper

Mérimée's account afterwards, heigho!—M. Thiers is a little brisk man towards sixty, with a round, white head, close-cropt and of solid business form and size; round fat body tapering like a ninepin into small fat feet, and ditto hands; the eyes hazel and of quick, comfortable, kindly aspect, small Roman nose; placidly sharp fat face, puckered eyeward (as if all gravitating towards the eyes); voice of thin treble, peculiarly musical;—gives you the notion of a frank social kind of creature, whose cunning must lie deeper than words, and who with whatever *polissonnerie* may be in him has absolutely no malignity towards any one, and is not the least troubled with self-seekings. He speaks in a good-humoured treble *croak* which hustles itself on in continuous copiousness, and but for his remarkably fine voice would be indistinct,—which it is not even to a stranger. 'Oh bah! eh b'en lui disais-j—' &c.—in a monotonous low gurgling key, with occasional sharp yelping warbles (very musical all, and inviting to cordiality and *laisser-aller*), it is so that he speaks, and with such a copiousness as even Macaulay cannot rival. 'Oh, bah, eh b'en!' I have not heard such a mild broad river of discourse; rising anywhere, tending anywhither. His little figure sits motionless in its chair; the hazel eyes with face puckered round them looking placidly animated; and the lips, presided over by the little hook-nose, going, going! But he is willing to stop too if you address him; and can give you clear and dainty response about anything you ask. Not the least officiality is in his manner; everywhere rather the air of a *bon enfant*, which I think really (with the addition of *coquin*) must partly be his character!—Starting from a fine Sèvres vase which Lady Ashburton had been purchasing, he flowed like a tide into pottery in general; into *his* achievements when minister and encourager of Sèvres; half an hour of this, truly wearisome, though interspersed with remarks and questions of our own. Then suddenly drawing bridle, he struck into *Association* (Lord Ashburton had the day before been looking at some of the Associated Workmen); gave his deliverance upon that affair, with anecdotes of interviews, with political and moral criticisms, &c., &c. For me *wenig zu bedeuten*, but was good too of its kind. One master of *Associés*, perhaps a hatter, 'ruled like a Cromwell,'—though by votes only; and had *banished* and purged out the opposition party, not to say all drunkards and other unfit hands: *tel régime de fer* was the *indispensable* requisite;—for which, and for other reasons, Association could never succeed or become general among workmen. Besides, it forbade *excellence*: no rising from the ranks *there*, to be a great captain of workers,—as many, six or seven of whom he named, had done by the common method. Then applicable only to hatters, chair-makers, and tradesmen whose market was *constant*. Try it in iron-working, cotton-spinning, or the like, there arrive periods when no market can be found, and without immense capital you must *stop*. Good thing however for keeping men from *chômage*, for 'educating' them in several respects. Thing to be left to try itself,—is not, and never can be, the true way of men's working together. To all this I could well assent; but wished rather it would all end, there being little new or important in it to me! At length, on inquiry about Michelet (for whom I had a letter), we got into a kind of literary strain for a little. Michelet stood low in T.'s esteem as an historian; lower even than in mine. Good-humoured contempt for Michelet and his airy syllabubs of hypothetic *songerie* instead of narrative of facts. 'Can stand *le poète* in his *place*; but not in the domain of truths'—a sentence, commented on and expanded, which indicated to me no great *aesthic* sovereignty on the part of M. Thiers,—leave him alone then ! Our conclusion was, M. Michelet was perhaps a bit of a *sot*;—M. Lamartine, who had meanwhile come in course too, being definable rather as a *fat* (a hard saying of mine, which T. with a grin of laughter adopted) :—and so we left Parnassus à la Française ; and M. Thiers, who could not stay dinner, took himself away. Our horses, in the meanwhile, had roved about saddled for two hours, and were now also gone. Nothing remained but to ' dress for dinner,' when at seven the two French gentlemen of distinction were expected.

Our two *distingués* were literary: one Mérimée, already mentioned, a kind of critic, historian, *linguis-*

tically and otherwise of worth ; a hard, logical, smooth but utterly barren man (whom I had seen before in London, with little wish for a second course of him); the other a M. Laborde, Syrian traveller ; a freer-going, jollier, but equally unproductive human soul. Our dinner, without Lady, was dullish,—the talk confused, about Papal aggression, &c.,—supported by me in very bad French (unwillingly), and in Protestant sentiments, which seemed very strange to my sceptical friends.   Joan of Arc too came in course, about whom a big book had just come out : of *De Laverdy*, neither of our friends had ever heard ! In the drawing-room with coffee it was a little better : a little better: a little, not much.   At last they went away ; and I, after some precautions and preparations, into bed,— where, in few minutes, in spite of noises, there fell on me (thank Heaven !) the gratefullest deep sleep ; and I heard or thought of nothing more for six hours follow-ing !—So ends the history of Saturday, 26th September. *Ay de mi !*

Sunday morning, short walk again ; glance into the Champs-Elysées and their broad avenue with omni-buses ;—I had to return soon for breakfast. My good sleep—though it ended at 5 A.M. and would not re-commence—had made me very happy in comparison. Breakfast,—baddish always, tea and coffee *cold*, &c. ; the Hôtel Meurice, spoiled by English and success, in general *bad*, though the most *expensive* to be found in Paris.   Lord Ashburton's bill (I incidentally learned) was about £45 a week : self, Lady Ashburton and two servants, maid and man !—After breakfast came Lord Granville ; talked intelligently about the *methods* of 'Glass Palace' (bless the mark!),—graphic account of Fox the builder thereof: once a medical student, ran off with master's daughter ; lived by his wits in Liverpool, lecturing on mechanics, &c. ; got into the railway ; became a railway contractor, ever a bigger and bigger one (though without funds or probably almost without) ; is now very great,—'ready to undertake the railway to Calcutta' at a day's notice, if you asked him : *he* built the glass soap-bubble, on uncertain terms :—very well described indeed. A cleverer man, this Lord Granville, than I had quite perceived before. After his departure, wrote to Chelsea, to Scotsbrig ; towards two went to walk with *Herrschaft* in the Tuileries Gardens ; garden very *dirty*, fallen leaves, dust, &c. ; many people out. To Place de la Concorde, opposite Lady Sandwich's windows (2, Rue Saint-Florentin) where Talleyrand once dwelt. Lady Ashburton, still suffering from cold, couldn't go to see her mother, went driving by herself,—the last time she was out at all during my stay. After a call by Lord Ashburton and me at Lady S.'s, we went, about 3 p.m., to ride ; the Champ de Mars our first whitherward.

Paris, Sunday.—All rather *rusty* ; crowds not very great ; cleanness, neatness, neither in locality nor population, a conspicuous feature. Champ de Mars all hung round with ugly *blankets* on Pont d'Iéna side; a balloon getting filled; no sight except for payment. Against my will, we dismounted at another entrance and went in. Horse-holder with brass badge vehement against another without : ' Sergent de ville ! '— at length *he* got possession of the horses, and proved a very bad 'holder.' Dirty chaos of cabriolets, &c., about this gate : four or five thousand people in at half-a-franc or, to the still *more* inner mysteries, a franc each. Clean shopkeeper people—or better, unexpectedly intelligent—come to see this ! A sorry spectacle : dusty, disordered Champ de Mars, and what it now held ! Wooden barriers were up ; seats on the old *height* raised for Feast of Pikes, which is terribly sunk now; instead of ' thirty feet ' hardly eight or ten, without grass, and much of it torn away altogether. Grassless, *graceless*, untrim and sordid, everything was ! An Arab razzia, with sad garrons and blanketed scarecrows of performers (perhaps fifteen or twenty in all) was going on ; then a horse race ditto; noisy music, plenty of soldiers guarding and operating. I moved to come away ; but just then they inflated a hydrogen *mannequin* of silk ; his *foot* quivered and shook, he was soon of full size, then they let him off, and he soared majestically like a human tumbler of the first grace and audacity, right over the top of the inflated balloon (I know not by what mechanism), perhaps 500 feet into the air, and then majestically descended on the other side : none laughed, or hardly

any, except we. Off again; find our horses with effort,
—man wants two francs, not one: a modest horse-
holder ! We ascend the river-side : dirty lumber on
all sides of path; *guinguette* (coarse, dirty old house,
ditto wooden balcony, and mortals miserably drink-
ing) :—across by Pont de Grenoble, into Passy, by
most dusty roads ; omnibuses, cabs, &c., meeting us
in clouds pretty often, and French cockney 'boxes' on
each side to Auteuil; finally into Bois de Boulogne,
which also is a dirty scrubby place (one long road
mainly of two miles or so, with paltry bits of trees on
each hand, and dust in abundance) ; there we careered
along at a sharp trot, and had almost all to ourselves,
for nobody else except a walker or two, a cab-party or
two at long intervals were seen. Ugly unkept grass
on each side ; cross-roads, one or two, turning off into
one knew not what; I found it an extremely sober
'Park'! One of the 'Forts' with great ugly chasms
round it, on our left. At length we emerge again into
Passy; see the balloon high overhead, people in it
waving their hats, *mannequin* (shrunk to a monkey)
hanging on below : a sudden wind then blew it away,
—for ever, one was glad to think. Arc de l'Étoile,
some Hippodrome just coming out, and such a be-
wildered Gulf-stream of people and cabs on the big
road townwards as I never saw before ! Lord Ashburton cautioned me to ride vigilantly, the people
being reckless and half-drunk : crack, crack, *gare !
gare à vous !* it was abundantly unpleasant ; at length

I proposed setting off with *velocity* in the aggressive manner, and that soon brought us through it. Dirty theatre, tea-gardens (where are singers, drink, &c.), with other more pleasant suburb houses, were nestled among the ill-grown trees,—why is this wood so ill-grown? At the corner of Place de la Concorde, 'Secours aux Blessés' stood painted on a signboard of a small house (police or other public house); a significant announcement; rain was now falling. Many carriages; almost all shabby. One dignitary had two servants in livery, and their coat-skirts were *hung over* the rear of the carriage, to be rightly conspicuous; the genus *gentleman* (if taken strictly) seemed to me extremely rare on the streets of Paris, or rather not discoverable at all. Perhaps owing to the *season*, all being in the country? Plenty of well-dressed men were on the streets daily; but their air was seldom or never 'gentle' in our sense: a thing I remarked.— Dinner of two was brief and dim; *épurées*, what they are? After coffee, English talk; winded up with (*obbligato*) readings of Burns, which were not very successful in my own surmise.—To bed, and, alas! no sleep, but tossing, fluctuating, and confusion till 4 A.M.; a bad preparation for next day.

Monday morning was dim, and at seven I was again awake; an unslept *ourie* man. Walk through the old streets, eastward and northward. Rue Neuve des Petits-Augustins, &c., &c., to Place des Victoires—places known to me of old: contrast of feelings seven and

twenty years apart: eheu, eheu! The streets had
all got *trottoirs*, the old houses seemed older and
more dilapidated: crowds of poor-looking people, here
and there a well-dressed man, going as if to his
' office' (bourgeois, in clean linen and coat); very
small percentage of such, and all *smoking*. Louis XIV.
in Place des Victoires: 'Comment?' said I to two little
dumpy men in white wide-awakes: 'Est-ce qu'on a
laissé *cela*, pendant la république?' They grinned a
good-humoured affirmation. Homewards by the Palais
Royal; said Palais Royal very dirty, very dim; hardly
anybody in it: *new* in the southern part; Louis
Philippe's Palace made into an exhibition place for
Arts et Métiers. Emerge then, after some windings
and returnings, into the Rue St. Honoré; heart of the
old Louvre and Carrousel almost gutted out, block of
half-demolished buildings still standing; very dusty,
very dim, all things. In the narrow streets and poor
dark shops, &c., such figures, poor old women, little
children, the forlorn of the earth. 'How do they
live?' one asked oneself with sorrow and amazement.
—Catarrh general still in our party, catarrh or other
illness *universal* in it. Better get home as soon as
possible?

After breakfast, with Lord Ashburton to call on
General Cavaignac, whom we understood to be in
town, of all Frenchmen the one I cared a straw to see.
Rue Houssaie where it joins as continuation to Rue
Taitbout, north from Boulevard des Italiens; there in

a modest enough locality was the General's house.
'Gone to the country (*aux départements*), uncertain
whither, uncertain when'; clearly no Cavaignac for
us! We drove away again, disappointed in mind,
tant soit peu. 'Lift the top from the carriage, let
me drive through the streets with you, and sit warm
and smoke, while you do business:' that was my
proposal to Lord Ashburton, who gladly assented:
agreed to wait at his 'club' (*Club* of Frenchmen
chiefly, and of some *étrangers*, near the boulevards,
—quite 'empty' at this time); home for a warmer
coat, coachman and lackey to doff the carriage-roof:
and after some waiting we all duly rally (at Rue de la
Paix I, at said club Lord Ashburton)—and roll away
eastward and into the heart of the city. Pleasant
drive, and the best thing I could do to-day. Boulevards very stirring, airy, *locomotive* to a fair degree,
but the *vehiculation* very light. Looked at the exotic
old high houses; the exotic rolling crowd. Barrière
St. Martin; turn soon after into the rightward streets,
shops, lapidary or other, Lord Ashburton has to call
at; I remain seated; learn we are near the Temple;
decide to go thither. Old, pale-dingy edifice, shorn of
all its towers; only a gate and dead wall to the street.
Policeman issues on us as we enter; stony eyes, vil-
lainous look, has never heard of Louis XVI., or his
imprisonment here. 'Non, monsieur!'—but from the
other side of the gate comes an old female concierge who
is fully familiar with it; she, brandishing her keys, will

gladly show us all. Building seems totally empty : a police station in some corner of it, that is all. *Garde Mobile* lived in it in 1848, before that it was a convent (under the Bourbons)·; Napoleon had already much altered it; filled up (*comblé*) one storey of it, in order to make a *pièce d'eau* (not quite dry) in the garden. Old trees still up to their *armpits* there : a very strange proceeding for a *pièce d'eau!* Damp, brown, and dismal, all these emptinesses ; grass growing on the pavements; big halls within (a grand royal hotel once, after the Templars ceased from it) ; on the second floor (once third ?) the royal *prison*-apartments, religiously kept, are still there. Marie Antoinette's *oratoire* ; the place of Cléry's scene of adieu : a grim locality indeed ! Garde Mobile had drawn emblematic figures with burnt stick, in a *few* instances they had *torn* the walls, and made ugly big gaps with their bayonets. Our old *concierge* called the primitive republicans (in reference to Louis) '*gueux*,'—she seemed of royalist disposition,—cut us off a bit of room-paper for souvenir, accepted our three francs with many courtesies, and so we left the Temple, a memorable scene in one's archives.

Bronze-dealer next, manufacturer rather,—the greatest (*soi-disant*) *de l'univers* : Lord Ashburton in want of such things went in, I with him, and we walked through various long suites, of *pendules, statuettes, chandeliers,* &c., &c.,—an ardent, greedy, acrid-looking person (he of ' l'univers ') escorting us ; almost frantic with the desire to *sell*, to a milord for money. A vehement lean creature, evidently of talent in his kind, and of an eagerness—I have not seen such a hungry pair of eyes. We bought nothing; I would not have had a gift of anything I saw there,—the best *de l'uni-vers*: '*tantis non egeo!*' Out at last, and I decided not to enter any other, but to sit outside and smoke. Next place, a still finer *bronze* concern ; *indisputably* de l'univers,—but I wouldn't enter ; sat smoking pleasantly in an old quaint street (Quartier du Temple somewhere) for three-quarters of an hour, and bought a glass of *vin ordinaire* (1d.) in the interim, and another for cocher, who seemed charmed and astonished. That suited me better than bronzes. But Lord Ashburton did buy a *pendule* and some fire or hearth apparatus here, all being so extremely good, and the chief man of the establishment, whom I soon after saw at the Hôtel Meurice delivering his goods, seemed to me again a decidedly clever, sagacious, courageous, broad and energetic man. *Mem.* I had been in a *Bookseller's* (on Saturday), the cut of whose face indicated some talent, and a similar *sincerity* of greed and eagerness. A reflection rose gradually that *here*, in the industrial class, is the real backbone of French society : the truly ingenious and strong men of France are *here*, making money,—while the politician, &c., &c., class is mere play-actorism, and will *go to the devil* by and by ! 'Assuredly,' as Mahomet says.—We returned by Marché des Innocents, by Rue St. Honoré and

many streets, which to look upon was a real drama
to me,—so many queer stone objects, queer flesh-and-
blood ones, seen just once and never again at all!
Home about five, to dine with Lady Sandwich at
seven; I flung myself on bed, and actually caught a
few minutes of sleep.

Lady Sandwich's dinner was wholly in the French
fashion, this was its whole result for me,—to see such
a thing *once.* Company, besides us two who entered
first: Marquis Villa-real, a thick Portuguese man with
big hoary head, and boring black eyes (glitter of black
glass), a sturdy man, long ambassador in England,—
spoke English—had he had anything to say for me:
M. and Mme. Thiers, madame a brunette of forty, pretty
enough of her kind, an insignificant kind, hardly spoke
with her; lastly, a Scotch Miss Ellice (' Bear's '); and
our two ' distinctions,' Mérimée and Laborde, with a
Comte (something) Roget, a poor thin man with two
voices, bass and treble alternating, who said almost
nothing with either of them. Kickshaws, out of which
I gathered a slice of undone beef, wines enough, out
of which a drop of good sherry and tumbler of *vin
ordinaire*; talk worth nothing, tolerable only had one
not been obliged to manufacture French. Women
and men together, all suddenly rise from table,
pushing back their chairs with *fracas*; then to the
drawing-room for coffee and talk with Thiers and
Mérimée, who said, or could say, nothing notable;
heartily glad to get away, with twenty drops of some

soporific liquid ('jeremy,' a laudanum preparation) from the good old lady which was to make me *sleep.* Eheu!—Mérimée sat again in the drawing-room at Meurice's; got upon German literature: 'Jean Paul, a hollow fool of the first magnitude;' 'Goethe the *best,* but insignificant, unintelligible, a paltry kind of scribe *manqué* (as it seemed)':—I could stand no more of it, but lighted a cigar, and adjourned to the street. 'You impertinent blasphemous blockhead!' this was sticking in my throat; better to retire without bringing it out! such was the sin of *the Jews,* thought I; the assay of so much that goes on still, 'crucify *him,* he is naught!'—for which they still sell 'old clothes.' Good-humoured banter on my return in, Mérimée being gone: then to bed,—and sleep, alas! no sleep at all!   A plunging and careering through chaos and cosmos, through life and through death, all things high and low huddled tragically together; now in my poor room at Scotsbrig (so quiet *there,* beside my poor old mother!), now at Chelsea, now beyond the moon: I did not sleep till six, and then hardly for an hour, such the noises, such my nerves.   The 'jeremy' (ten drops of it) had rather done me mischief, the other ten I poured out of window.   Towards morning one practical thought rose in me, that I could get *home again in a day;* that I had no work here, and ought to get home!   Out after eight, up Rue de la Paix, down towards Obelisk of Luxor again; bought an *Indicateur des Chemins de Fer.*   It was settled at breakfast that Lord Ashburton should go with me *on Thursday*,—the Lady to stay behind till Saturday, while her cold mended, and then come. *Très bien.* Lady Sandwich has a *second* dinner for us to-day; out of which I apologise ; to dine simply at *four*, and will keep myself peaceably at home. [Pause *here* : have to go the Strand with an umbrella! Monday, 6 Oct., 1851.]

Tuesday, 30 September, after breakfast (*then, I think*) call on the Brownings. Very sorry they that I am bound for home perhaps to-morrow, at any rate next day; will come to them to tea 'if possible.' At Meurice's, Mérimée again to take Lord Ashburton to some show of ancient armour : I decline to go ; stay there, and lounge in talk with Lady Ashburton, who knits. 'Attaché to French Embassy,' name forgotten or never known, thin, half-squinting, insignificant, brown-skinned young Parisian ;—I go out to call on Lady Sandwich; dinner in prospect there, and lamentations over my and everybody's sickness. Dine at four, on frugal starved beef, with one glass of sherry; Lord Ashburton to dine below with certain Bruces (Lord Aylesbury's son and *femme* who is Sidney Herbert's sister) who are just come : enter said Lady Bruce, pretty but *unbedeutend*; enter Bruce, big nose, English noisy say-nothing ; enter finally an Englishman who knows me, whom I cannot recollect to know, who proves at last to be *Sheridan* (Mrs. Norton's brother) : talkee, talkee, *nichts zu bedeuten.* I withdraw to

Browning's before seven. Great welcome there; and tea in quiet; Browning gives me (being cunningly led to it) copious account of the late 'revolutions' at Florence,—such a fantastic piece of Drury-lane 'revolution' as I have seldom heard of. With all such 'revolutions' may the devil swiftly fly away! Home soon after ten; remember nothing of what I found there;—to bed, and happily get some reasonable sleep. Weather has now broken into showers. Lady Sandwich's dinner (an *English* party in honour of us) has consisted mainly of Sir (is he that ?) Henry Bulwer, whom I never saw and care little about seeing.

Wednesday morning, damp walk; Nero's *collar and string* (gift for my wife), at the top of Rue de la Paix: cigars a little farther on, one or two,—very *bad*, dear as in England. Settled *now* that Lord Ashburton is to go with me to-morrow, through in one day; the Lady to wait 'till Saturday,' when probably she will be able to follow. *Très bien.* Donothingism for a while; then out to see Champ de Mars again; Hôtel des Invalides by the way; curious *hawker* (in good clothes, like a kind of gentleman) selling steel pens on Pont Royal: he wrote like a Butterworth,—poor soul, no better trade! *Invalides* and barracks in front near by very striking. Multitudes of *blind* old soldiers. Promenade des Aveugles; place nothing like so *clean* as Chelsea; cannons round it, chimney tops, &c., shaped (I thought) like a kind of fantastic *helmets*; figure of Napoleon in inner court:—very well.

Through dull streets, with some trees, to École Militaire and grand review in Champ de Mars. Poor Champ de Mars, in a very dilapidated, unswept, and indeed quite ugly condition! Federation ' 30 feet' of mound is sunk to eight or ten (as I said above), is torn through in many places, is untrimmed, sordid everywhere,—the place (perhaps 100 acres or more) is altogether dusty, disorderly, waste and ugly. If Federation slope were to be completed, trimmed, and kept *green* with the trees on it; if *any* order or care were shown.—But there is none of that kind, there or anywhere. What strikes you in all public places first is the dirt, the litter of dust, fallen leaves or whatever there may be. Review going on, worth little: finer *men* than common about the streets, with these strange *bellows*-shaped red trousers (tight over the hips, tight at ankles, intermediately *wide* as petticoats), with their strait pinched blue coats and ridiculous flower-pot caps; good middle-sized, well-grown men many of them; they were marching, going on in *detail*, some resting, not many together anywhere: hardly worth above a glance or two. Passy and Chaillot looked very beautiful across the river. Troops now began to take up position and *fire*,—burn the Republic's gunpowder. I went my way; inquired of an oldish soldier (not Invalid) about the populous heights to westwards : it was ' Sèvres '; St. Cloud not quite visible here; this is the *Pont d'Iéna* (old soldier, very civil and talkative). I *cross* by Pont Iéna ; ascend

† B B

through dirty little tea-garden groves into Passy, sit down there among wilderness of stones (new *unused* mason stones), and smoke, looking over a pleasant view of some wing of Paris, the noise from Champ de Mars growing louder and louder—to the waste of the Republic's powder. Passy, Chaillot, suburban village street; very quiet, in spite of an omnibus or two; exotic of aspect, worth walking alone. Arc de l'Étoile again; still enough to-day when there is no Hippodrome. Rain begins in the Champs Elysées; call on Lady Sandwich; home to dinner, by the arcades, in decided rain. Comte (something) Roget is there; has been speaking of Abbés, Abbé Gondy, &c.; is getting himself delicately quizzed, I perceive. '*Jeunesse dorée, jeunesse argentée,*—des bottes,'—in fine M. le Comte, who is a very weak brother, hastens to take himself away, feeling not at ease here. Dinner (*bad* mutton-chop,—useless wretched 'cookery' all along, to *my* poor experience), then half dress a little, a dinner is to be here at seven. Thiers and the two *inevitables* (Mérimée and Laborde); I decided to vanish to Brownings in the interim. At Brownings vague talk, kind enough; take leave, and home soon after nine. Prints: I had been surveying two large batches of Bookseller's Prints, 'on approb.;'—marking the defects, &c. Did not go up to the three strangers all at once; duly by degrees shook hands with the two inevitables (who stayed late, clatter-clattering); Thiers, in about half an hour, glided out without any speech with me. I am told that he is jealous that I respect him insufficiently! Poor little soul, I have no pique at him whatsoever; and of the three, or indeed of known Frenchmen (Guizot included) consider him much the best man. A healthy Human Animal, with due *beaverism* (high and low), due vulpinism, or *more* than due; in fine a *healthy* creature, and without any 'conscience,' good or bad. Whereas, Guizot—I find him a solemn *intriguant*, an Inquisitor-Tartuffe, gaunt, hollow, resting on the everlasting No, with a haggard consciousness that it ought to be the everlasting Yea: to me an extremely detestable kind of man. So I figure him,—from his books and aspect, and avoided to speak with him while he was last here. Heaven forgive me if I do the poor man wrong; practically I have only to *avoid* him, that is all. To poor Thiers I have sent compliments (if such be *due* at all) since my return; part with him in peace.

The inevitables are not interesting; at length they go their ways: and now it palpably turns out, Lord Ashburton is *not* going to-morrow morning, feels better, and ought to stay for Lady Ashburton! Heavy news for my poor fancy (shuddering at a French journey); but how could I deny that the measure was perfectly reasonable; that, in fact, the poor ailing lady *ought* to have some escort? I must go myself, then; must part and shave this night, be called to-morrow at 6¾: 'adieu, madame!' Lord Ashburton walks with me while I smoke in Place Vendôme; will see me on the

morrow (but doesn't) ; lends me two gold sovereigns :
Good night !   Packing, shaving, fiddling hither and
thither : it is past one o'clock before I get to bed ;
and then there are many *noises* (some strange enough)
to start and again start me : at length, in spite of *fate*,
sink into chaotic sleep, and lie so till Mason ('groom
of chambers,' valet long known) call me : quarter to
seven : up, and not a minute lost !

Thursday morning (2 Oct. 1851). Swift, swift !
The little brown valet has coffee ready ; I can eat only
a cubic inch of bread, half-*drink* a small egg ; drink
nearly all the hot milk : that is my five-minutes' breakfast in the deadly press of hurry ; then into a *fiacre*,
laquais de place volunteering to attend me,—and so
away ! Early French streets ; some 'Place de Lafayette ' (so far as I could read), then Terminus, still
in good time,—but such a bustle, such a fuss and uproar for half an hour to come ! Tickets, *dear* (some
£2 12*s.*), and difficult extremely, then *sliding* of your
luggage *en queue* along a lead counter (to be weighed),
and quarrels about it. Ohone, ohone ! laquais and
fiacre cost me $3\frac{1}{2} + 1\frac{1}{2} = 5$ francs. Luggage (*mistaken*, I believe after all) is $1\frac{1}{2}$ franc + endless, maddening botheration. At length you *are* admitted,
hardly find a place ; and so away ! Eight of us inside : two John Bulls (one with toothache and afraid
of air) ; one fat Frenchwoman, very sad-looking ; then
I ; opposite, *young* John Bull, and snappish old-
young English lady ; at the extreme right, two French

exhibitioners : have to fight for *air*, but get it,—then hold my peace as much as possible : ‘ Madame, cela finira ; cela ne durera pas à tout jamais ! ’ We are quiet to one another, and no incivility occurs. ‘ Auteuil,’ said my French neighbour on the right, an oldish, commonplace, innocent man ; then ‘ Montmorenci ; ’ country very beautiful here ; grows gradually less so ; ‘ Pontoise,’ and still uglier flat bare country, gradually after which quite flat, bare, ill-tilled and ugly, and so continues. ‘ At Arras ’ (you can *see* nothing of it, or of anything : a mere open barren flat, and a meagre little barrack of a station-house built), get a bun and glass of vin ordinaire,—this was all my food till England. ‘ Amiens ’ (nothing visible) ; ‘ Lille ’ (ugly waste station-house). On, on : oh, let it end ! Country all *flat ; flax* with ditches : *haricots* in upright bundles with a stick in each ; *spade* husbandry (man digging), careful culture hereabouts ; pleasant-looking villages on the higher ground towards the sea ; some trees, very feeble ; broad level railway course, often straight as a line : not one tunnel from Paris. Short battering shower or two, then again bright weather. Thank Heaven, Calais *at last.* Passport showing ; crowded botheration, steamer overflowing (German, Italian, French), in the end we do get under way,—have seen *nothing* of Calais but the harbour and some of the steeple-tops : is not that a beautiful way of travelling ?

Our passage was of two hours, rather pitching,

cold wind, once a violent shower of rain: 'Hoahh—ohh!' frequent and sordid; couldn't think of smoking; *stood* mainly. Stewards abundantly humane; one poor German lad half-dead; two hundred of us or more,—Dover in the damp, gusty twilight; and at length squeeze out. 'Commissioner of Gun Tavern,' one *can* get refreshment: along then! Brandy and water and beef-steak, in the dirty coffee-room of Gun Tavern,—extremely welcome in fine, and beneficial. India captain talking as he ate, foolish old Lancashire steam machinist (from Lago Maggiore region) answering loudly, foolishly. Commissioner has *done* my trunk: 'two-franc piece' (what you please),—no likelihood of starting 'for an hour yet,' so *many* are we. Get my wetted (*not* dried) topcoat. Somebody has stolen three good cigars; happily nothing else. Station house, and place myself; can't *see* trunk, have to believe it right (and it proves so). Fat French woman lands beside me again. Young English-Belgian tourists (seemingly), three young men, one ditto woman: silly all, and afraid of air. Off, at last, thank Heaven! By the shore, cliffs, and sea to Folkestone; *we* have no lamp (so *many* in train); after Folkestone, thanks to beef-steak and extremity of fatigue, I fall *asleep* (never the like in a railway before); half-waken twice, to pull down the window (which is always pulled up again straightway); awaken wholly, and it is London Bridge! Admirable silence, method and velocity here. They keep us standing some ten minutes,

tickets got, trunks are all laid *out*, in an enclosure
under copious light; ‘ Tiens, je vois déjà ma malle ! ’
exclaims Monsieur : as might I, and others. Near midnight, through muddy rains, am home safe,—scarce
credible !—and have, as it were, *slept* ever since. Oh
the joy of being home again, home and silent ! No
Ashburton come *yet* : weather wet. *Finis.* 7 Oct.,
1851.

LETTERS WRITTEN BY THOMAS CARLYLE

TO

VARNHAGEN VON ENSE IN THE YEARS 1837–57

EDITED BY RICHARD PREUSS

The letters here published for the first time do not require more than a few introductory words. As testimonies of Carlyle's mind and genius, they speak for themselves.

The originals have been found among the manuscript treasures of the Royal Library at Berlin, where the whole literary inheritance of Varnhagen has been deposited since his death in the year 1858. Of his own letters Varnhagen, usually so careful in such matters, had taken no copies; and it is doubtful whether it be possible to find the originals, or whether they exist at all.

It was a happy idea of Varnhagen to send, in the year 1837, the first four volumes of his collection entitled 'Denkwürdigkeiten meines Lebens' to Carlyle. It seems that he wished to have them

C C

reviewed in England. At least Carlyle devoted to the 'Denkwürdigkeiten,' as well as to the former writings of Varnhagen relating to his wife Rahel, a long article in the 'London and Westminster Review' (1838). Subsequently the connection became important for both these men. After the death of Goethe Carlyle's personal relations to Germany were almost confined to occasional and withal rare meetings with Germans living in London. He received, from time to time, letters and messages from Germany, but they were, as he wrote to Emerson, of no great moment. When the message of Varnhagen came, the 'History of the French Revolution' was about to be published, and the trouble of supervising the press, as well as the preparation of his lectures on the German literature, may have retarded the answer to Varnhagen's letter. But at length he wrote; and thus the apostle of German genius and German literature in England entered into direct communication again with a German writer, and with that writer who was in the very centre of the literary life in Germany at that time. Thence a continuous correspondence arose, yet which was maintained by occasional messages from both sides. Varnhagen sent to Carlyle the later volumes of his 'Denkwürdigkeiten' and other German books the latter was in need of; Carlyle sent to Varnhagen his writings and autographs of English authors and public men, for autographs became more and more

the great passion of Varnhagen.   On two occasions
the two men met each other in the course of years:
at first in 1852, and again in 1858, not long before
the death of Varnhagen, both times at Berlin, whither
the historian of Frederick the Great was led by the
wish to see the residence of his hero with his own
eyes.

Hearty thanks are due to Mr. James Anthony
Froude, the friend and literary executor of Carlyle,
for his kind readiness in authorising the publication
of these letters.

I

5 Cheyne Row, Chelsea, London: December 31, 1837.

My dear Sir,—Will you accept, after too long delay, my hearty thanks for your kind and estimable gift, which, a good many weeks ago, on returning hither out of Scotland, I found awaiting me here? The name Varnhagen von Ense was long since honourably known to me; in the book 'Rahel's Gallery,' as in a clear mirror, I had got a glimpse of the man himself and the world he lived in; and now, behold! the mirror-image, grown a reality, has come towards me, holding out a friendly right hand in the name of the ever dear to both of us! Right heartily I grasp that kind hand, and say again and again, ' Be welcome, with thanks.'

If it were suitable or possible to explain amid what complexity of difficulties, engagements, sicknesses, I struggle to toil along here, my slowness in answering would not seem inexcusable to you. I wished to read the book first. A book unread is still but the *offer* of a gift; I needed first to take it into me, and then tell you with proper emphasis that it had in very truth become mine. Not till these late days was the leisure and the mood for such an enjoyment granted me. The two volumes of ' Denkwürdigkeiten ' remained like a little kindly inn, where, after long solitary wandering in bad weather, I should find repose and friends. Once more I say to you, and now with proper significance, Many thanks.

Insight, liveliness, originality, the hardy adroit spirit of a man who has seen and suffered and done, in all things acquitting himself like a man, shines out on me, in graceful coherence, light, sharp, decisive, from all parts of this as of your other books. It is a great, and to me a most rare, pleasure in these times to find that I agree wholly on all important matters with a writer; that in many highest cases his words are precisely such as I should wish to hear spoken. But, indeed, your view of Goethe being also mine, we set out as it were from a great centre of unity, and travel lovingly together towards all manner of regions. For the rest, nothing pleases me more than your descriptions of facts and transactions, a class of objects which grows continually in significance with me, as much else yearly and daily dwindles away, in treating which a man best of all shows what manner of man he is. I read with special interest your Doctor Bollmann,[1] a name not altogether new to me; I could read volume after volume of such autobiography as that you give us— such Halle universities, such Battles of Wagram,

---

[1] The reference to Justus Erich Bollmann is to be found in the fourth volume of the *Denkwürdigkeiten und vermischte Schriften*, by Varnhagen. There is also published an excellent essay about him by Friedrich Kopp in the *Deutsche Rundschau*, vol. xviii. (1879), entitled 'Justus Erich Bollmann und die Flucht Lafayette's aus Olmütz.'

such Fichtes, Wolffs, Chamissos, and the high, tranquil-mournful, almost magical spirit of your Rahel shining over them with a light as of stars! You must not cease; you must continue. That we might *see*, eyes were given us; and a tongue, to tell accurately what we had got to see. It is the Alpha and Omega of all intellect that man has. No poetry, hardly even that of a Goethe, is equal to the true image of reality—had one eyes to see that. I often say to myself, the highest kind of writing, poetry or what else we may call it, that of the Bible for instance, has nothing to do with fiction at all, but with beliefs, with facts. Go on, and prosper.

If you see Herr Criminaldirector Hitzig, pray remember me very kindly to him. Your friend Chamisso is also one I love. Dr. Mundt will mourn with me that the brave Rosen,[1] his friend and mine who brought him hither, has been so suddenly summoned for ever away. He is one whom many regret. Do you know Friedrich Rückert? If you stand in any correspondence with him, I will bid you tell him that I got acquainted altogether unexpectedly with his 'Hariri' last summer, and rejoiced over it for weeks as over a found jewel.

[1] Considerable Orientalist and Sanscritist, born 1805 at Hanover, was called at the age of 22 to teach the Oriental languages at the London University, laid down his professorship for want of satisfaction in it, and died 1837 in London, before he could finish the principal work of his life, the edition of the *Rigveda*. His early death caused general sympathy.

Perhaps you sometimes write to Weimar; if so, pray offer our peculiar regards, my wife's and mine, to Madame von Goethe. I sent Dr. Eckermann a packet and letter, six months ago, to which there is yet no answer. His 'Gespräche'[1] and your remarks on them were right welcome.

No such book had I seen for years; it set me searching, tho' with little effect, thro' Sylvestre de Sacy and others; it remains a distinct acquisition for me that I shall never part with.

His Chinese Song-book I have been enjoying in these very weeks. He is a man whose heartiest friends must lie wide-scattered in such an era as ours, and ought to speak out as they have opportunity.

I have been writing a Book on the French Revolution, which will perhaps get to Berlin by and by. German Literature diffuses itself here and in America, rapidly, lustily, without further effort of mine. Its consequences, as I calculate, will be great and beneficial, on the new generation now rising into activity. *Deutschland* will reclaim her great Colony; we shall become more *Deutsch*, that is to say more *English*, at same time.

The *Deutsche Stamm* is now clearly in the ascendant; seems as if it were destined to take the main part of the earthly globe, and rule it for a time!

---

[1] Vols. i. and ii. of the *Gespräche mit Goethe*, by Eckermann, were published 1836. The essay Varnhagen wrote thereupon is to be found in vol. vi. of his *Denkwürdigkeiten und vermischte Schriften.*

Tapferkeit, their characteristic according to Goethe, deserves to do it.[1]

With true esteem, with thanks and affectionate wishes, I subscribe myself in hopes of meeting again some time, my dear Sir,

Heartily yours

THOMAS CARLYLE.

II

London : March 10, 1838.

My dear Sir,—Some two months ago I wrote to you in grateful tho' late acknowledgment of your two volumes of 'Denkwürdigkeiten,' which work I had then read, as others here have since done, with great satisfaction.

The bearer of this note is Mr. Woodhouse, a worthy English gentleman, proceeding. towards Vienna ; desirous of knowing what is best in Germany and among the Germans. Permit me to recommend him to you. He is a stranger to *Deutschland* as yet, but deserves to know it better.

Perhaps if Dr. Mundt is still in Berlin, he could, for my sake, be of some furtherance in this matter. At all events, please to accept, thro' Mr. Woodhouse, my salutations and hearty assurances of continued regard.

Believe me always, yours with true esteem,

THOMAS CARLYLE.

---

[1] Compare with this the letter to Froude written in September 1870 (*Thomas Carlyle, a History of his Life in London*, 1834–1881. By James Anthony Froude, London, 1884, vol. ii. p. 400).

III

Chelsea, London : Nov. 7, 1840.

My dear Sir,—A fair traveller from your country, who has done us the honour and pleasure of a visit, reminds me that I ought to write, that I ought to have written long weeks ago. Weeks, or even months : for on looking at your last note I am shocked to discover that it must be almost half a year since it, and the new volume accompanied by it, arrived here! Why I have shamefully delayed so long were now hard to say. Certainly it was not for want of thankfulness ; neither was it for the rather common reason, that I had not read the book and so knew not how to speak of it. The new volume of the ' Denkwürdigkeiten ' was eagerly read in the first days after its arrival here, and with a pleasure which is still vividly present to me. Alas, you are a sickly man like myself ; you know well enough, I doubt not, what *Procrastination* means ! One of our poets calls it the ' thief of time.' After long months one is suddenly astonished, some day, to find how much of life, and of the best uses of life, it has stolen from us.

The most striking piece in this fifth volume was, to me, the ' Congress of Vienna.' All was good, and very good ; but this best. At the risk of speaking things which, in a rapid hollow time like ours, were perhaps as well unspoken, I must express my real

D D

admiration (that is the word) of the talent, skill, and faculty of many sorts displayed in such a composition. That is what we call the *art* of writing—the summary and outcome of many arts and gifts. The grand secret of it, I believe, is *insight*—just estimation and understanding, by head, and especially by heart. Give a man a narration to make, you take in brief the measure of whatsoever worth is in the man. The thing done lies round him, with length, width, depth, a distracted chaos; he models it into order, sequence, and visibility; justly, with whatever force of intelligence is in him. So far could *he* see into the genesis, organisation, course and coherence of it; so truly and far, no trulier and farther: it is the measure of his capability, of his *Taugend*, and even, if you like, of his *Tugend*. I rejoice much in such a style of delineation; I prefer it to almost all uses which a man can make of the spiritual faculty entrusted him here below. Let us understand the thing done; let us see it, and preserve true memory of it: a man has understanding given him, and a pen and ink, chiefly for that. In the name of the present and of future times, I bid you continue to write us ' Memoirs.'

Your proposed visit to London did not take effect last year. In another year perhaps you may execute it. You will find some persons here right well-affected towards you; much to see and consider; many things, I may suppose, which at first, and some which to the last, will afflict and offend you. We are near two millions in this city; a whole continent of brick, overarched with our smoke-canopy which rains down sometimes as black snow; and a tumult, velocity, and deafening torrent of motion, material and spiritual, such as the world, one may hope, never saw before. Profound sadness is usually one's first impression. After months, still more after years, the method there was in such madness begins a little to disclose itself.

I read few German works at present; know almost nothing of what you are doing. Indeed, except your own writings there turns up little which a lover of German literature, as I have understood the word in old years, would not as soon avoid as seek. In these days I have read a new volume of Heine's with a strange mixture of feelings. *Heine über* Börne—it is to me the most portentous amalgam of *sunbeams* and brutal *mud* that I have met with for a long while. I remember the man Börne's book, in which he called Goethe the *graue Staar* that had shut into blindness the general eye of Germany. Heine seems to have given up railing at Goethe; he, Heine himself, it seems, has now become a 'Column of Luxor,' *aere perennius*, and a god does not rail at gods. *Eheu! Eheu!*

If you stand in any correspondence with Dr. Schlesier of Stuttgart, will you take occasion to signify, with many thanks on my part, that I have received his third volume of 'Gentz's Writings'; that I did make some attempt to get the book *reviewed* here, but, having now no connection with that department of things, could not find a proper hand to undertake the business. Indeed, I apprehend Gentz has altogether passed here. I can remember him as a popular pamphleteer with a certain party in my early boyhood; but the party has now disappeared, the ideas of it have disappeared; and nobody will now recollect Gentz in the old light, or recognise him in a new. To myself I must confess he hitherto will by no means seem a hero. The only portion of his writings that I have read with any entertainment is that historical piece delineating the prologue to the Battle of Jena. What you somewhere say about him I can read; hardly what any other says. A lady here, daughter of the late Sir James Mackintosh, remembers him at Vienna: 'a man in powdered ceremonial hair, with a red nose,' seemingly fond of dining! *Edidit monumentum!*

The fair Sophie kindly undertaking to carry any parcel, I send you a little pamphlet of mine published last year. *Chartism*, whether one hear the word or do not hear it, is the great fact of England at present.

Did any one ever write an adequate life of your Frederick the Great? Is there anywhere a legible life of Luther, so much as an attainable edition of his *Tischreden*? I fear the answer is 'No' in all these cases.

Farewell, dear sir; be, I do not say happy, but nobly busy, and think of us here as friends.

Sophie promises to see us a second time to-morrow. I do not rightly know her name yet, but she has a bright *gemüthlich* face, and laughing eyes of that beautiful *German grey* !

Believe me, yours ever truly,

T. CARLYLE.

IV

Chelsea, London : May 16, 1841.

My dear Sir,—Some six weeks ago, while I was just running off into the country, your very welcome and most friendly letter reached me here. An ugly disorder, which they call *Influenza*, had altogether lamed me, in the cold weather of spring ; the doctors, and still more emphatically my own feelings, declared that I could not shake the drug of it off except in the quiet of the fields. Always, after a certain length of time spent in this enormous never-resting Babel of a city, there rises in one not a wish only, but a kind of passion, for uttermost solitude : were it only some black, ever-desolate moor, where nature alone was present, and manufacture and noise, speech, witty or stupid, had never reached. I prolonged my excursion, which at first was only a visit to Yorkshire, into the South of Scotland, my native region, where brothers of mine, where an aged, good mother still live for me. I myself, to all other persons, am now as good as a stranger there. It is a mournful, solemn, nay, almost preternatural place for me now, that birthland of mine ; sends me back from it *silent*, for there are no words to speak the thoughts and the *unthinkables* it awakens ! Arriving here, ten days ago, your Berlin books, one of the most interesting gifts, lay all beautifully arranged on a table for me. I had heard of their safe arrival in my absence, and here they lay like a congratulation waiting my return.

You forbid me to *speak* of this altogether extraordinary gift; accordingly I shall say nothing of it, how much so ever I must naturally feel, except that, under penalty of my never *asking* you again about my book, you must not *purchase* for me any more than these ! No, that would never do; for I shall want perhaps to ask about many books. I will put them on my shelves, having once read them thro'; there let them stand as a peculiar thing, a memorial to me of many things. All my days I have laboured and lamented under a fatal lack of books; as indeed England generally and London itself would astonish you in that particular; think only that in London, except it be the garbage of new novels and such like, there is no library whatever from which any man can borrow a book home with him. One library alone, in our huge *empire*, that of the British Museum here, is open to the public, to read *in it*; thereat first I went to attempt reading, but found that in a room with 500 people I could do no good as a reader. A German, a Frenchman, can hardly believe the existence of such a state of things; but it is a lamentable fact. We are a strange people, we English : a people, as I sometimes say, with more *inarticulate* intelligence and less of articulate than any people the sun now shines on. Speak to one of us, speak to almost any one of us, you will stand struck silent at the contractedness, perhaps Cimmerian stupidity of the *word* he responds ; yet look at the *action* of the man, at the combined action of twenty-eight millions of such men. After years you begin to see through their outer *dumbness* how these things have been possible for them ; how they do verily stand in closest continual communication with many a power of nature, clearest insight into that ; how perhaps their very dumbness is a kind of force. On the whole, I grow to admire less and less your *speaking* peoples. The French are a speaking people, and persuade numbers of *men* that they are great ; but coming to try veracious nature, the ocean for example, Canada, Algiers or the like, nature answers, 'No, Messieurs, you are little ! ' Russia again, is not that a great thing, still speechless ? From Petersburg to Kamschatka the earth answers, ' Yes, I love the English too, and all the Teutons, for their silence. We *can* speak, too, by a Shakespeare, by a Goethe, when the time comes. Some assiduous whisking 'dog of knowledge' seems to itself a far cleverer creature than the great quiet elephant or noble horse ; but it is far mistaken !

However, this of the lamentable want of books in

London (owing to that 'outer stupidity' of the English) has now brought about some beginning of its own remedy. What I meant to say was, that the generous Varnhagen *need* not send me any more books, because any good book, German or other, has now become attainable here. Some two years ago, after sufficiently lamenting and even sometimes execrating such a state of matters, it struck me, Couldst not thou, even thou there, try to mend it? The result, after much confused difficulty, is a democratic institution called 'London Library,' where all men, on payment of a small annual sum, can now borrow books; a thing called here 'Subscription Library,' which in such a city as London, appetite growing by what it feeds on, may well become by-and-by one of the best libraries extant. We are democratic, as I said, or rather we mean to be; for as yet only the elect of the public could be interested in the scheme. Prince Albert, good youth, is patron, by his own free offer; has given fifty pounds of money, and promises 'a stock of German books.' Varnhagen's are already there. *Faustum sit.*

You give an altogether melancholy account of your health; in which, alas, I can too well sympathise! It seems to me often the one misery in this world. But the supreme powers send it: we are to work under such condition; we cannot alter that condition. Perhaps there is even much good in it: I often feel so. Your response to the poor pamphlet *Chartism* is that of a generous human heart, *resonant* to all human things, never so remote from it. We are struggling as thro' thick darkness, in this England of ours, toward light and deliverance as I do believe. Adieu, my dear Sir; better health of body to you, and no worse healthy brotherliness of soul.

With affectionate esteem, yours always,

T. CARLYLE.

V

Chelsea, London: Dec. 19, 1842.

My dear Sir,—For several months now I have been a great defaulter; defrauding you of a most indispensable reply to a kind message, and myself of a great pleasure in imparting it! How this has been, by what foolish combinations of sickliness, idleness, excessive work, you, who alas are yourself too often a sick man, will perhaps well enough understand. Suffice it now, better now than still later, very penitently and very thankfully to say that your most welcome gift, with the kind written remembrance in it, arrived safe here, in due course; that I have read the books, especially your own part of them, a good while ago, with agreeable results then and since, and that now, when you are home again (as I hope) refreshed and recruited by the bath waters and summer recreations, I knock again at your town door with a grateful salutation.

Your 'Denkwürdigkeiten' are again, as ever, the delightfullest reading to me. Truly, I think, were I an absolute monarch I should decree among other things, that Varnhagen von Ense be encouraged, ordered and even compelled to write and ever to continue writing Memoirs! It is authentically my feeling. Always alas, as one grows older, one's appetite for books grows more fastidious; there is now for me very little speculation and almost nothing of the so-called Poetry that I can bear to read at all: but a man with eyes, with a soul and heart, to tell me in candid clearness what he saw passing round him in this universe—is and remains for ever a welcome man. Speculations, poetries, what passes in this or the other poor human brain,—if it be not some most rare brain of a Goethe or the like: this is often a very small matter; a matter one had rather *not* know. But what passes in God's universe; this only is a thing one does wish to know, if one adequately could! In truth, I have not for years read any writings that please me, solace and recreate me as these 'Denkwürdigkeiten' do. It is beautiful to see such a work so done. A Historical Picture of the living present time; all struck off with such light felicity, such harmonious clearness and composure; such a deep, what I could call *unconscious* soul of Method lying under it :—the work of an Artist! Well; I will thank you; and wish you long heart and strength to continue, for my own sake and the world's; for the sake of this Time, and perhaps still more of the Times that are coming.

Your Russian Kartoptschin is a terrible fellow; a man in the style of Michael Angelo! One begins to understand how what I often call 'dumb Russia' may be a kind of dumb Rome, one of the greatest phenomena on the Earth present, with such souls in it here and there. We have to thank you, at least I have, for showing us a glimpse of actual Russia face to face for the *first* time. By your help I got a real direct look at the wild Poet-soul, Puschkin; and said to myself, Yes, there is a Russian man of genius; for the first time, I *see* something of the Russians! We begin here, the better heads of us, to have a certain true respect for Russia with all its 'Barbarism' real and imaginary; to understand that tho' the Russians have all Journalists in the world against them, they have Nature, Nature's laws and God Almighty partly in their favour! They can drill wild savage peoples and tame waste continents, tho' they cannot write Journalistic Articles. What a contrast with our French friends! *They* can prove by the precisest logic before all men that they were, are and probably will always be in possession of the true light: *Voilà*, this is the key to all arcana, *this* of ours. And then take a look at them in Algiers and elsewhere!

My own studies and struggles, totally ineffectual as yet, have lain principally for a long time back in the direction of Oliver Cromwell and our great Puritan Civil War, what I call the 'Apotheosis of Protestantism.' I do not count with any certainty that I shall ever get a book out of it: but in the meanwhile it leads to various results for me; across all the portentous rubbish and pedantry of two centuries I have got a fair stout view, also, of the flaming sun-countenance of Cromwell,—and find it great and godlike enough, tho' entirely *unutter*able to these days. Our Histories of him contemporary and subsequent are numerous; all stupid, some of them almost infinitely stupid. The man remains imprisoned, as under Aetna Mountains of rubbish; unutterable, I suppose, for ever. But the meaning of this preamble was that I had an inquiry to make of you. Whether, namely, there exists in German any intelligent and intelligible Book about the military antiquities of Gustavus Adolphus's time? Much in our Cromwell's methods of fighting &c., remains obstinately obscure to me. I understand only that it was the German and Swedish method; the chief officers of our Civil War, especially great multitudes of Scotch, had served in the Thirty-Years' War. Often have I reflected, in gazing into military puzzles of that period, 'Would that I had Varnhagen here, the soldier and thinker, to tell me what this means!'

I decide on asking, if there is any German Book, at least. But I fear there is none. We have a late

'Life of Wallenstein' by a very intelligent Scotch Soldier, Colonel Mitchell, but Mitchell too says he cannot understand *how* they fought with their pikes and muskets or matchlocks; in short, I find he knows no more of it than I do.

There is a 'Life of Jean Paul'[1] come to me from over the Atlantic; by one Mrs. Lee, of Boston; an entertaining little book and curious as coming from the other hemisphere. I think of sending you a copy by some opportunity, if I can find one. Pray write to me by and by; do not imitate my sluggishness!

Yours ever, with true regard,

T. CARLYLE.

VI

Chelsea, London: den 5. Febr. 1843.

My dear Sir,—Many thanks again for your kind present of Books; for your two kind letters, the latter of which arrived with Asher's[2] book-parcel, duly, a few nights ago. The only unfriendly news you send is that of your own health which I wish you had been able to make a little pleasanter to me! Summer weather at the baths, and no permission to enjoy it

---

[1] *Life of Jean Paul Frederic Richter.* Compiled from various sources. Together with his autobiography. Translated from the German. In two volumes. Boston, 1842.

[2] The meritorious German bookseller, who since 1830, at Berlin, successfully laboured to further the book trade with foreign countries, and has deserved well especially of the great English libraries. He died 1883, on a journey, at Venice.

except thro' carriage windows, is very sad work. And you are still a prisoner in Berlin, or nearly so ;—yet, thank heaven, not an idle one, not a discontented one : this too is something to be thankful for. We have to take the Light and the Dark as they alternate for us here below ; and try to make the right use of both. I say often of myself that if I had suffered no ill health, I should have known nothing. The stars shine out, as Friedland's did, when it is grown rightly *dark* round us ! Yet I hope to hear, as the summer advances, that you emerge again, and see good under the sun. Nay, so long as you can continue writing, with whatever pain it be, how many sons of Adam are there, who ought to *pity* you; who are not rather called to envy you ? I know not if I ever reported with what pleasure I read that little Delineation of the Prussian Field-Marshal Schwerin.[1] One has pleasure in it because it *is* a 'Delineation,' which so many books only pretend to be : one *sees* a certain section of Human Life actually painted, rendered credible and conceivable to one. That last Battle is clear to me as if I had fought in it: there is a kind of gloomy dumb tragic strength in the Phenomenon, as in some old Norse-Mythics, for me,—as if I looked into the old Death-Kingdoms, whereon Living Prussia, with what it can say and do, reposes and grows ! Those long ranks of speechless Men

---

[1] *Leben des Feldmarschall Grafen von Schwerin, von Varnhagen*; was published 1841.

standing ranked there, with their three-cornered hats and stiff hair-queues and fighting apparatus; dumb, standing like stone statues to be blasted in pieces with cannon-shot :—there are 'inarticulate meanings' without end in such a thing for me! Surely I much approve your further biographic projects; and bid you '*Frisch zu!*' How true also is that of Goethe in his advice to you :[1] I have felt it a hundred times;—indeed it is properly the grand difficulty with my own poor *Cromwell* at present; that he lies buried so deep; that his dialect, thought, aim, whole costume and environment are grown so obsolete for men. What an English Puritan properly *meant* and struggled for in the seventeenth Century : I say to myself 'Is all that dead? Or is it only *asleep* (not entirely with good consequences for us) ; a thing that can never die at all?' If it be *dead*, we ought to leave it alone! 'Let the dead bury their dead' is as true in Literature as elsewhere. Hence indeed so few *Histories*, and so many *Pedantries* and mere Sham Histories,—which if men were resolute enough, they would verily fling into the fire at once and make an end of!

[1] In the essay 'Varnhagen von Ense's Biographien,' in the sixth volume of *Ueber Kunst und Alterthum* (1827). The words of Goethe Carlyle here refers to are the following: ' We wish that he [Varnhagen] may proceed, with his biographical representations, more and more to the eighteenth century, and promote, by delineating the individualities and the spirit of the time with which they stood in action and reaction, clearness of the whole state of things. Clearness necessitates insight, insight creates tolerance, tolerance alone is able to procure a peace active in all parts and talents.'

Stuhr, as you predict, is heavy; but I find him solid and earnest, I believe I shall find it well worth while to travel thro' him.[1] One's *desire* to know about the old days is so unquenchable; the average of *fulfilment* to it grows at length so very low! Stuhr is very far indeed above what I have to call ' far ' in late times.

Some fortnight ago, I sent off the 'Life of Richter' by the channel you pointed out. There was not another copy readily procurable; so I sent you the one we had ourselves been reading here. There was a Mitchell's ' Life of Wallenstein ' added, which perhaps you may find partly interesting even in its very short-comings. Mitchell is an honest man ; but his indigna-tion against much inanity that he has to witness here throws him into somewhat of a cramped antagonism now and then. He is distinguished here by his deadly enmity to the bayonet, which he declares to be a total chimera in war,—false, damnable, heretical, almost in the old ecclesiastic sense! My stock of autographs which I have had much pleasure in gathering for you is of much more bulk than value! Hardly a half dozen of men very interesting to you will you find here ; the rest are transitory notabilities,—on many of whom as they are like to be entirely unknown out of

---

[1] We conclude from the inquiry made in the preceding letter that, under the numerous works of the Prussian historian Peter Feddersen Stuhr, here is meant *Die Brandenburgisch-Preussische Kriegsverfassung zur Zeit Friedrich Wilhelms des grossen Kurfür-sten* (Berlin, 1819).

their own Parish, I have had to mark some brief commentary in pencil. Pray use your *Indian rubber* there, where you find needful: for it is of the nature of the speech to a trusted friend, not of *litera scripta*. Perhaps even thro' the Trivial, you with your clear eyes will get here and there a glimpse into our English Existence: the great advantage is, that you can and ought to *burn* some nine-tenths of the bundle so soon as you have looked it over. As occasion offers I will not forget to gather you a few more autographs: Byron, Fox, Pitt I do not yet give up; indeed the first of those, with some others, are already promised me.

Your reading of the Austins is altogether correct. Mrs. Austin came first into vogue among us by translating Puckler Muskau (if that is the right spelling) and has risen ever since by her sunny hopeful vivacious character, and a good share of female tact and the like. Her husband, as you say, is truly painful,—a kind of *Prometheus Vinctus*, bound *not* by any Jupiter! The man is faithful, veracious, energetically almost spasmodically laborious; but of an egoism which has, alas, proved *too* strong,—which has made him unhealthy, unhappy; which, as I say, 'has eaten *holes* in the case of it.' Poor Austin,— a brave man too: but able to bring it no farther than hard isolated *Pedanthood*! Nay, as Sir Toby in Shakespeare has it, 'because *thou* art *virtuous*, shall there be no more cakes and ale?'

F F

I am very busy; and hope to tell you about what (it is a poor Volume, perhaps preparatory to something farther) in a month or two. Adieu, my good Friend: better health to both of us; unabated heart to both of us.

Yours ever truly,

T. CARLYLE.

VII

Chelsea, London: May 1, 1843.

My dear Sir,—Almost a month ago your three beautiful volumes of 'Memoirs' were safely delivered to me here, and in all ways cordially welcomed. I reckon it a healthy sign of your German Public, in spite of all its confusions, that it demands a new supply of such Writings : there is everywhere a great heart of truth living silent and latent amid the noise and tumult of world-wide Inanities literary and other; this we shall always know, and quietly trust in this.

Last week there was consigned to your Berlin-London Bookseller here a new volume of mine [1] with your address on it ; probably in a fortnight it may be looked for. I now, by the direct conveyance, write to announce it ; enclosing a few more Autographs, which have come to me since your last packet. None of them is like to be of almost any interest; but they

---

[1] *Past and Present*, written and published 1843.

are gathered here without trouble, and I say always, you can at worst burn them. From time to time when such an object turns upon my path, I will not fail to lift it ; to send it over sea, to the man of all living men who can extract most meaning out of it, for his own behalf and ours !

Since the finishing of that Book, I have been reposing myself with various *imaginary* kinds of work ;—among others a daily spell at reading Danish, with a view to get acquainted with the old Norse world. Müller's ' Sagabibliothek,' I had hoped, was in German ; but, alas, it proves to be in Danish ; and I have to learn that new dialect first, which turns out to be an almost ridiculous mixture of Scotch, and broken *Deutsch*, artfully disguised ; the whole broken down, seemingly *so as to give the speech-organs a minimum of trouble* ! I get into it without difficulty ; but find Müller unluckily to be no perfect oracle after all. ' Nials Saga ' in Icelandic is also here ; and the abstract of it in Müller gives me great curiosity to penetrate into a sight of it, and of the strange old world it belongs to. We are without due helps in English for introducing ourselves to old Scandinavia ; nor do I find hitherto in German any effectual notice of such. Do you know the magazine ' Bragur ' ; and what is the worth of it ? Has anybody written or translated, or in any way made accessible a solid work on that old province of things, in German speech ? Geyer's Swedish History in its German dress is already ordered from the bookseller : I have also read with attention the German Version of one Strinnholm a Swede on the 'Wikingszüge,'—it is something, not much. This ; and some nine or ten Books of travels in Iceland, from not one of which can I gain the smallest distinct insight even as to what specially the outward look of the Island is !—If in your circle, you happen to know any real Master in Scandinavian things, you could perhaps question him for me, on some convenient occasion : perhaps even a German Book-catalogue, if I knew which, might instruct me in several things.

There was one other matter, of the smallest possible weight, about which I have often forgotten to ask you a small question. In the supplement to Creuzer's 'Symbolik,' written I think by one Mone (which I found to be but a stupid book) there is account given of an ancient German Body having been dug up from some morass, I think in the neighbourhood of Paderborn, in which, or some such museum, says Mone, the Body yet lies; due account of the business having been given in printed 'Transactions' or the like, to which he refers. If I remember rightly the date is 1817. But I have not Mone's book at hand ; and, as you see, the matter has got somewhat dim for me. The purport of my request is, that if there was any Pamphlet published about it, any Paper in some Society's Transactions, or other attainable Article descriptive of this singular affair, you would indicate it to me. This poor old Cheruscan brother man, apparently some horrible miscreant, plunged down to be *tanned* in peat-bogs, and then to be dug up into daylight again after 2,000 years : this is a thing I shall never forget. This is almost all that I now remember of Mone and his grey dreary book. In Dublin Museum, I believe, there is the analogous figure of an antique nearly naked Celt, dug out of bogs, in like manner ; but this, from my account of it, seems much less notable than the Cheruscan.

I ought earnestly to caution you against taking much or any *trouble* about all this, but I am afraid, that will be almost of no avail ! In verity, these matters are so unimportant to me, you can hardly take *too little* trouble with them ; and if I find, as is still to be dreaded, that you have taken too much, why then, in that case, I will not employ you again ! Actually that shall be your punishment.

To-day, however, in my haste, I must bid you Adieu, in hope of meeting again, on paper at least, before long. Poor Schelling ! I really fear you are *right* regarding him ! As for us, by God's help, Dringen wir *vorwärts*.

Yours ever,

T. Carlyle.

VIII

Chelsea : Dec. 4, 1843.

My dear Sir,—Will you accept from me this new packet of mostly worthless *Autographs*, if perchance it may amuse you for an hour? The collecting of it, as opportunity spontaneously turned up, has been a real pleasure to me, not a trouble or employment in any sense. We will keep the lion's mouth still open; and when I find any contribution accumulated there, I will continue to send it you.

Several of these autographs, I think, are duplicates : but you can burn the second or the first, whichever you find the more worthless, and retain the other. The best part of them, as you will perceive, came to me from Mr. Lockhart, Sir Walter Scott's son-in-law, Editor of our chief Review,[1] a man of sound faculty and rather important position here,— who has lately made acquaintance with your writings, and is glad to do any civility to such a man.

It is now about three weeks since a new Gift of Books from you arrived safe, thro' the assiduous bookseller Nutt. Many thanks for your kindness, which never wearies! They are beautiful volumes, the outside worthy of the interior, these of your own : they stand on my shelves, in a place of honour; and, as I look at them or re-examine them, shall remind me of many things. Nyerup too seems an excellent

---

[1] *Quarterly Review.*

work of its kind ; and shall be well read and useful to me one day. I wanted precisely such a lexicon, for those 'Norse Mythics.' The business has had to postpone itself for the present; but is by no means finally dismissed ; nay it is likely to return, on occasion, for a long course of time. I often feel it to have been a great mistake this that we Moderns have made, in studying with such diligence for thousands of years mere Greek and Roman *Primordia*, and living in such profound dark inattention to our own. Odin seems to me as good a divinity as Zeus, the Iomsburg is not a whit less heroic than any Siege of Troy ;—the Norse conceptions of this universe, the Norse operations in this universe, were as well worth singing of, and elaborating, as some others ! But Greeks and Romans, I suppose, did not found Colleges for studying the *Phœnician* languages and antiquities ? In how many ways are we hidden as with night-mares, we poor Modern Men !

After long sorrows and confused hesitations, I have at last sat down to write some kind of book on Oliver Cromwell and the English Civil Wars and Commonwealth. It is the ungainliest enterprise I ever tried; grows more and more bewildering, the closer I look into it : many times I have wished it had never come athwart me ; stolen already various years of ugly labour from me. But in many enterprises years of sore labour are to be sunk as under the foundations. I say and repeat to myself: St.

Petersburg is a noble city; and there had to perish 170,000 men in draining the Neva bogs, before the building of it could begin; under the first visible stone of Petersburg there lie 170,000 lives of men! Courage! I must not forget to thank you for the good 'Stuhr': some gleams of military illumination I did get from him, which is more than I can say of several more pretentious personages.

The Musca volitans [1] is not unknown to me; I had, for some five years, and still occasionally have, a very pretty one,—which I call the 'French Revolution,' that book having brought it on me! Ill health is a most galling addition to one's burdens. But here too we must say, Courage, Courage! You have long been a sufferer under this foul Fiend; and you have wrenched some good hours from it too, and have some right brave work to show for yourself nevertheless. *Festina lente!* that is the important rule. May I hear that you are better; that you are again victorious and remember me! And so adieu, dear Friend, from

Your affectionate,

T. CARLYLE.

IX

5 Cheyne Row, Chelsea, London: April 20, 1844.

My dear Sir,—I am deeply in your debt, for books and most friendly messages; I have had two parcels both of which have come safe, and been duly wel-

---

[1] *Mouche volante,* a disease of the eyes.

comed and enjoyed. The 'Marschall Keith' pleases me greatly, reminds me of the 'Schwerin' and other things I had before. We have now got the entire act[1] into our London Library, and even our young ladies are busy reading it. Of all this I should have sent you notification long ago! Alas, I was waiting for some expected autographs; I was waiting for this and that. At length enters a young American friend just about setting off to Berlin: By him I on the sudden send you off Bulwer's new book on Schiller, which has stood ready for you these several weeks; this with my love, and excuses,—my *Letter* shall follow, when the autographs please to arrive. Here are three, of no value.

Get well in this beautiful weather; let us all get well, and be busy, and good to one another !

In great haste, ever truly yours,

T. CARLYLE.

The 'three autographs' are not, at the moment, discoverable !

X

Chelsea : Febr. 16, 1845.

My dear Sir, — I am delighted to hear from you again, to taste of your old friendliness and forgiveness again. I have behaved very ill,—or rather seemed to behave, for the blame is not wholly mine, as the

---

[1] The *Biographische Denkmale*.

G G

penalty wholly is. These many months I have not, except upon the merest compulsion, written to any person. Not that I have been so busy as never to have a vacant hour,—alas, very far from that, often enough ;—but I have been, and am still, and still am like to be, sunk deep ; down in Chaos and the Death kingdom ; sick of body, sick of heart; saddled with an enterprise which is too heavy for me. It is many long years now since I began the study of Oliver Cromwell, a problem for all ingenuous Englishmen ; it is four or five long years since I as it were committed myself to the task of doing something with it : and now, on fair trial, it proves the likest to any *impossible* task of all I ever undertook. The books upon it would load some waggons, dull as torpor itself every book of them ; the pedantries, dilettantisms, Cants, misconceptions, platitudes and unimaginable confusions that prevail upon it,—drive one to despair ! I have read, and written and burnt ; I have sat often contemplative, looking out upon the mere Infinite of desolation. What to do I yet know not. I have Goethe's superstition about 'not turning back;' having put one's hand to the plough, it is not good to shrink away till one has driven the furrow thro' in some way or other ! Alas, the noble seventeenth Century, with a God shining thro' all fibres of it, by what art can it be presented to this poor Nineteenth, which has no God, which has not even quitted the bewildering *pretension* to have a God ? These things hold me silent, for of them it is better not to speak; and my poor life is buried under them at present.

However, I suppose, we *shall* get into daylight again, sooner or later! After a good deal of consideration, I decided on gathering together all that I could yet find of Oliver's own writing or uttering; his 'Letters and Speeches' I now have in a mass, rendered for the first time legible to modern men: this, tho' it must be a very dull kind of reading to most or all, I have serious thoughts of handing out, since men now *can* read it;—I would say, or in some politer way intimate, 'There, you unfortunate *Canaille*; read them! Judge whether that man was a "hypocrite," a "charlatan" and "liar," whether *he* was not a Hero and god-inspired man, and you a set of sniggering "Apes by the Dead Sea." This you perceive will not be easy to say! All these things, however, plead my excuse with you, who know well enough what the like of them means in a man's existence; and so I stand absorbed in your thoughts, and am pitied by you, and tenderly regarded as before!

Your beautiful little Books came safe to hand above a week ago. The reading of them is like landing on a sunny green island, out of waste endless Polar Seas, which my usual studies have resembled of late. I like Derfflinger very well; and envy you the beautiful talent of getting across a wide dim wilderness so handsomely, delineating almost all that *is* visible in it as you go! Your Elector of Brandenburg,

Derfflinger's Elector, was an acquaintance of my Oliver, too; this is a new point of union. I had read Lippe [1] already; but grudged him not a second reading, neither is this perhaps the last. I have known the man always since Herder's Biography by his Widow; and regarded him with real curiosity and interest. A most tough, original, unsubduable lean man! Those scenes in the Portuguese War which stood all as a Picture in my head were full of admonition to me on this last occasion. I said to myself, 'See, there is a man with a still uglier enterprise than thine; in the centre he too of infinite human stupidities; see how he moulds them, controuls them, hurls them asunder, stands like a piece of human Valour in the middle of them;—see, and take shame to thyself!' Many thanks to you for this new Gift. And weary not to go on working with great or with small encouragement in that true province of yours. A man with a pen in his hand, with the gift of articulate pictural utterance, surely *he* is well employed in painting and articulating worthy acts and men that by the nature of them were dumb. I on the whole define all Writing to mean even that, or else almost nothing. From Homer's 'Iliad' down to the New-Testament Gospels,—to the 'Goethe's Poems' (if we will look what the essence of them is),

---

[1] Graf Friedrich Wilhelm Ernst von Schaumburg-Lippe, Portuguese field-marshal, called Herder, 1771, to Buckeburg as counsellor of the consistory.

—all writing means Biography; utterance in human words of Heroisms that are not fully utterable except in the speech of gods! Go on, and prosper. Tho' all kinds of jargon circulate round the thing one does, and in these days no man as it were is worth listening to at all upon it; yet the *Silences* know one's work very well, and do adopt what part of it is *true*, and preserve that indestructible thro' eternal time! Courage!

I have sent you here a few Autographs; they are worth almost nothing; they came without trouble, and will testify at least of my goodwill. If I had any service useful for you, very gladly would I do it.

You ask what Books &c. you can again procure for me? At present no Books; but there is another thing perhaps,—tho' I know not certainly. The case is this. Booksellers are about republishing a miserable little 'Life of Schiller' by me; and want a *Medal* of Schiller which they could engrave from. A good likeness; an autograph in addition is hardly to be looked for. I have here a small cameo copied from Danecker's Bust, by much the finest Schiller's-face I have seen. But perhaps there is no such Medal? Do not mind it much, I pray you! And so farewell and wish me well!

T. CARLYLE.

XI

Chelsea, London: April 7, 1845.

My dear Sir,—About a week ago I had your very kind letter with the Autograph of Schiller, which latter I shall take care to return you so soon as it has served its purpose here. The Medallions, and the Portrait of Schiller will arrive in good time for their object; we shall certainly be able to make out a likeness of Schiller from the combination, unless *our* part in it be mismanaged; yours has been performed with all imaginable fidelity! I could regret that you give yourself such a quantity of trouble to serve me; really a far too liberal quantity of trouble! —but I suppose you find a satisfaction in it; so I must let you have your way. To-day is my extremity of haste; with Printers chasing me, and paper litter of every description lying round me in the most distracting way, I must restrict myself to the one little point of business which your letter indicates: that matter of the 'Behemoth.' Your great Frederick is right in what he has written there, at least he is not wrong,—tho' I suspect he has but consulted Book Catalogues, or some secondhand Criticism, rather than the Work itself which he speaks of. 'Behemoth' is the name of a very small book of Thomas Hobbes, Author of the 'Leviathan,' as you have guessed: I think the big 'Leviathan' was published about 1650 or shortly after; and this little 'Behemoth' not till about 1670, tho' probably written long before. I had a copy of it, and read it twice some years ago; but at this moment it has fallen aside, and I must speak from memory. It is properly a *historical Essay* on the late Civil War, which had driven Hobbes out of England; it takes a most sceptical atheistic view of the whole Quarrel; imputes it all to the fury of the Preaching Priests, whom and indeed all Priests and babbling Religionists of every kind Hobbes thinks the Civil Power ought to have coerced into silence, or ordered to preach in a given style. In this manner, thinks he, the troubles had all been prevented; similar troubles may again be prevented so. He speaks little about Cromwell; rather seems to admire him, as a man who did coerce the Priests, tho' in a fashion of his own;—this leads me to suspect that your king had never seen the actual book, but spoke of it from hearsay. It is a most rugged, distinct, forcible little Book, by a man of the Creed and Temper above indicated; I remember it gave me the idea of a person who had looked with most penetrating tho' unbelieving eye upon the whole Affair, and had better pointed out the epochs and real cardinal points of this great quarrel than any other contemporary whom I had met with. I know not whether this will suffice for Herr Preuss's object and yours: but if you need more precise instruction, pray speak again; it is very easy to be had

to any extent. Nay I think it would not be difficult
to pick from the Old-Book stalls a copy of the book
itself: but indeed there is a new Edition of all
Hobbes' works lately published, in which the
'Behemoth' is duly included,—Sir William Moles-
worth's 'Edition of Hobbes;' which is probably in
one of your Public Libraries by this time.

I send you an Autograph of Thomas Babington
Macaulay, a conspicuous Politician, Edinburgh-Re-
viewer, Rhetorician, and what not, among us at
present. The note is addressed to me:[1] the subject
is perhaps worth mentioning. An old foolish story
circulates concerning Oliver Cromwell: how when

[1] We are enabled to give the said letter of Macaulay to Carlyle.

Albany: March 31, 1845.

Dear Sir,—I should be most happy to be of the smallest use to
you. But I fear that Mr. Mackintosh's memory has misled him.
He is under the impression that the famous saddle letter got into Sir
Edward Harley's hands, and that Sir Edward Harley shewed it to
Sir Harry Vane. This, he thought, was mentioned in the extracts
which Sir James Mackintosh made from the Welbeck papers.
There certainly is among those extracts a concise account of Sir
Edward Harley's life by one of his sons, but not a word touching the
letter. In truth the story is incredible. For Sir Edward was a
strong Presbyterian, bitterly hostile to the military Saints, and closely
connected with Denzil Hollis. If Cromwell had found such a letter,
the last man to whom he would have given it would have been
Harley; and, if Harley had got hold of such a letter, the last man to
whom he would have shown it would have been Vane. But I believe
the whole story of the letter to be a mere romance.

If you have the smallest curiosity to look over the Welbeck papers
or any other part of Sir James Mackintosh's collection, I shall be
truly glad to give you any help in my power. Mr. Mackintosh, I
have no doubt, would permit me to send you any volume which you

the king, in 1647, was negotiating between the Army
and the Parliament, he had promised to make Oliver
an Earl and Knight of the Garter; how Oliver did
not entirely believe him; got to understand that he
was writing a letter to his Queen, which was to go
off on a certain afternoon, sewed into the pannel of
a saddle, by a Courier from an Inn in London: how
Oliver thereupon, and his son-in-law, on that certain
afternoon, *disguised themselves as troopers*, proceeded to
the specified Inn, gave the Courier a cup of liquor, slit
open the saddle, found the Letter, and there read,—
'Fear not, my Heart; the *garter* I mean to give him
is a hemp rope.' Whereupon &c. &c. This story,
of which we have Oil Pictures, Engravings, and a
general ignorant belief current among us, I have
for a long time seen to be mere *Mythus*; and had
swept it, with many other such, entirely out of my
head. But now a benevolent gentleman writes to
me that, for certain, I shall get evidence about it, in
Sir James Mackintosh's papers,—sends me even a long
memoir on the subject. Macaulay has Sir James's
Papers at present: I forward to Macaulay the long

might have occasion to examine.   I fear, however, that you would
find little relating to times earlier than the Restoration.

Believe me, my dear Sir, yours very truly,

T. B. MACAULAY.

To the date of this letter Carlyle has written with pencil the
following note:—

'The Albany is a set of houses included within gates, within
regulations,—and all let as lodgings to opulent Bachelors here. Old
Indians, official persons, and such like are to be found there.'

memoir; requesting *him* to burn it, if, as I conclude, he has and can have no evidence to confirm the story. This is his answer. It is astonishing what masses of dry and wet rubbish do lie in one's way towards the smallest particle of valuable truth on such matters! I was in Oliver's native region two years ago; and made sad reflexions on the nature of what we call 'immortal fame' in this world!

Peel is considered to have done a great feat in getting a Grant of Money (a much increased Grant) for the Catholic College of Maynooth in Ireland. I do not wonder your King is in a great hesitation about setting up Parliaments in Prussia. I would advise a wise man, in love with *things*, and not in love with empty talk *about* things, to come here and look first! Adieu, my dear Sir,—in haste to-day.

Yours always truly,

T. CARLYLE.

XII

Chelsea: June 8, 1845.

My dear Sir,—I am still kept terribly busy without leisure at any hour: but no haste can excuse my neglecting to announce the safe arrival of your bounties, which arrive in swift succession, and ought to be acknowledged in word as well as thought.

The tiny Package of the Schiller Valuables had survived without damage the hazards of its long journey: it arrived here, after not much delay, several weeks ago,—just as the Printing of the Book was about completed : still in time. We admire much the new Portrait of Schiller. It was put at once into the hand of the Publisher ; who with all alacrity, set about engaging ‘ the best Engraver,’—whose name I do not know ; whose quality I much insisted on ; and whom, accordingly, I suppose to be busy with the operation even now. Hitherto I have heard nothing farther ; my Publishers live far off in the heart of the City and its noises ; and all my locomotions at this period direct themselves towards the opposite quarter. But of course I expect to see a Proof before they publish : if the Artist do his duty, it will not fail of welcome from all parties. I would thank you and the kind Madam von Kalb[1] for all your kindness : but you will not accept even of thanks. I suppose this must be the real likeness of Schiller, in fact ; whosoever spreads this abroad, to the gradual extrusion of the others, is doing a good thing ! We have hung up the little Medallions on the wall, where they shall many times remind us of you.

Your ‘ Life of Blücher ’ came next ; which shall solace my earliest leisure ;—and which in the meanwhile does not lie idle, but gets itself read with acceptance in the house. I forwarded the copy to Mr.

---

[1] Fräulein von Kalb, who was, since the death of her mother Charlotte von Stein, lady of honour at the court of Berlin. In her possession was the miniature whose reproduction adorns the second edition of Carlyle’s *Life of Friedrich Schiller.*

Lockhart: I had by chance seen him the night before. He is not, and has not been, so poorly in health as your news had reported: a man of sharp humours, of leasible nerves; he complains somewhat, but is recovering;—a tough, elastic man. It is a strange element for a man, this town of ours; and the voice of what is called 'Literature' in it gets more and more into the category of *Jargon* if you be a little in earnest in this world! Were there not something better *meant* than all that is *said*, it were a very poor affair indeed. 'Verachtung, ja Nichtachtung': that really is the rule for *it*.

My poor book on Cromwell will, if the Fates permit, get itself disengaged from the Abysses by and by. It is very torpid, after all that I can do for it; but it is authentic, indisputable; and earnest men may by patience spell out for themselves the lineaments of a very grand and now obsolete kind of man there! What else is the use of writing? To explain and encourage grand dumb acting, that is the whole use of speaking, and Singing, and Literaturing! That or nearly so. Good be with you, my dear Sir. With many thanks and regards,

Yours ever truly,

T. CARLYLE.

XIII

Chelsea: June 13, 1845.

My dear Sir,—This morning the Bookseller called with a Proof of the 'Engraving of Schiller,' and with this Autograph, which he has now done with. The Engraving seemed to be tolerably good, but you will have an opportunity yourself of judging before long. As to the Autograph, knowing its value I am impatient to get it returned; and, on considering, fancy that an instant despatch by the Post may perhaps be the safest way :—however, I will consider that farther; at all events, I now straightway seal it up with your address, that it may be ready for whatever conveyance, and in some sense off my hand. Our weather has grown hot as Sahara; my press of confused business rolls along more bewildering than ever,—and has to transact itself in this tumult of tumults, as if a man should sit down to collect his scattered thoughts in the inside of a kettle-drum! It will be over by and by.

Yours ever truly,
T. CARLYLE.

In great haste,—by a sure hand, the Herr Plattnauer. This Saturday, 28 June, 1845.

T. C.

XIV

Chelsea, London : August 19, 1845.

My dear Sir,—Once more I am to trespass on your good nature for a little bit of service you can do me. A distinguished lady here, the lady Harriet Baring, has seen lately, in the house of some country friend, an ' Illustrated Life of Frederick the Great,' [1] just imported from Germany, a copy of which she is very desirous to possess. It is ' in one stout volume 8vo, the woodcuts are beautiful'; recently published; where, by whom, or of whose authorship I cannot tell! This is somewhat like the Interpreting of Nebukadnezzar's Dream, the Dream itself not being given : however, I hope your sagacity will be able to divine what is meant. It is evidently some ' Pracht-Buch' for Drawing room Tables: ' Leben Friedrichs, mit Holzschnitten';—the Woodcuts, moreover (or perhaps they were not *wood*-cuts at all) were ' in the manner of Ratsch.' Does this define it for you? *Wood*-cuts or not, they were interspersed among the Letterpress,—part of a page printed, part engraved.

If you can find with certainty what Book it is, and get me a Copy well bound, and send it over by the Berlin and Fleet-Street Bookseller, I shall be really

---

[1] Evidently is meant *Geschichte Friedrichs des Grossen*. Geschrieben von Franz Kugler. Gezeichnet von Adolf Menzel. Leipzig, 1840.

obliged. One might have it bound here; but the foreign binding will be more piquant. It should be done *anmuthig*, yet with much modesty : we will trust to your taste for that. On the outside of one of the *boards* (of course not on the *back*) there should be legible, within a border, the letters ' H. M. B. ' (which mean Harriet Montague Baring) and 'Addiscombe' (the place of residence). These are rather singular duties to impose upon you ! Nevertheless I will trust to your goodness for doing them even with pleasure. And pray observe farther: I cannot consent to the operation at all unless you leave the whole *money* part of it to be settled by myself with the bookseller here; that is an absolute condition, a *sine quâ non*.

Another lady has employed me in another somewhat singular thing of the Book kind,—which also, when your hand is in, I may as well ask you to do. It is to send a copy of the established ' Domestic-Cookery Book ' of Germany ! We wish to see what the Germans live upon; and perhaps to make incidental experiments of our own out of that. Any *gnädige Frau* acquainted with her duties will direct you what the right Book is. It need not be bound ; it is for use : to get the right Book is the great point. I hope you will so far approve this International Tendency, and new virtuosity on the part of high persons here, as to lend due help in the matter ! ' Absolute condition,' or *sine quâ non*, as in the former case.

I sent by a private hand, some two months ago, a couple of Copies of 'Schiller's Life,' with the Autograph you had kindly lent me. My Messenger reported that you were gone to the Baths; where I suppose you still are.   I hope, well?

In November you will get Cromwell's Letters; which I hope you will be able to read. I have had a really frightful business of it with that book, which grew in my hands into rather unexpected shape;— which still detains me here, now that all the world has quitted London. Accept many salutations and kind wishes from

Yours ever truly,
T. CARLYLE.

XV

Chelsea: Octr. 22, 1845.

My dear Sir,—You have again, as you are on all occasions doing, deserved many thanks from me. The German Books, all right and fit according to the requisition, were announced to me as safe arrived, three weeks ago, while I was in Scotland on a visit to my native place there.   They were sent straight to the fair hands to whom they now belong; and due thanks, the real ownership of which was *yours*, were paid me by return of Post.   The 'Friedrich der Grosse,' I find, was perfectly correct; not less so, I will hope, the 'Geist der Kochkunst!'   In fact you have very much obliged me by your goodness in this matter; and now if the Bookseller will send his account, it will complete the favour; and this important little matter, more important than some greater ones, will be well and kindly finished.

A few days after I wrote last, there came to me, from Lewis, your Book on 'Hans von Held.' Lewis had been unwell; had hoped always to bring the Book, and never till then decided on sending it. For this Book also I will very heartily thank you. It is like a Steel Engraving; has vividly printed on my mind the image of a *Man* and his Environment; and in its hard outlines, bound up by the rigours of History and Authenticity, one traces indications enough of internal harmony and rhythm. As in the Tirynthian walls, built of dry stone, it is said you may trace the architectural tendencies that built a Parthenon and an Iliad, of other materials! I found much to think of in this life of Held: new curiosities awakened as to Prussian life; new intimation that the soul of it as yet lay all dumb to us English, perhaps to the Prussians themselves. They begin to seem to me a great People: a kind of German-English, I sometimes call them; great *dumb* Titans,—like the *other* Mecklenburger that have come to this side of the Channel so long since.

In my Scotch reclusion I read Preuss's two Books on 'Friedrich,' [1] which you sent me a long time ago.

___

[1] *Friedrich der Grosse, eine Lebensgeschichte*, Bd. 1-4 (Berlin, 1832-4), and *Friedrich der Grosse als Schriftsteller* (Berlin, 1838).

The liveliest curiosity awoke in me to know more and ever more about that king. Certainly if there is a Hero for an Epic in these ages,—and why should there not in these ages as well as others ?—then this is he! But he remains still very dark to me ; and Preuss, tho' full of minute knowledge and seemingly very authentic, is not exactly my man for all purposes: In fact I should like to know much more about this king; and if of your own knowledge, or with Herr Preuss's help, you could at any time send me a few names of likely Books on the subject, they would not be lost upon me.

About the middle of next month, the ' Cromwell,' which is waiting for a Portrait, and also for the return of London Population from the Country, is to make its appearance ; and your Copy shall have the earliest conveyance I can find. You will of course try to read it ; and if you can get across the rind of it, will find somewhat to interest you. *Glück und Segen* always !

Yours most truly,

T. CARLYLE.

XVI

Chelsea : Novr. 13, 1845.

My dear Sir,—Again accept many thanks for your kind letter, for your kind punctuality in sending me that little Note of Monies, which completes our small book-operation, and perfects your service to me in regard to it. Here is Bookseller Nutt's receipt for the amount; and so we conclude with the Scotch wish on glad occasions, ' May never worse be among us ! '—

Your commission for the Schiller Portraits was very easily executed. I have made the Bookseller send you six, that you might have two still on hand since four were already disposed of: they are put into a copy of the little book itself, and are to leave London, by Nutt's Parcel, on Tuesday next, four days hence. I hope they will come all right; and be a momentary pleasure to your friends and you. I have not been able to see them myself; but Chapman the Bookseller is a punctual man. About the beginning of December he will send you, by the same conveyance, a copy of the ' Cromwell ': a rather bungling Engraver is busy with a Portrait of the old Puritan Hero,—which I am somewhat afraid he will spoil. Our Artists are, for most part, properly *Mechanics* ; and excel, if at all, only in that latter department !—

We have *Preuss's* big book in our library here, tho' not quite accessible at present. I design to consult it and others by and by. *Archenholz* [1] is an old friend of mine; the first book I ever read in German,—many years ago now !—By the way, would you on some good occasion send me a complete list of all your writings ? We have most of them here in

---

[1] *Geschichte des siebenjährigen Krieges*, von F. W. von Archenholz, published first in *Berliner historisches Jahrbuch* of 1789.

our London Library, a favourite reading for all manner of intelligent men and women : but I think they are hardly all here, and we ought to have them all. Pray do not forget this.—I have lately been reading Bülow-Cummerow [1] on Prussia : a somewhat commonplace, longwinded, watery man : out of whom, however, I glean some glimpses of Prussian life, which are very strange to me. Almost the *converse* of ours ; full of struggle, full of energy and difficulty ; so like and so unlike !

Our wanderings here are not yet concluded. The day after to-morrow we go down to the Sea-Coast in Hampshire, for a week or two of winter sunshine, and the sight of kind friends, in a climate much superior to London at this season. One of our gracious Hosts is the Lady to whom that *Friedrich* Book of Prints you sent us has gone.—I should have told you long since that my Wife made friendship with Miss Wynne, of whom we hope to see more in time coming.

And now for the present, Farewell. I will wish strength and good-speed ; courageous resistance to the Winter, and to all other enemies and obstacles, of which a man finds always enough !

With true regard yours always,

T. CARLYLE.

---

[1] *Preussen, seine Verfassung, seine Verwaltung, sein Verhältniss zu Deutschland*, von Ernst Gottfried Georg von Bülow-Cummerow. The book was published 1842, first gift of the freedom from censorship, granted by order of the cabinet dated 4th October, 1842, to books above 320 pages.

XVII

Chelsea, London : Decr. 16, 1846.

My dear Sir,—Yesterday there went from Mr. Nutt's shop, imbedded, I suppose, in a soft mass of English Literature,—a small box bearing your address; which I hope may reach you safely, in time for a New-year's remembrance of me. It is a *model of the Tomb of Shakespeare*, done by one ingenuous little artist here ; which may perhaps interest you or some of your friends, for a moment. I understand the likeness in all respects to be nearly perfect,—which indeed is the sole merit of such a thing ;—a perfect copy of the old monument, as it stands within Stratford Church for these two centuries and more :—only with regard to that part of the Inscription, ' Sweet friends, for Jesus' sake,' &c. to these lines, which in the model have found room for themselves directly *under* the Figure of Shakespeare, you are to understand that, in the original, they lay on the floor of the Church, some three feet *in advance* of the Figure ; in fact, covering the dust of the Poet; the Figure itself standing, at the head of the grave, against the wall.—And so enough of it ; and may the poor little Package arrive safe, and kindly bring me before you again !—

I have been silent this long while, only hearing of you from third parties ; the more is the pity for me.

In fact, I have not been well; travelling, too, in Scotland, in Ireland; much tumbled about by manifold confusions outward and inward; and have, on the whole, been silent to all the world; silent till clearer days should come. I have still no fixed work; nothing in the dark chaos that it could seem *beautiful* to conquer and *do*;—no work to write at; and as for reading, alas that has become, and is ever more becoming, a most sorry business for me; and often enough I feel as if Caliph Omar, long ago, was pretty much in the right after all; as if there might be worse feats than burning whole continents of rhetorical, logical, historical, philosophical jangle, and insincere obsolete rubbish, out of one's way; and leaving some living God's-message, real *Koran* or 'Thing worth reading,' in its stead! These are my heterodoxies, my paradoxes, of which too I try to know the limits. But in very deed I do expect from the region of *Silence* some salvation for myself and others; not from the region of *Speech*, of written or Oral Babblement, unless that latter very much alter soon! *Cant* has filled the whole universe,—from Nadir up to Zenith,—God deliver us!

Preuss's 'Friedrich' has not yet reached hither, except thro' private channels; but I mean to make an effort for sight of it by and by. I have the old 'Œuvres de Frédéric' beside me here; but without chronology and perpetual commentary they are entirely illegible.—' Zinzendorf '[1] received long since, and read : thanks!

Yours ever truly,

T. CARLYLE.

XVIII

Chelsea, London : March 3, 1847.

My dear Sir,—Some ten days ago your new volume of ' Denkwürdigkeiten ' was safely handed in to me ; I fancy it must have been delayed among the ice of the Elbe, for the note accompanying it bears date a good while back. Thanks for this new kindness : a valued Gift, to be counted with very many other which I now owe to you.—Some time before, there had arrived your announcement that the little *Tomb of Shake-speare* had made its way across the impediments and, what was very welcome to me, that you meant to show it to Herr Tiek. Surely, there is no man in all the world that deserves better to see it! Will you say to him, if he knows my name at all, that I send him my affectionate respects and salutations ; that, for the last twenty years and more, he has flourished always in my mind as a true noble ' Singing-Tree ' in that German land of *Phantasus* and *Poesis*, that I, and very many here, still listen to him with the friendliest regards, with true love and reverence, and

---

[1] Varnhagen von Ense, *Leben des Grafen von Zinzendorf*, in the 5th volume of the *Biographische Denkmale*, 1830.

bid him live long as a veteran very precious to us. Your king did no act that got him more votes from the instructed part of this Community, than that of his recalling Tiek in the way he did, to a country where he was indeed *unique*, and which had good reason to be proud of him.

I have read the new volume of ' Denkwürdigkeiten ' ; and am veritably called to thank you, not in my private capacity alone, but as a speaker for the Public withal. If the Public thought as I do on such matters,—that is to say, if the Public were not more or less a blockhead—the Public would say to itself, ' This is the kind of thing that before all others is good for me at present ! *This*, to give me an account of memorable actions and events, in more and more compact, intelligent, illuminative form, *evolving* for me more and more the real essence of said actions and events,—*this* is Literature, Art, Poetry, or what name you like to give it ; this is the real problem the writing-man has to solve for me, at present.' Truly if I had command over you, I should say, ' Memoirs, and ever new Memoirs ! ' There are no books that give me so lively an impression of modern Facts as these of yours do. Withal I get a view as if into the very heart of Prussia thro' them ; which also is highly valuable to me. I can only bid you *persevere*, give us what is possible ; and must reflect with regret that one man's capabilities in such respect are limited and not unlimited.—Last week too I have read, with the liveliest interest, your Book on *Blücher*, which I had not sufficiently studied before. A Capital Book; a capital rough old Prussian *Mastiff* set forth to us there! I seem to see old Blücher face to face; re·cognise his supreme and indispensable worth in that vast heterogeneous Combination,—which also to him was *indispensable*; for in a common element, one sees, he might very easily have spent himself, as hundreds like him have done, to comparatively small purpose; but that huge inert mass was always there to fall back upon, to be excited and ever anew excited, till it also had to kindle and flame along with him. '*Kerle, Ihr sehet aus wie Schweine!*' and then these scenes, as at Katztadt, 'Napoleon just behind me, say you?' or to the enthusiastic Public on the streets of Halberstadt, '*So mögt Ihr denn alle— —!*'—I have laughed aloud at such naïvetés, every time they have come into my mind since. Thanks again and again for painting us such pictures, a real possession for all men.

Probably you are aware there is a kind of trans-lation going on for your Works, for our behoof, at present? One Murray, a principal Bookseller here, has decided on picking out two volumes from you, for a Series of Books ('Home and Colonial Library,' or some such name) which he is going on with, in these years. The Translator is of the —— Firm, which is partly known to you;—respectable, he and his Enterprize, and to be welcomed in the meanwhile; but I cannot but heartily wish he and his party had let the matter alone; for precisely in those days I had in private set another young man, of much superior talent, upon the same adventure, and had got a bookseller too—when this announcement of the Murrays and —— brought us to a sudden stop. Meanwhile, as I say, the thing is not to be regretted; the thing is to be welcomed in its place and time; will do good in the meanwhile, and prepare us by and by for better.

Of my own affairs I can report no alteration hitherto. I remain contentedly idle; shall doubtless feel a call to work again by and by, but wait *unbeschreiblich ruhig* (as Attila Schmelze [1] has it) for that questionable consummation! I am very serious in my ever-deepening regard for the 'Silences' that are in our Existence, quite unheeded in these poor days; and do, for myself, regard Book-writing in such a time as but a *Pis-aller*. With which nevertheless one *must* persevere! Adieu, my dear Sir; enliven me soon by another letter.

Yours ever,

T. CARLYLE.

Chelsea, London: March 3, 1847.

---

[1] *Des Feldpredigers Schmelze Reise nach Flätz, mit fortgehenden Noten; nebst der Beichte des Teufels bei einem Staatsmanne.* Von Jean Paul, 1809. The little book seems to have been much in favour in Carlyle's house, for also his wife alludes to it in a letter written from Liverpool the 23rd July, 1845. Above the date she writes: 'First day in Flätz' (cf. *Letters and Memorials of Jane Welsh Carlyle*, vol. i. p. 310).

XIX

Chelsea, London : Nov. 5, 1847.

My dear Sir,—It is a long time since I heard from you ; a long time since I wrote to you,—a still *longer* indeed ; so that, however I may regret, there is no room for *complaining* : it is my own blame ! Your last letter found me in Yorkshire ; wandering about the country, as I long continued to do, in the brightest Autumn weather ; I did not get the *Schiller book*[1] into actual possession till my return home, some little while ago ; when I found there had a second volume also arrived. Many kind thanks to you for such a Gift. For its own worth, and for sake of the Giver, it is right welcome to me. I finished the second volume last night ; my most interesting book for many months past : in great haste, I send you forthwith a word of hasty acknowledgement ;—in great eagerness for the Sequel too ! The book does not say who is Editor ; have not You yourself perhaps some hand in it ? Whoever the Editor may be, the whole world is bound to thank him. Never before did one *see* Schiller ; the authentic homely Prose Schiller, out of whom the Hero Schiller as seen in Poetry and on the Public Stage hitherto, had to fashion himself and grow ! And truly, as you say,

---

[1] Schiller's *Briefwechsel mit Körner*, whose first edition was then published.

they are one and the same. For the *veracity*, and real unconscious manliness of this poor hungry Schiller of Prose, fighting his battle with the confusion of the world, are everywhere admirable. No cant in him ; no weak sentimentalism ; he has recognised the rugged fact in all its contradictoriness ; looks round, with rapid eager eye, upon his various milk-cows of finance, 'This one will yield me so much, that so much, and I shall get thro' after all ! '—and *is* climbing towards the Ideal, all the while, by an impulse as if from the Gods. Throughout I recollected that *Portrait* you sent me ; with its big jaws, loose lips, hasty eager eyes,—all as in loose onset and advance, 'Forward ! Forward !' Poor Schiller, there is something that one loves extremely in that ragged careless aspect of him ; true to the very heart : a veritable Brother and Man ! Körner too I hear universally recognised as a Tüchtiger ; full of sense, of friendly candour and fidelity : it is rarely that one reads such a Correspondence between two modern men. Thanks to you all for giving it to us ; thanks to *you* individually for sending it me at once.

I would fain send you some news of myself ; but alas, that is a very waste Chapter, not fit for entering upon, to-day ! I have no work on hand that can be *named* ; I feel only that the whole world of England, of Europe, grows daily full of *new meanings*, which it well beseems all persons of intelligence to try if they *can* read and speak. For the rest, I am very solitary; by choice and industry, keep solitary: the world here, especially the world of 'Literature' so called, is not my world. In fact I begin very greatly to despise the thing they call 'Literature,'—and to envy the active ages that had none of it. A waste sea of vocables: what salvation is there in that? Ranke's failure [1] does not surprise me: If I were a Prussian, or even German, I would decidedly try *Friedrich*. Adieu, my dear Sir: be kind and write again soon.

Yours ever truly,
T. Carlyle.

XX

Chelsea : Decr. 29, 1848.

My dear Sir,—It is a long sad time since I have written to you, or could expect to hear any word directly from you: for indeed I have been, and still am, in an altogether *inarticulate* condition; writing to nobody; in the highest degree indisposed to writing or uttering of myself in any kind ! You do not doubt but many kind thoughts and remembrances have crossed the sea to you, all this while; nor do we want evidence of the like on your part; nay, from Miss

---

[1] The *Neun Bücher preussischer Geschichte*, which were published 1847 and which, at the time of their first appearance, received a good deal of unfavourable criticism. Cf. the disapproving judgment of Varnhagen in *Briefe Varnhagens an eine Freundin*, Hamburg, 1860, p. 70 *sq*.

Wynne and otherwise, we have pretty accurately known how you were going on, and have generally had some image of you kept lurid and vivid in our circle here. Forgive my silence—silence is not good altogether, when there are kind hearts that will listen and reply! The advent of the New Year admonishes me that I should open my leaden lips, and speak *once* more,—were it but as Odin's Prophetess, from the belly of the Grave! In the language of the season, I wish you a right brave New Year, and as many of them as your heart can still victoriously port in such a world. *Courage! En avant!* I will start up too, some day, and march along with you again, I doubt not.

Some weeks ago your little Pamphlet on the question of German Unity (*Schlichte Reden*) came to me, a welcome little word, which I read with entire assent. This was your message hitherward ; and now, the other day, I despatched for you a little old Book of mine which they have been republishing here ;— a book of no moment; which probably you already have received : let this be a small memento from me, when you look upon it. Whether I shall ever write another book in this world has often seemed uncertain to me of late ; but I believe I shall have to try it again before long, or else do worse !

What a year we have had since February last! The universal breaking down of old rotten thrones, and bursting up of street-barricades ; enfuriated Sansculottism everywhere starting up, and glaring

like a world-basilisk into the empty *Wan-Wan* that
pretended to be a god to it. ' What *art* thou, accursed
contemptibility of a Wan-Wan ? '—It is to me the
most sordid, scandalous and dismal sight the world
ever offered in my time ; and if there were not in the
dark womb of that ' abomination of desolation ' a ray
of eternal light for me, I should think (like poor
Niebuhr) the universe was going out, and pray for my
own share, ' From me hide it ! '   But withal I discern
well, none more loyally.   It is a *sacred* phenomenon,
a fulfilment of the eternal prophecies, the beginning
of a new birth of the world.   A general ' bankruptcy
of Imposture ' (so I define it) ; Imposture, long known
by the wise for what it was, is now known and
declared for such to the foolish at the market-cross,
and *admits* openly that it is a bankrupt piece of scan-
dalism, and requests only time to gather up its rags,
and walk away unhanged.   How can I lament at
this ?   Dismal, abominable as the sight is, I cannot
but intrinsically rejoice at it.   And yet what a Future
lies before us, for centuries to come,—if we had any
thought within us, which very few have.

The feeling here among considerate persons is,
that Germany, in spite of all the explosions of nonsense we have seen, will certainly recover some
balance; and march, like a brave country,— *not* towards
Chaos, as some others seem to do !   We can understand that it is all the *dirty*, the foul and mutinous
folly that comes *first* to the top : but Germany deceives

us all if there be not abundant *silent* heroic faculty in the heart of it;—and indeed it is to England and Deutschland that the Problem seems to me now to have fallen : and a dreadful Problem it is,—*in*soluble by the Southern genius, as we see. God assist us all !

I am ever your affectionate Friend,

T. CARLYLE.

Goethe and the Frau von Stein : but that deserves a chapter by itself ! I read *your* copy. With pleasant wonder, which has not yet subsided into clear appreciation.[1]

[There is a 'Memorandum' joined to this letter, on a separate bit of paper :]

My wife, for above a year past, is acquainted with your works done on paper *by the scissors* ; works that fill the female fingers with despair,—the female heart with desire to *possess* for itself a few specimens. Can you kindly think of this, some after-dinner ?—T. C.

---

[1] *Goethes Briefe an Frau von Stein*, herausgegeben von Adolf Schöll, 1848-51. At the same time Carlyle wrote about this book to his friend Miss Charlotte Williams Wynne, who is often mentioned in these letters :—' I have read little yet—Goethe is quite Wertherian—and the Frau von Stein, a consummate flirt, seems to have led an edifying life,—what did the poor Herr von Stein say to it ? ' ' This is a coarse view,' says Miss Wynne in her letter to Varnhagen, to whom she communicates it, ' but so like Carlyle that I give it.'

XXI

Chelsea: Decr. 24, 1850.

My dear Sir,—At the winter solstice, when Christmas Carols are about breaking out, and men are remembering old friends, I again write to you. For many months past, I have been too sickly and dispirited to write to any one; indeed, of late, the burden of life falls so heavy on me, and things in this strange epoch are so intricate around and in me, I feel it a kind of necessity to hold my peace, and contemplate the Inextricable without attempting to *name* it at all. I do confidently hope to reacquire the use of speech, and with it much human joy at present very much forborne :—in the meanwhile I can say: old friends are only the more dear and sacred to me that I have to look at them as if I were already in Hades,—as if they and I had no portion but in Eternity, and our speech to one another, for the present, were as that of Gods, a mute symbolical one! Perhaps you understand all this, out of your own experience too; at any rate, I know you will forgive it, and look kindly on it as you do on all things.

We regularly hear of you thro' Miss Wynne and otherwise; we had Berlin visitors not long since, and looked direct upon faces that had lately looked on you. Many kind and pleasant messages have we

L L

had, and none that was not kind and pleasant, from Herrn Varnhagen; for all which, accept gratitude if we have nothing better!—The other evening Miss Wynne was with us; and we hoped to have persuaded her again to-morrow; but she decides to pass this Christmas day, the first after her Father's death, in solitude and silence. Which also we reckon to be good.—You will be rejoiced to learn that, since this final consummation and winding up of her many toils and sorrows, her health appears decidedly to begin improving; and friends look forward with assurance towards better days for this excellent and amiable person. Of Milnes,[1] Bölte,[2] &c. I say nothing; for I suppose you hear of them much oftener than I do, at this season of the year.

But let me state my special errand before my paper end. I have a favour to ask on this occasion;

---

[1] Monckton Milnes, afterwards (since 1863) Lord Houghton.

[2] The lately (November 1891) deceased German authoress Amely Bölte, who, while she lived in London, was intimate with Carlyle and his wife. Engaged by Carlyle to collect autographs for Varnhagen, with whom she was in correspondence since 1844, and, after his death, published his letters to her in a book entitled *Varnhagens Briefe an eine Freundin*, Leipzig, 1860. Carlyle gives her in a note to the *Letters and Memorials of Jane Welsh Carlyle* a character not altogether flattering: 'This was a bustling, shifty little German governess, who, in a few years, managed to pick up some modicum of money here, and then retired with it to Dresden, wholly devoting herself to literature.' His wife's opinion, given in a letter written to him August 13, 1843, is more kindly: 'In the evening I had Miss Bölte till after tea . . . she is really a fine manly little creature, with a deal of excellent sense, and not without plenty of German enthusiasm, for all so humdrum as she looks.' (Vol. i. p. 234 *sq.*)

and I know you will do in it for me what you can,—
my only apprehension is that you put yourself about
to do *more*. Beware of that latter extreme; and hear
in brief what the matter is. A certain Herr Neuberg[1]
who has lived long in England, and has now revisited
Germany (a Würtemberger, I think), is resident at
Bonn this winter; and I think meditates some
journey to Berlin soon. He is a man of unostenta-
tious but truly superior character; a most pious,
clear, resolute, modest and earnest man; with
excellent insights and faculties; well acquainted both
with our literature and yours, and indeed knows
England and English affairs better probably than
any stranger you have met. This Neuberg, who was
twenty years a merchant in this country, and then,
finding himself possessed of a competence and totally
without enthusiasm for more, decided to give up business, and live henceforth among intellectual objects,
—appears to have produced some small volume
for the Press (I think it consists mainly of translations from *me*, upon the subject of Work); and this
chiefly is his errand to Berlin at present. In which
matter it is naturally clear to him of how much
service you, whose works, qualities and position are

---

[1] Joseph Neuberg, born 1806 at Würzburg (not a Würtemberger
therefore, but a Bavarian), died 1867, friend of Carlyle, translated
Heroes, Hero-worship and the *Heroic in History*, and the first four
volumes of *Friedrich II.* into German, and gathered out of his works
Beiträge zum Evangelium der Arbeit. Cf. about him the *Deutsche
Rundschau*, 1884, vol. xli. p. 144 *sqq.*

well known to him as to everyone, might be; wherefore he modestly insinuates, not a request, but a hint or wish that I would introduce him. Being a man whom I so much esteem, and who has really so much sense and practicality, and deserves so much esteem, there is no refusing him this favour: accordingly, either by post from Bonn, or more probably direct from hand in Berlin, you will likely soon receive a card of mine introducing Neuberg and his little errand; whom I will only ask you to *receive* for my sake and to treat farther according as the circumstances seem to yourself to direct. His Manuscript, I believe, is of no great length, and will probably be very clearly written: if you pleased to run your eye over it, and give him any advice, he would be very grateful for it (as should I), and would receive it with a truly intelligent and modest mind. But, once more, let this be, I entreat you, just as the case directs; for neither N. nor I will be so unfair as to make any request about it, or entertain any expectation upon it. With regard to the man himself, I much mistake if you do not find him a rather pleasant incidental acquaintance, with conversation which will entertain you well on various subjects;— and as such I will beg you to welcome him; leaving the rest to follow, or not to follow, as the law of the phenomenon prescribes.

And so adieu, my dear Sir; with many wishes and regards, suitable at this season and at all seasons.

I hope to write again, about many other more interesting matters; I even hope to hear from you again. We are full of 'Papal Aggression,' 'Crystal Palace,' and other nonsense of which I say nothing just now. Yours ever truly,

T. CARLYLE.

XXII

Chelsea: Octr. 29, 1851.

My dear Sir,—Mr. Neuberg intimated to me, the other night, that he is about returning to Germany, probably to Berlin among other places, and that he will take charge of any packet of 'Autographs' or other small ware, which I may have to send you. By way of acknowledgement for your great kindness to Neuberg, if not for infinitely more solid reasons, I ought to rouse myself, and constitute him my messenger on this occasion! He is deeply sensible of your goodness to him; and surely so am I, to whom it is not the first nor the hundred-and-first example of your disposition in that respect. Many thanks I give you always, whether I express them in words or do not at all express them. This I believe you know; and so we need not say more of it at present.

There were other letters I had laid up for you; which seem, in some household earthquake, to have been destroyed, at least they are undiscoverable now when I search for them: but by the present sample I

think you will infer that they were not good for much,
—hardly one or two by persons of any note or
singularity, whom you are not already acquainted
with, so far as *handwriting* can bring acquaintance :
such were those now fallen aside, such are these now
sent ; if they yield you a moment's amusement in
your solitude, and kindly bring you in mind of a
friendly hand far away, they will do all the function
they are fit for.   About a fortnight ago I despatched,
without any letter enclosed, a volume I have been
publishing lately, Biography of a deceased Friend of
mine.[1]   This also I hope you have got, or will soon
get, and may derive a little pleasure from.   It will
give you a kind of glimpse into modern English life ;
and may suggest reflexions and considerations which,
to a *human* reader like yourself, are not without value.
I wrote it last summer when we were all in Babel uproar
with the thing they called ' Crystal Palace,'—such a
gathering of jubilant *Windbeuteln* from all the four
corners of the world as was never let loose on our poor
city before !—in which sad circumstances all serious
study was as good as impossible ; and, not to go quite
out of patience, one had to resolve on doing something that did not need study.   Thank the gods, we
are now rid of that loud delirium, of street-cabs,
stump-oratory, and general Hallelujah to the Prince
of the Power of the Air,—what I used to call
the ' *Wind-dust-ry* of all Nations ' ;—and may the

----

[1] *The Life of John Stirling* (1851).

angry Fates never send the like of it again in my time !

In the end of July I ran off to try a month of *Water Cure*, which has done me no ill, and not traceably very much good ; after which I went to my native region in Scotland, then to Lancashire &c. on my way homewards, nay was even a week in Paris ; —and at last, for a month past, am safe at my own hearth again, beautifully *silent* in this deserted season of the Town-year ; and on the whole am much more content with my lot than I have been in the past noisy months. Silence, solitude : I find this withal an indispensable requisite in life for every faithful man ; and have often thought of ancient oriental *Ramadhan* &c. with a real regret, and pity for the modern generation. No devout mortal but will long to be alone from time to time ; left utterly to himself and the dumb universe, that he may listen to the Eternal voices withal, that the whirlwinds of dusty terrestrial nonsense may from time to time precipitate themselves a little.

What my next task is to be ? That is the question ! If I were a brave Prussian, I believe I should forthwith attempt some Picture of Friedrich the Great, the *last* real *king* that we have had in Europe, —a long way till the *next*, I fear—and nothing but sordid loud anarchy *till* the next. But I am English, admonished towards England ;—and Friedrich, too, is sure enough to *be* known in time without aid of mine.

—And so I remain in suspense; have however got Preuss's big book, and decide to *read* that again very soon. I am much at a loss for *maps* and good *topographies* on that subject: if you could select me a very recommendable name or two, it might be of real help. We have huge map-dealers here, a wilderness of wares; and can get any German thing at once, if we will know *which*. *Item*, I have been reading again (for curiosity merely) about Catharine II. :—you who know Russian might guide me a little there too. Catharine is a most remarkable woman ;—and we are to remember that, if she had been a *man* (as Francis I., Henry IV., &c.), how much of the scandal attached to her name would at once fall away. Doubtless you have read Kropomisky's 'Tagebuch': is it good for anything? Are there *no* Histories but Castera's and Took's? Any news on that subject would be welcome too, some time when you are benevolent to me. Adieu, my dear Sir, and do not forget me !—

T. CARLYLE.

We have lost Miss Wynne's latitude and longitude in these her travels. If she comes to Berlin, remind her punctually of that fact.—Milnes, as you perhaps know, is at last wedded; just returning from his marriage-jaunt: a very eligible wife he got.

XXIII

Chelsea, London : June 6, 1852.

My dear Sir,—Since you last heard of me, I have been reading and inquiring not a little about Frederick the Great; and have often had it in view to write to you, but was always driven back by the vague state of my affairs in that quarter. For all is yet vague; I may say chaotic, pathless;—and on the whole, my studies (if they deserve that name) have hitherto served less to afford me direct vision on the subject, than to shew what darkness still envelopes it for me. Books here are pretty abundant upon Frederick, for he has always been an object of interest to the English; but on the whole not the right Books,—the right Books, materials and helps are not accessible here, and indeed do not exist here even if one could (which I cannot) sit in the British Museum to read them. On the other hand, importation of books from Germany, I find, is intolerably tedious and uncertain :— in that, I have to admit that my real progress, in proportion to my labour, is quite mournfully small; and after struggling with so many dull reporters, *Preuss* (in all forms), *Ranke, Frédéric* (Œuvres de, in two editions), *Voltaire, Lloyd* (Tempelhof [1]

---

[1] Lloyd's *History of the late War in Germany between the King of Prussia and the Empress of Germany and her Allies*, containing 'reflections on the general principles of war . . .' London, 1781–9,

still unattainable), *Jomini, Archenholtz, Retzow,* not to speak of *Zimmermann, Nicolai, Denina,* &c. &c., 'reporters' enough,—I find the thing reported of still hovering at an immeasurable distance, and only revealing itself to *me* in fitful enigmatic glimpses, not quite identical with any of the 'reports' I have heard!—Add to which, I have no definite *literary* object of my own in view, to animate me in this inquiry; nothing but a natural human curiosity, and love of the Heroic, in the absence of other livelier interests from my sphere of work at present: you may figure I have not been a very victorious labourer for the last seven or eight months.

Nevertheless, I decidedly grow in love for my Hero, and go on; and can by no means decide to throw him up at this stage of the inquiry. That I should ever write anything on F^{ic} seems more and more unlikely; but perhaps it would be good that my *reading* upon him, which has been a kind of intermitting pursuit with me all my life, should now finish and complete itself at last. Accordingly friend Neuberg, I believe, has now another small cargo of Books on the road for me; nay other wider schemes of inquiry are opening: one way or other, I suppose, I ought to play the game out.

From Raymann's 'Kreiskarten,' and Stieler's

<hr>

was published in a German translation 1783-1801 by Tempelhof, whose notes became the principal source for Archenholtz's *History of the Seven Years' War.*

maps, joined to an invaluable old *Busching* [1] which has come to me, I get, or can get, fair help towards all manner of *topography* : on the other hand, I greatly want some other kind of Book or Books which should give me with the due *minuteness* and due *indubitability* a correct basis of *Chronology* ; in all former inquiries, I had some Contemporary set of Newspapers, 'Analyse du Moniteur,' 'Commons Journals,' private Diary or the like, to serve me in this respect ; but here I have yet found nothing, and do much want something, the result being always an indispensable one with me, and preliminary to all other results. Had faithful Preuss done the Œuvres de F[c] according to what I think the right plan, all would have been safe in this particular, in the hands of so exact a man : but unfortunately he has looked on F[c]'s works as *literature* (which they hardly are, or not at all are) and not as Autobiographic Documents of a World-Hero (which is their real character) ; and then tying up every little ounce-weight of different ware into a bundle of his own,—we have a most perverse regularity of *method* ; the book, in spite of its painful unrememberable annotations, very often unintelligible to the earnest reader ; not to be read in any way except with all the volumes about you at once ; and yielding at last a

[1] Anton Friedrich Büsching, the establisher of the political-statistical method of geography. His principal work, *Neue Erdbeschreibung*, of which he himself wrote the first eleven volumes,—that is to say, Europe and a part of Asia, in the years 1754-92—was continued after his death.

result which is quite bewildering,—not a living hero and the shadow of his history, but the *disjecta membra* of him and it. From these Œuvres, were they even completed, there will be no Chronology easily attainable.—If you know of any such book as would serve me in this particular, or can hear of any, I will beg you to let me know of it. Also (after all my Büschings and Raymanns) I should be very thankful for a little Topographical Dictionary of Prussia, or even of Germany (if not too big): Büsching's 'Indexes' being hitherto my only help in this respect. Character of place, sequence of time, Topography and Chronology,—these are the warp and woof of all historical intelligibility to me.

Another book which I want still more, if there be such a book, is some *Biographical* Dictionary, or were it even an authentic old 'Peerage Book' such as we have in England,—or even a distillation of old Army-lists and Court Calendar,—some Prussian Book, I mean, or general German Book, which would tell me a little who these crowds of empty names *are*, at least which of them is meant, when one hears them mentioned. This is a quite frightful want with me. There are such multitudes of different Schwerins ('of Schwerins,' I somewhere heard), all of them unknown to me, so many Brandenburg-Schwedl-Brunswick-Bewerns, half-dozens of Dukes of Würtemberg, &c. &c. —it becomes like a Walpurgis-Nacht, where you can fix some of them into the condition of visual shadows at least! The very Margraves of Baireuth and Anspach are and continue mere echoes to me.—The Duchess of Saxe-Gotha too (F^e's and Voltaire's), I have asked on all sides who or what she is and nobody can so much as show me the colour of a ribbon of her! Voltaire's 5,000 letters (100 times *too many*) I find as imperfectly *edited* as any; indeed they are three-parts utterly illegible already, for want of editing,—and must end by being flung out, as portions of Chaos or the utterly Dark, for most part before very long, I apprehend. It was F^k alone that first sent me into that black element, or beyond the very shores of it; and I confess I had no idea how dark and vacant it had grown.—If you can think of any guide or guides for me, in this important particular at once so essential and so completely unprovided for, surely it will be a great favour. Of course there are guides better or worse, to an inquiring stranger; and the worst of them, if only authentic and intelligible, would be a kind of heaven to me in this enterprise.

Did you see the Selection from Sir Andrew Mitchell's Correspondence, two thick volumes which appeared here some years ago? Doubtless they are in some of your Berlin libraries. The Editor, one Birret, is a man of some energy and talent; but said to be very vain and ill-natured; and is, beyond doubt, profoundly ill-informed on the matter he has here undertaken. There is a letter, from a poor English soldier, acting as servant to Marshal Keith, which gives some poor glimpses of Keith in his last moments, and of the terrible mewing of Hochkirch: you must see this poor *Tebay's* letter (that is the name of him) for your second edition of 'Keith'; if you have it not at hand, pray apply to me for a copy, which will be very easily got. It seems there are large masses of Mitchell Correspondence still unprinted in the British Museum, and various MSS. of Frederick included in them; which, however, I believe, have been seen by Raumer and other Prussians. I read *Mirabeau*,[1] and still have him; but except Mauvillon's[2] volume on the Prussian soldiers, I found the rest mainly a huge and to me quite questionable *lecture on Free-trade à la Cobden*; —well worth its reading too, for Mirabeau is Mirabeau wherever one finds him. I have often pictured to myself the one interview of Vater Fritz and Gabriel Honoré on the stage of this world !

But, on the whole, I must now tell you of a project that has risen here of a little tour to Germany itself on our part; of which the chief justification to me,—tho' the *female* mind withal has other views in it,—would be to assist myself in the inquiries after Frederick. To look with my eyes upon Potsdam, Ruppin, Rheinsberg, Küstrin, and the haunts of

---

[1] *Sur la monarchie prussienne sous Frédéric le Grand* (1787).

[2] Mauvillon, who collected the materials for Mirabeau's book, himself wrote the chapter about the tactics of the Prussian infantry. Later he made a German translation of the *Monarchie prussienne*, of which the printing was not finished till after his death (1794).

Frederick; to see the Riesengebirge country and the actual fields of Frederick's ten or twelve grand battles : this would be a real and great gain to me. Hohenfriedberg, Soor, Leuthen, I could walk these scenes as truly notable ones on this Earth's surface ; footsteps of a most brilliant, valiant and invincible human soul which had gone before me thro' the countries and left indelible trace of himself there. Then at Berlin, one could see at least immensities of *portraits*, Chodowieski Engravings &c. &c. which are quite wanting in this country ; as well as all manner of books to be read or to be collected and carried home for reading ;—not to mention oral inquiries and communications, or the very sight of friends who might otherwise remain always invisible to me ! In short, I think it not unlikely that we may actually come, my Wife and I, this very summer ; and try the business a little ; for there are Homburg or other watering places in the game too, and we really both of us need a little change of scene, after so many years of this Babel. The drawbacks are sad in- capacity, especially on my part, for sleeping, for digesting, for porting the conditions of travel,— which are sport to most people, and alas are death to poor us ! However, if the motive energy *were* suffi- ciently great ? We can both of us speak, or could soon learn to speak, a kind of Deutsch-Kauderwälsch, which might be intelligible to the quick-eared ; and for me, I have a certain readiness in bad French as well. Miss Wynne eagerly urges the attempt, on hygienic grounds ; others urge, and in fact, there is a kind of stir in the matter, which may perhaps come to something.

Will you, at any rate, be so kind as to describe to me a little what you reckon the resources of Berlin in regard to my F^c speculations might be?—Berlin, I conclude, must be the headquarter in regard to all that ;—and mention especially what the *proper time*, both in regard to climate and to the presence of instructive persons, might be for visiting your city. People speak of Berlin heats, and sand, and blazing pavements, and again of Berlin sleets and frosts : a still more important point would be the possibility of lodging in some open-aired and above all, *quiet* place ; doubtless all this is manageable,—with a *maximum* quidem, and also with a *minimum*. Till your answer comes, I will stir no farther.

Miss Wynne, home from Paris this good while, seems as well as ever, and quite beautiful again. We all salute Varnhagen.

Yours always,
T. CARLYLE.

XXIV

Dresden : Septr. 25, 1852.

My dear Sir,—Here I actually am in Germany, and have been there three or four weeks ; in my great haste and confusion I despatch a line to announce that small fact to you,—and farther that I hope to be in Berlin itself (and to see you, if I am lucky) about Tuesday or at farthest Wednesday next. I have come up the Rhine from Rotterdam; have been at Ems, Homburg, Frankfurt, Weimar, &c.: this afternoon we go towards Schandau, Lobositz; and after Lobositz, direct to Berlin,—I suppose by Zittau and Frankfurt a. O.

My wife is not here; she is safe at home,—where I wish I too were! Neuberg alone accompanies me; one of the friendliest and helpfullest road-companions man ever had. I have of course seen many interesting things; in fact I have prospered well in all respects, *except* that *I can hardly get any sleep*, in these noisy bedrooms, in these strange beds: in fact it is now four weeks since I had a night of sound sleep; I am obliged to help myself along with broken sleep, in about half the natural quantity, — which circumstance necessarily modifies very much the objects I can hope to attempt with success in this journey of mine. To gather some old books (on the subject of F^k), to see Portraits and Places, this is nearly all I can aim at, as matters go.

Berlin is to be my last station; from Berlin I go home by the shortest route, and at the quickest rate of steam conveyance. I calculate on staying there perhaps a week; longer if I c^d get a lodging where sleep were possible; but of that I fancy there is no hope! I am habitually a bad sleeper; cannot do with noises, &c. at all: and the arrangements for sleep, in all German places where I have tried, are eminently unsuitable hitherto.—If you or any of your people could advise where *a quiet bedroom* was to be had in Berlin, that would be one of the valuablest favours! At all events, leave a line for me 'Berlin, Poste restante'; that I may know at once whether you are in Town; and where to find you.—And now for the Sächsische Schweiz, and other confused journeyings!

Yours always truly,
T. CARLYLE.

XXV

Chelsea: Janr. 15, 1854.

My dear Sir,—Your 'Bülow's Leben,'[1] with the kind letter in it, has come safe to hand: many thanks for so welcome and friendly a Gift, which so many others, a long list now, have preceded! It lay waiting for me here, on my return from a short sad visit I had made to Scotland, whither I had been called on the mournfullest errand,—the death of my aged, dear and excellent Mother, whose departure I witnessed on Christmas day; a scene which, as you can well believe, has filled me with emotions and reflexions ever since, and cannot for the rest of my life be forgotten. I have kept myself very silent,

---

[1] Varnhagen von Ense, *Leben des Generals Grafen Bülow von Donnewitz*, Berlin, 1854.

and as solitary as possible, ever since my return; looking out more earnestly towards new labour (if that might but be possible for me), as the one consolation in this and in all afflictions that can come. In the evenings of last week, three of them at least, I have read *Bülow*, as an agreeable halting-place for my mind; and was very sorry last night when it ended upon me, as all things have to do.

You have given us a flowing Narration, in your old clear style; painted out a stormy battling Life-Pilgrimage, with many interesting particulars in it. Bülow was not much other than a Name to me before; but I possess him now on much closer terms: the man and the scene he worked in are very vividly brought out in this Book. Both in face and in character, I find him an intensely Prussian Physiognomy; really very interesting to me,—with his strange old Swedenborgian Father, his wild Brothers, and all his peculiar environments and personalities. Almost a type Prussian, as I said; reminding me of much that I saw, and guessed, among your military people, while among you.—Was that Tauentrien a kinsman of Frederic's Governor of Breslau? A most ridiculous figure he makes in that proposed duel with Bülow!—

I have gone thro' great quantities of the dreariest Prussian reading since I saw you; but cannot boast to myself that Prussia or Vater Fritz becomes in the least clearer to me by the process.

Human stupidity (with the *pen*, or with other implements in its hand) is extremely potent in this Universe! How I am to quit this Fritz after so much lost labour, is not clear to me; still less how I am ever to manage any Picture of him on those terms. Mirabeau, so far as I can see, is the only man of real *genius*, that has ever spoken of him; and he only in that cursory and offhand way. In the end, I suppose I shall be reduced to Fritz's own letters and utterances, as my main resource, if I persist in this questionable enterprise. If I had been able to get any *sleep* in Germany, my own eyes might still have done a good deal for me; but that also was not possible: the elements were too strong for so thin a skin; I was driven half-distracted after five or six weeks of that sort,—and to this hour the Street of the *Linden*, and with it all Berlin, is incurably reversed to me; and I cannot bring the North side out of a *southern* posture in my fancy, let me do what I will. I remember Lobositz, however; I remember Kunersdorf too in a very impressive manner; and wish I had gone to Reinsberg, to Prag, to Leuthen &c. &c.

My wife had a pleasant Note from Miss Wynne at Rome the other day: Rome seems full of interest to the two fair Tourists, and they are doing well,—in the middle of a large colony of English visitants, if other interests should fail. It is a very welcome hope of ours, at all times, to see Miss Wynne settled within easy reach of us again.

You must recommend me to Mademoiselle Solmar [1] very kindly, if you please : her kind politeness to me I often think of, with real regret that I was not in a condition to profit by it more : such goodness, coupled with such gracefulness,—what but five weeks of want of sleep could have rendered it of small use to a foreign wayfarer !

We are busy here, babbling about Turk wars, Palmerston resignation-reacceptances, Prince-Albert interferences &c. &c.,—with very trifling degree of wisdom, and to me with no interest whatever. London, England everywhere are swelling higher and higher with golden wealth, and the opulences which fools most prize ;—London in particular is stretching itself out on every side, at a rate which to me is frightful and disgusting ; for we are already two millions and more ; and our new populations are by no means the beautifullest of the human species, but rather the greediest and hungriest from all ends of the Earth that are flocking towards us. We must take our destiny. ' Unexampled prosperity,' fools call it,—by no means I.

Yours ever with thanks,
T. Carlyle.

Neuberg requested me lately to ask if you had

---

[1] A friend of Varnhagen at Berlin, who died a few years ago at a great age.

got a copy of his 'Heldenverehrung,' and to bid you demand one appointed, at Decker's,[1] if not.—Adieu.

XXVI

Chelsea, London : Aug. 12, 1857.

My dear Sir,—About ten days ago, there came to me a very pretty message from Berlin : a note from you in the incomparable hand so familiar to me of old, and a beautiful little book,[2] which entertained me greatly for several evenings after. I am truly glad to get a word from you, in assurance of the old disposition towards me, and marking that you are still well and active; such things grow ever more precious as one grows more solitary in this world,—inexorable *time* more and more exercising his sad privilege upon us! Do not forget me; nor will I you,—amid the wrecks that go on around us.

The book is altogether delightful reading : I have sent it on, the instant it was finished here, to my Wife, who has run into Scotland during the heats, and who I dare say is busy now upon it. Nothing can be more gracefully thrown off; with perfect clearness too, so far as the circumstances permitted. It gives me

---

[1] The *Geheime Ober-Hofbuchdruckerei* of Decker, who published the German translations of Carlyle's writings.

[2] It is the book of Varnhagen's niece, Ludmilla Assing, entitled: *Gräfin Elisa von Ahlefeld, die Gattin Adolphs von Lützow, die Freundin Karl Immermanns. Nebst Briefen von Immermann, Möller und Henriette Paalzow. Berlin 1857.*

curious glimpses into the latest chapter of your Berlin Histories, which was quite dark to me before. Immermann, &c. I had heard of; but only as rumours of Names; I never read anything of Immermann,—nor does this narration give me much appetite to him: he plays but a sorry figure here. On the whole, a tragic Female History throughout; things all gone awry in that and other departments, and no immediate prospect of their coming right again! But the *Gräfin* herself is very beautiful, in her sorrows and otherwise; a fine clear Being,—clear, sharp, as if she were made of *steel.* Perhaps there are other good books upon that *Freischaar* of Lützow's, and the human aspects of the *Befreiungskrieg* in Prussia? They would be welcome to me, if they are at all like this present one,—had I gone into a little leisure again. The last letter in the book, about digging up the friend's body, and bringing it home to natal earth,—has a grim pathos, and silent *Tapferkeit* and *Redlichkeit* that goes into one's very heart.—Ask the fair authoress if she has not other books perhaps, of the like quality, lying in her heart! You can assure her, with my respectful homages, that I find this one a book extremely well worth writing, and well worth reading.

For months and years past I have been sunk as man seldom was, in the dismallest *Stygian* regions, struggling with this unblessed Task of mine, which I have often thought would kill me outright. You called it a *gewaltiges* subject; I have often bethought me of that term,—and that if I had been twenty years *younger*, it might have suited better! but now, there is no help;—struggle thro' to the farther side, or else drown: that is the condition.— We are now at last fairly *at Press*; slowly printing,—I flying slowly ahead. In another twelvemonth (if all can hold out) there may be three volumes ready,— down to Decr. 1745;—and the worst part of the job done. *Taliter qualiter*, dreadfully *taliter* indeed!— At present I am in very great want of books, Magazines, Essays, or any real Elucidations by persons of veracity and insight, about the two Silesian wars (1740, 1744). 'Guerre de Bohème,' 'Espagnac,' (Marshal Saxe) and the terrible imbroglio called ' Helden-, Staats- und Lebens-Geschichte,' are almost my only resources hitherto.

Miss Wynne, you doubtless know, is at Heidelberg. My Wife was sadly ill the whole of last winter; and is still too weak. Milnes is looking towards Heidelberg too, he tells me. Weather is very hot; News from India, &c. &c. : *good* news in fact are scarce.

Yours ever truly,

T. CARLYLE.

XXVII

Chelsea ——, Oct. 7, 1857.

My dear Sir,—Many thanks for your two notes to me,—for your kind thought in regard to that matter of 'Voltaire at Frankfurt.'[1] I already had a copy of that excellent little tract,—fruit of your goodness to me at its first appearance;—and have again studied it over, more than once, since these investigations began. It lies bound up with other interesting pieces of a kindred sort; ready for use when the time comes. But you are not to think this second copy wasted either; the little pamphlet itself I have already turned to good account for my interests;—and the fact of its being sent me on those terms has a value which I would not willingly part with.

How often have I wished that I had you here 'as a Dictionary'! but there is nothing such attainable in these latitudes:—the truth is, I should have *come to Berlin* to write this book: but I did not candidly enough *take measure* of it, before starting, or admit to myself, what I dimly felt, how '*gewaltig*' an affair it was sure to be! In that case, I had probably never attempted it at all. Nobody can well like his own performance worse than I in this instance, but it must be finished *taliter qualiter*. Nay, on the whole

---

[1] Reprinted in vol. viii. of *Denkwürdigkeiten und vermischte Schriften*, von K. A. Varnhagen von Ense, after his death (1858), published by Ludmilla Assing (1859).

it needed to be done : the English are utterly, I may
say disgracefully and stupidly *dark* about all Prussian
and German things ;—and it did behove that *some*
Englishman should plunge, perhaps on his mere
English resources, into that black gulph, and tear up
some kind of human footpath that others might
follow.—At any rate, I hope to get it *done* ; and that
will be reward enough for me, after the horrible imprisonment I have had in it so long.

The 'Edinburgh Review' on Goethe I have not
seen : somebody told me it was by ——, whom you
may remember : 'Hat nichts zu bedeuten,' there
or here.   Nor Lord Brougham's speculations on
the *Great Friedrich* any more ;—the speculations of
Lord Brougham's horse are as well worth attending
to.   And indeed are about as much *attended to* by the
best kind of people here !   For I am happy to say,
there is, sparingly discoverable, a class among us of a
silent kind, much superior to that vocal one ;—and
many a 'Palmerston,' 'Crimean War,' &c. &c. as
mirrored in the Newspapers and in the heads of these
Stillen im Lande would surprise you by the contrasts
offered.   What they call 'Liberty of the press' is
become a thing not beautiful to look at in this country, to those who have eyes !

The Indian mutiny is an ominous rebuke.   It
seems probable they *will* get it beaten down again,
but I observe those who know least about it, make
lightest of it.   What would Friedrich Wilhelm have

said to such an ' army ' as that black one has been *known* for thirty years past to be !—Miss Wynne has returned to us ; bright as ever. Adieu, dear Sir, take care of yourself thro' the grim months.

Yours ever truly,

T. Carlyle.

The little Ahlefeld book (tell Madame) is a great favourite here, as it deserves to be, with all who see it.

LETTER OF THOMAS CARLYLE TO KARL EDUARD VEHSE (*born* 1802, *died* 1870),

AUTHOR OF 'GESCHICHTE DER DEUTSCHEN HÖFE SEIT DER RE-
FORMATION,' 48 VOLS., HAMB. 1851-58, 'SHAKESPEARE ALS
POLITIKER, PSYCHOLOG UND DICHTER,' 2 VOLS., HAMB. 1851,
AND OTHER BOOKS.

5 Cheyne Row, Chelsea, London: Octr. 11, 1853.

My dear Sir,—Since I saw you last year in Dresden, I have been reading a great many of your books; finding in them, as all the world does, abundant entertainment, and endless matter for reflexion. It is very surprising to me how you have contrived to amass such a quantity of floating information on things seldom formally recorded; and how correct it all is; at least how correct our British part of it, is, which I naturally take as a sample of the whole. You do often name your authorities, which is a great satisfaction to every careful reader; if you had in all cases done so, it would among other advantages have saved you the trouble of this Note, which I had long had it in view to venture upon writing to you, containing the two following inquiries :—

1. Can you tell me, in what book or books that account of George the First's Death is to be found,—

with all the tragic particulars between Velden and Osnabrück;—and in general what *is* the chief book for the secret history of George the First? In English I remember only *Horace Walpole*, and *Coxe*; in German I have got the *Herzogin von Ahlden*, which you often refer to, and *Aurora von Königsmark*: but, I think, you must have had some better book than any of these.

2. In one of your Histories,—I think that of the Prussian *Hof*, but have unfortunately mislaid all reference to it,—you quote from the ambassador Mitchell a sentence which I never can forget; to the effect: 'If the English would give up talking (in their Parliaments &c.) and were led on by such a man (as Friedrich the Great), what might they not accomplish!' These are not the words; but that is the sense; and I am extremely anxious, and shall indeed thank you much, if you can have the goodness to tell me *where* in Mitchell the passage is to be found. As was said, I can now find no reference to it in any of my Notebooks; I did not find it in our English book of the 'Mitchell Papers,' nor is it in Raumer that I can see; nor did I yesterday succeed in hunting it up out of your own book on the Prussian Court: at the same time I have the liveliest remembrance of reading it in one of your books; so that, being really anxious to get hold of the thing, I am obliged to send my question to you in this vague shape (not quite so bad as Nebuchadnezzar's dream, but too like that celebrated production of the human mind!)—and must appeal to

your charity to summon out your own better remembrance, on my behalf.   I think the words must
certainly be in the 'Preussische Hof,' or, failing that,
there is only the 'Hannoverische' to be looked to.
Please discover for me, if you possibly can.

It is only this *second* question that I am essentially
concerned in ; but if you can answer the first also, it
will of course be welcome,—tho' in that case, who
knows if it will be the *last* I may ask of you in the
progress of my reading !

Believe me, Dear Sir, sincerely yours,

THOMAS CARLYLE.

SOME NOTES OF VARNHAGEN ABOUT CARLYLE'S FIRST VISIT TO BERLIN, 1852.

CARLYLE

Tieck erzählte mir, er sei über Carlyle, als dieser ihn hier besuchte, äusserst verwundert, ja betroffen gewesen. Sein Aussehen war kläglich, trotz seiner roten Backen, seine Kleidung äusserst vernachlässigt, sein Benehmen bäurisch. Und es sei sichtbar gewesen, dass diess nicht unbewusst so gekommen, sondern er habe sich was drauf eingebildet. Bald im Anfange des Gesprächs habe Tieck den Namen Coleridge genannt, da sei Carlyle in ein unbändiges Lachen ausgebrochen, in ein Lachen, das sich als ein erzwungenes zu erkennen gab und ganz beleidigend wurde. Auch fragte Tieck ihn mit kaltem Ernst: 'Warum lachen Sie denn?' worauf Carlyle plötzlich innegehalten, und mit ernstem Ton und Miene gesagt, o nein! er wisse recht gut, dass über Coleridge viel Ernstes zu sagen sei u.s.w. Nun galt erst recht die Frage, warum er denn gelacht? Allein darauf erfolgte keine Antwort. Närrische Eitelkeit! Ueber seine Reise- und Wirthshausklagen, dass es hier keine ruhige Stube gebe, kein Gardinenbette, dass wir nicht die Bücher über Friedrich den Grossen haben, wie er sie grade möchte, dass er dem Zweck seiner Reise zuwider hier nichts sehen, nichts hören gewollt, über seine verrückte Ansicht von der Bedeutung des grossen Königs etc. zuckte Tieck mitleidig die Achseln, und meinte, es wäre besser, Carlyle schriebe nicht über ihn.[1]—Tieck sprach deutsch mit Carlyle; sein Englisch, sagte er, habe er zu sehr vergessen.

(VARNHAGEN. Hdschrftlch).

Jan. 1854.

CARLYLE

1852.

In Berlin speiste Carlyle auch bei dem Banquier Magnus, der viele ansehnliche Gäste seinetwegen eingeladen hatte, unter andern auch den Geheimen Regierungsrat Wiese und ähnliches frömmelndes Gelichter. Es kam die Rede auf Göthe, und nachdem viel zu seinen Ehren gesprochen und seine Grösse bewundernd von allen anerkannt worden, konnte

---

[1] Aehnlich dachte der Historiker Heinrich Leo, der am 10. Februar 1853 an Varnhagen schrieb: 'Von Carlyle's Friedrich II. habe ich nie *viel* erwartet, so begeistert ich sonst für dieses Mannes Arbeiten, namentlich für die erste Partie seines Present and Past und für seinen Cromwell, bin. Auch die Geschichte der franz. Rev. hat vortreffliche, hochherrliche Seiten, nur zu sehr Laterna magic.—Aber für Preussen und preussische Herrlichkeit haben Engländer, selbst germanisirte Engländer, gradezu den Sinn nicht,—wie anglisirte Deutsche (z. B. Bu. [Bunsen]) vollständig verlieren. Carlyle's Friedrich wird, wie ich glaube, eine Abhandlung des Blinden werden von der Farbe, statt der Natur künstliche Gespreiztheit wie natürlich.'

Wiese sich nicht enthalten, mit andächtigen Mienen und Gebärden vorwurfsvoll zu beklagen, dass ein so grosser, so begabter Geist den Segen des Glaubens nicht gehabt, seine Kräfte nicht dem Herrn zu Ehren verwendet habe. Mehrere stimmten in diesen angeschlagenen Ton lebhaft ein. Carlyle war schon unruhig geworden und hatte schon allerlei böse Gesichter gemacht. Endlich legte er beide Arme stark auf den Tisch, und vorwärts gebeugt begann er in seiner schwerfälligen langsamen Weise und in seinem ungeschickten Deutsch mit lauter Stimme : ' Meine— Herren ! Weiss—denn—keiner von Ihnen—die alte —Geschichte,—dass Jemand die Sonne gelästert hat, —weil er—seine Cigarre—nicht—an ihr hat anzünden —können ? ' Die Anwesenden schwiegen erschrocken, und sahen mit Beschämung, dass sie in diesem Engländer sich geirrt hatten.

(VARNHAGEN VON ENSE).   Hdschrftlch.

Diese Geschichte ist bereits aus Lewes' Life of Goethe bekannt; Lewes erfuhr sie in Berlin von einem Künstler, dessen Namen er nicht nennt.

LETTERS OF JANE WELSH CARLYLE TO AMELY BÖLTE, 1843–1849.

5 Cheyne Row: December 23, 1843.

Unmenschliche!—Are you become so inoculated with the commercial spirit of this England, that you will no longer write to me but on the debtor-and-creditor principle?   Am I no longer to have any privileges—moi? no longer to receive two or three or even four letters for one, in consideration of my worries and my indolence?   So *you*, at least, seem to have resolved!   But thank heaven there are still generous spirits among my correspondents who despise such balancing of accounts: who rain down letters on me 'thick as autumnal leaves' without asking even whether I read them!—And you think no shame of yourself, cold-blooded calculating little German that you are?—Well then, open your ledger and set down now in black and white: 'Mademoiselle Bölte debtor to Mrs. Carlyle—in one letter to be paid immediately—*no credit given*.'

What are you doing and thinking, and wishing, and hoping,—for in Devonshire I suppose people can still *hope*—even in December—here the thing is im-

possible. On the dark dismal fog which we open
our eyes upon every morning, there is written as on
the gate of the città dolente, *alias* Hell: 'Lasciate
ogni speranza voi che entrate.' And many things
besides speranza have to be thrown overboard as well.
To keep one's soul and body together seems to be
quite as much as one is *up to under* the circumstances.
I attempt nothing more. As there is nothing which I
so much detest as *failure* where I have *willed*, so I
take precious care never to will anything as to which
I have a presentiment of *failing*. My husband is
more imprudent, he goes on still *willing* to write this
'Life of Cromwell' under the most desperate apprehension that it will 'never come to anything'—and
as if people had the use of their faculties in all states
of the atmosphere! And so he does himself a deal
of harm and nobody any good. He came into this
room the other morning when I was sitting peaceably
darning his stockings, and laid a great bundle of
papers on my fire, enough to have kindled the
chimney, if it had not been, providentially, swept
quite lately—the kindling of a chimney (as you in
your German ignorance may perhaps not be aware)
subjecting one here in London to the awful visitation
of three fire-engines! besides a fine of five pounds!
I fancied it the contents of his waste-paper-basket
that he was ridding himself of by this summary
process. But happening to look up at his face, I
saw in its grim concentrated self-complacency the

astounding truth, that it was all his labour since he returned from Scotland that had been there sent up the vent, in smoke! 'He had discovered over night' he said 'that he must take up *the damnable thing* on quite a new tack!' Oh a very *damnable thing* indeed! I tell you in secret, I begin to be seriously afraid that his 'Life of Cromwell' is going to have the same strange fate as the child of a certain French marchioness that I once read of, which never could *get* itself *born*, tho' carried about in her for twenty years till she died! A wit is said to have once asked this poor woman if 'Madame was not thinking of swallowing a tutor for her son?' So one might ask Carlyle if he is not thinking of swallowing a publisher for his book? Only that he is too miserable, poor fellow, without the addition of being laughed at. In lamenting his slow progress, or rather non-progress, he said to me one day with a *naïveté* altogether touching, 'Well! They may *twaddle* as they like about the miseries of a bad conscience : but I should like to know whether Judas Iscariot was *more* miserable than Thomas Carlyle who never did anything *criminal, so far as he remembers*!' Ah my dear, this is all very amusing to *write* about, but to *transact*? God help us well thro' it! And, as the Kilmarnock preacher prayed, 'give us all a good conceit of ourselves,' for this is what is chiefly wanted here at present! If my husband had half the *conceit of himself* which shines so conspicuous in some witrers I could name, he would 'take it *aisy*' and regenerate the world with rose-water (*twaddle*), as *they* do, instead of ruining his digestive organs in the manufacture of *oil of vitriol* for that purpose!

Your little friend Miss Swanwick called here the other day, looking ineffably sweet! almost *too* sweet for practical purposes! 'That minds me' (as my Helen says) I received by post a little while since a letter in a handwriting not new to me, but I could not tell in the first minutes whose it was. I read the first words: 'Oh those bright sweet eyes!' I stop amazed, 'as in presence of the Infinite!' *What* man had gone out of his wits? In what year of grace was I? What was it at all?—I looked for a signature—there was none! I turned to the beginning again and read a few words more: 'There is no escaping their bewitching influence!' 'Idiot!' said I, 'whoever you be!' having now got up a due matronly rage! I read on however. 'It is impossible that such eyes should be unaccompanied with a benevolent heart; could you not, then, intercede with the possessor of them to do me a kindness? The time of *young ladies* is in general so uselessly employed that I should think you would really be benefitting—Miss Swanwick [!] in persuading her to—translate for me those *French laws on pawnbroking*!' Now, the riddle was satisfactorily solved! The 'bright sweet eyes' were none of *mine* but Miss Swanwick's; and the writer of the letter was

Robertson, who you may remember I told you raved about those same eyes—to a weariness! My virtuous-married-woman-indignant *blushes* had been entirely thrown away! It was too ridiculous! But could you have conceived of such stupidity—even among authors—as this of beginning a letter to one woman with an apostrophe to the eyes of another?

My German friend has returned from Germany safe and sound, and brought me thence a highly curious *gage d'amour*, which is causing a sort of general panic among my admirers. Old Sterling in particular is furious at it and likens it to the Devil's tail (where he saw the Devil's tail, whether at the 'Times' newspaper-office, or in what other unholy place, I did not like to ask). The thing is the most splendid, most fantastical, altogether inconceivable—bell-rope! Made for me by the hands of Plattnauer's countess-sister. A countless number of little *Chinese pagodas*, of scarlet network festooned with white bugles, are threaded on a scarlet rope, ending in a ' *voluptuous* ' scarlet tassel, which again splits itself away into *six* little bugle-tassels! For three days and three nights I was in the dreadfullest perplexity what to do with it! To ring up one's *one maidservant* with *such* a bell-rope would have been an act of inconsistency all too glaring! besides I should have been always fearing when I pulled it that I should bring a shower of *bugles* about my ears! So I decided finally to give it a *sinecure*-place beside the drawing-room-door, where there is no bell-wire but only a brass-headed nail to suspend it from! 'Don't you admire it there?' I asked my husband after it was hung up. 'Oh yes,' said he, 'certainly!—as a splendid solecism! as one admires a *beautiful idiot*!'

But it strikes me that considering your demerits, my dear, I am here writing you an absurdly long letter! The fact is that I have not, I find, got *quite* rid of what somebody described as 'that damned thing called the milk of human kindness'—and I bethink me that on Christmas day you will be feeling sad more or less. When one is far from one's own land and own friends, those *anniversaries*, however they may be cheered for one by present kindness, always bring the past and distant strangely and *cruelly* near and make one long as one *dares not long every day* to be as one has been! A word of encouragement and sympathy from a *fellow-sufferer* under these *anniversary-feelings* may be some little comfort to you, at all rates it is such comfort as I have to give, and if I had any better you should have it with a blessing—and so this is why I write just to-day; because I mean that you should read my letter on Christmas.

Give my kindest regards to Mr. and Mrs. Buller and a kiss to Theresa, who I hope is striding thro' all departments of human knowledge in *seven-leagued boots* and carrying all the cardinal virtues along with her!

I send you a little thing for good luck to your new

year.   And so I commend you to Providence and your own sound little judgment, which is a very good deputy for Providence on this earth,—and remain with sincere good wishes very kindly yours,

JANE CARLYLE.

Bay House : Wednesday (1845).

Ah my dear little friend !   I am so sorry for the disappointment that is awaiting you ! and yet,—should I like that you were not to feel some disappointment on finding me no longer there to welcome you back ? Certainly not.   I shall have been here a fortnight on Saturday—how much longer we remain depends on others than me—for *me*, I never can do long well in idleness—unless indeed in the idleness of Seaforth-House, which feels to be a sort of preparation for future exertion, a gathering of new strength from touching the bosom of Mother Earth.   But at Seaforth-House (?) it is not so much *idleness* as *indolence*—and the difference is immense.   The one is a repose for the faculties, the other a strenuous waste of them.— Mr. Charles Buller is here—no other visitor for the present besides ourselves.

Lady Harriet is perfectly kind to me and I *admire* her more and more, but do not feel to be more intimate with her.   I fear she is too *grand* for ever letting herself be *loved*—at least by an insignificancy like me.   I *could* love her immensely if she looked to care for it.

I have a very stupefying headache to-day and am afraid of having to betake myself to bed, but I would in the first place send you this scrap that you might have some shadow of a welcome from me on your return.

By and by I shall be back, and then !

Ever your affectionate
JANE CARLYLE.

5 Cheyne Row : [1848].

My Dear,—Having constituted yourself a little Providence for your friends you must take the consequence of being applied to in all sorts of contingencies. But you are a rash, *slap-dash* Providence and your interventions often miscarry thro' this over-zeal. So I pray you not only to come to my aid with your good intentions, but to do it with a *certain* practical deliberation. My maid is going away and I must have another. The reasons for my parting with her need not be stated here—enough that she is to go— and I must again endure the horrors of a household-revolution, a hateful thought, just now, whilst I am still confined to the house, and good for so little in it.

By communicating my want to the tradespeople or by putting an advertisement in the newspapers I might have plenty of servants sent me *to look at,*—but such over-plenty ! and a chance whether *one* would be found among them worth the trouble of investigating—and this year I have not poor Christie to receive the whole swarm and send *me* only such as seemed to have some feasibility for my purposes.

Miss Wynne has a Welsh-woman out of a situation of whom she spoke to me some time since, in case of my hearing of a place for her ; but she does not think her adequate to *my own* service—tho' she says so much good of her that I have begged her to let me at least judge of her with my own two eyes.

It would be a kindness to me, then, if you would inquire among your acquaintance if what Mr. Buller calls ' a treasure ' be known to any of them. You should know by this time the sort of person I need— and such a one is more likely to be heard of among your poorer acquaintance than the rich ones. A servant out of a *fine house* would not content herself in mine, nor could I ever reconcile myself to the ways of such a one.

If you hear of any, write to me and tell me her particulars *before* sending her here—for there is great awkwardness in refusing any one *sent,* when one don't like her on examination.

There are *Servants' Homes* and Places I believe where one can have choice on paying something. But I am not well enough to venture out yet on such errands. My cough has been worse of late days and I have had mustard blisters on and been bothered considerably.

Lady Harriet was here yesterday and met Miss

Wynne at the parlour door. I never saw two such tall women in my room together.

Ever affectionately yours,

JANE CARLYLE.

Epsom : Sunday, Febr. 18, 1849.

My dear Amalie,—I am still here, with no particular wish to return to London. Nevertheless as we live in a conditional world with duties to do better and worse—and 'forms of Society' to attend to, and above all a lot of silver spoons to look after, it behoves me to go back to-morrow. Then the first business requiring my attention may have to be transacted with you yourself. I shall call for you to-morrow betwixt 2 and 3 P.M., when I hope it will not be inconvenient for you to receive me for a few minutes. Don't get into any apprehensions that I am empowered to make any proposal to you of either legitimate or illegitimate nature, having no superfluity of lovers on hand at present, while people are so universally occupied with politics.

But times may mend for us women—one lives in hope.—Meanwhile it is an innocent little concern of a daily soreness I have to speak about; you having always plenty of that sort of things which it is a convenience to yourself as well as to others to dispose of. N.B.—Beauty to be dispensed with.

Affectionately yours,

JANE W. CARLYLE.

Friday, March [1849].

You *divined* perfectly right, Dear, as to the *intention* part of it ; Lady A. was to ' take me with her to Addiscombe ' and we were to have gone yesterday, to stay till Monday or Sunday, as I meant to have told you in time to spare you a vain journey on Sunday.

But Lady A. felt too unwell yesterday for making a journey in such bitter cold—so put off till to-day, and to-day I have another note from her putting off into the vague. I am thankful ; tho' I should have stood to my engagement I was wishing greatly I had not made it—this weather taking all spirit of enterprise out of me.

Thanks for the offer of Music, but I found the only concert of that sort I ever tried dreadfully wearisome, and besides a concert-room in this weather ! Oh my dear ! ' Dinna speak o' it ! '

Yesterday on my way to Oxford Street in quest of *warm* stockings I called on your milliner—but saw nothing to excite my cupidity. Besides, the things seemed to me much about the usual shop-price !

Thanks for all your ' delicate attentions.' I rather wish you *had* been ' a man,' for if anything could rouse a spirit in one it would surely be the getting oneself ' eloped with,' and I think *you* understand me better than any male lover ever did—hang them all !

Your affectionate
JANE CARLYLE.

[August 6, 1849.]

Thanks, Dear. I send the address to Countess Pepoli by this post, and yours,—and she can communicate with you on the not-young lady herself— or await my return on Monday if she likes that best.

As for Figgy—do not name that little viper to me again! And if you wish to avoid serious difficulties *material* as well as moral you will let her and her concerns alone. I find everybody furious at what is considered your impertinent and ill-intentioned interference with her—for she herself makes herself a merit with the others of *showing you up*! She took the last—I must say very ill-advised—letter you wrote her to Captain Robinson and said, ' See here what an impertinent and most improper letter Miss Bölte has written to me. I mean to write to her that she is to send me no more such letters and that my mind is quite made up to go to India '—and she writes to Henning (he had all the letters here yesterday) that she is quite satisfied that going to India is best, &c. &c.—to buy a certain dog for her she had seen in the Park ; and to get her a new dress. Pray keep from mixing yourself further in the concerns of such a little traitor or it will be the worse for you. Lady A. is highly indignant at the unauthorized use made of her name. *I* also might be a little indignant at having mine used in inciting the wretch to open rebellion. But that you are the most indiscreet little woman in the world is no news to me! I did not mean to have told you anything of all this till I could do it *vivâ voce,* but having to write at any rate I may as well put you on your guard, and advise you to give over meddling in what you cannot mend.

Ever yours affectionately,

JANE CARLYLE.

All you say to Figgy out of mistaken compassion is repeated to Henning and Capt. Robinson &c. and you are made to look a sort of Demon lying in wait for her soul.   So pray be quiet if you can.

5 Cheyne Row: Aug. 14, 1849.

My poor little woman !—I can quite understand your intention ' to scream '—I have the same feeling myself very often—a notion to *scream* for four and twenty hours without stopping ! — not over the treachery of one good for nothing Figgy but over the treachery of the species generally—and indeed over what Mr. Carlyle calls ' the whole infernal caudle of things ' !   What *I* object to you is not so much what I call your *indiscretion* as a certain *heedlessness of judgement*—thro' which you fly at helping everybody in every difficulty without having first satisfied your-self that the difficulty *is soluble,* or the person *capable of having it solved*—for you know the proverb, ' one man may take a horse to the water but twenty cannot make it drink.'   And where one tries to lead a girl without truth or affection like Figgy by noble ways

to noble aims, it is a labour which a little consideration of the laws of nature might have spared one.
All the trouble you take for an unhelpable person is
so much out of the pocket of some other who could
have been helped. But you have heard enough of
Figgy for the present I should think—I shall merely
add that I have taken upon me to send those letters
of hers to Lady Ashburton (desiring to have them
back) that she might see how little the correspondence
was of *your* seeking—and how detestably the girl
had behaved to you. Her guardians talked much of
their determination to put an end to your 'interference' with her. I said the girl had done that
herself I should suppose, when she carried your letter
to Capt. R. and declared she would '*order* you to
write to *her* (!) no more in such a foolish strain'—
that if you found her worth interfering with *after that*
you must be fit for Bedlam!

Capt. R. was going to write to you, they said—
whoever writes to you and whatever they say : I
advise you to hold your peace altogether, if per-
missible — if you must answer something, to make
your words as few and cold and impassible as you
can.

I did something after your energetic fashion last
night ; Miss Heerman came to me at seven, to say she
must decide about the other situation to-day—I liked
her appearance and manner very much, and so did
Mr. Carlyle. So rather than let her slip thro' their

fingers, I put on my things, tired as I was with my journey, and *walked* off with her thro' the dark lanes to Countess Pepoli at Kensington. She was in a great quantum of indecision, but promised to settle the matter in the morning—and she did—at eleven she came here, having first been to Miss Heerman, to tell me she had engaged her. I hope it will answer on both sides. I wish Capt. S. had got her—he thinks his fat lump sadly ignorant.

The habit-shirt is a great hit!—the very sort of thing I have wanted for long—something that would cover my neck, which looks very bad at this date, and at the same time not give one the appearance of having a sore throat. Thank you heartily for your pains.

My maid was so glad to have me back and had everything so clean ! A real jewel she is ! For *her* too I have to thank you every day. *I*, you see, am one of *the helpable*, so you had better stick to helping *me* in my various needs. I will go to see you some morning, if the weather mend before Sunday.

Ever affectionately yours,
JANE CARLYLE.

PRINTED BY
SPOTTISWOODE AND CO., NEW-STREET SQUARE
LONDON